CW01186594

Britain and the Crisis of the European Union

Britain and the Crisis of the European Union

David Baker
Formerly Associate Professor of Politics, Department of Politics and International Studies, University of Warwick, UK

Pauline Schnapper
Professor of British Studies, Institut du Monde Anglophone, University of Sorbonne Nouvelle, France

palgrave
macmillan

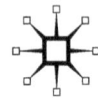

© David Baker and Pauline Schnapper 2015

All rights reserved. No reproduction, copy or transmission of this publication may be made without written permission.

No portion of this publication may be reproduced, copied or transmitted save with written permission or in accordance with the provisions of the Copyright, Designs and Patents Act 1988, or under the terms of any licence permitting limited copying issued by the Copyright Licensing Agency, Saffron House, 6–10 Kirby Street, London EC1N 8TS.

Any person who does any unauthorized act in relation to this publication may be liable to criminal prosecution and civil claims for damages.

The authors have asserted their rights to be identified as the authors of this work in accordance with the Copyright, Designs and Patents Act 1988.

First published 2015 by
PALGRAVE MACMILLAN

Palgrave Macmillan in the UK is an imprint of Macmillan Publishers Limited, registered in England, company number 785998, of Houndmills, Basingstoke, Hampshire RG21 6XS.

Palgrave Macmillan in the US is a division of St Martin's Press LLC, 175 Fifth Avenue, New York, NY 10010.

Palgrave Macmillan is the global academic imprint of the above companies and has companies and representatives throughout the world.

Palgrave® and Macmillan® are registered trademarks in the United States, the United Kingdom, Europe and other countries.

ISBN 978–1–137–00519–9

This book is printed on paper suitable for recycling and made from fully managed and sustained forest sources. Logging, pulping and manufacturing processes are expected to conform to the environmental regulations of the country of origin.

A catalogue record for this book is available from the British Library.

A catalog record for this book is available from the Library of Congress.

To Dr Philippa Sherrington (1968–2011), a wonderful educator and committed European

To Dr Julie Boch (1969–2011), a brilliant academic and dear friend

Contents

List of Figures	x
Acknowledgements	xi

Introduction	1
A multi-faceted crisis	2
Britain and Europe in the new global environment	6
Notes on theory and methodology	10
Intergovernmentalism and historical institutionalism	11
Comparative and historical political economy	13
Outline	15

1 The Political Economy of the Eurozone Crisis	17
The Eurozone: A crisis waiting to happen	20
The Eurozone crisis: An analytical chronology	24
Phase one: From Maastricht to Meltdown	24
Phase two: The sovereign debt crisis	26
Solutions become problems	29
European integration: From embedded liberalism to variegated neoliberalism	34
Conclusion: Winner takes all, but at what cost?	37

2 British Preferences in the European Union: Unsung Success	42
Consequences of a late entry, 1945–1979	44
Conservative governments, 1979–1997	47
The New Labour years	52
The Convention and the constitutional treaty	56
Conclusion	60

3 Euroscepticism in Britain: Cause or Symptom of the European Crisis?	61
British euroscepticism	62
Divisions about Europe, 1945–1988	66
Blair and New Labour: An end to divisions?	71

The Conservative Party after 1997: The drift towards hard euroscepticism	79
Public opinion since the late 1990s	85
Conclusion	89

4 The Crisis of Democracy in the United Kingdom — 91
- Disillusionment and the strains in the political system — 93
- Fragmentation and polarisation — 95
- The effect of national and global trends — 99
- The rise of populist parties — 101
- The political use of referendums — 105
- Devolution and the possible end of the British state — 109
- Conclusion — 112

5 Britain and the Political Crisis in the European Union — 113
- An ongoing academic debate — 114
- Disenchantment with Europe — 117
- Consequences of the financial and economic crisis — 120
- Attempts to respond to the 'democratic deficit' — 125
- Domestic crises and the fear of globalisation — 129
- Conclusion — 132

6 Britain and the Economic Crisis of the European Union — 134
- The view from London — 135
- British exceptionalism in the European Union — 137
  - Nation and Atlanticism: The exceptional community — 138
  - Nationhood and sovereignty — 140
- An alternative for Britain in the global economy? — 142
  - Hyperglobalism — 144
  - Open regionalism — 148
  - Intergovernmentalism — 151
- Hyperglobalism: Winner takes all? — 153
- Cameron's diplomacy in Europe and the failure of Tory statecraft — 157
- Semi-detachment or 'Brexit'? — 162

Conclusion — 165
- Continuity and change in the dynamics in the European Union — 166
- The crisis of governance and legitimacy — 169
- The British situation — 170

Britain on the sidelines	175
Where next? The known unknowns	176
Notes	185
Bibliography	191
Index	224

Figures

3.1 UK public opinion on the EC/EU, 1972–2010   86
5.1 Survey results on the perception of the EU   122
5.2 Pew Research poll results of the survey on the EU 122

Acknowledgements

David Baker wishes to thank Andrew Gamble, Mark Blyth, Charlie Lees, David Seawright, Ben Rosamond and Joel Wolfe. He also wishes to thank especially his wife Su Baker for putting up with his excessively late working hours and strange fascination with British Conservative Party euroscepticism.

Pauline Schnapper would like to thank colleagues and friends who have either read and commented on parts of this work or otherwise contributed to her thinking on the issues discussed, especially Emmanuelle Avril and Anand Menon. She is also grateful to Mark Bevir and the Center for British Studies, University of California in Berkeley, for hosting her in 2013–2014. Eric Guilyardi has, as ever, provided invaluable moral support throughout.

Introduction

This book focuses on the effects of political and economic crises on the European Union (EU) and on the seemingly endless debate in the UK over the UK's position within the EU. It analyses the way the sovereign debt crisis, in particular, has fuelled the further rise of radical euroscepticism in the UK against the backdrop of a deepening crisis in the British political system and wider questioning of the European project across the EU. The widening rift between the UK and the EU is seen as occurring at a time when, paradoxically, the EU has, in many respects, become closer to the traditional model of intergovernmental cooperation and market-led solutions encouraged by successive British governments. Long described as an 'awkward partner' (George 1998) and in spite of Tony Blair's half-hearted attempts to engage with his partners between 1997 and 2007, the UK under a coalition government has become further estranged from other member-states and EU institutions with, we argue, potentially damaging consequences for the UK and the future of the EU itself.

Underlying this process has been a clash between two geopolitically dominant visions of Europe and political economy, one centred on Germany within the EU, based on pooling sovereignty and institutionalising rule-bound centralised economic oversight, and the other, strongly promoted by Conservatives of various kinds in the UK, ranging from pragmatic reclaimed national sovereignty (enhanced intergovernmentalism) to an ultra-free market hyperglobalism seeking freedom from EU membership (Baker et al. 2002).

One significant symptom of this has been the increasing influence of the British right in UK–EU relations, with the rise of the United Kingdom Independence Party (UKIP) and the side-lining of pro-European voices in an increasingly radicalised and eurosceptic Conservative Party, especially since the issue of immigration became intertwined with the issue of Europe. The resulting shift of the Conservative Party to the right caused David Cameron to withdraw from the centre-right grouping in the European Parliament; offer an in/out referendum on EU membership if elected in 2015; threaten to unilaterally restrict economic migration from Eastern European states, which would be in breach of European law and bring the UK into direct confrontation with its partners; and threaten to withhold part of the £1.7 billion extra budget payments caused by a recalculation of the UK's Gross National Income (GNI).

A multi-faceted crisis

Since this is principally a study of how the global political and economic crises have impacted on the EU and the UK and how these crises have then interacted, a concept of crisis is essential. Crisis is derived from the Greek *krisis* meaning a 'decision' taken at a time of intense difficulty or danger, when vitally important judgements and actions must be made and taken. Marx saw such crises as a recurrent and hugely damaging part of capitalism's development, while Joseph Schumpeter reformulated this to make capitalism's 'creative destruction' a positive factor in its development.

A political crisis is often a turning point or watershed intensifying political activity. In any system-wide crisis, after short-term emergency measures marked by a loss of direction, fear and widespread cognitive dissonance comes a period of intense soul-searching over who or what is to blame, and fierce debate over whether or not it is necessary to make fundamental changes to the system, or simply restore the status quo. Any system-wide crisis such as the present 'Great Recession' creates the potential political space for radical new thought and actions and opens at least some citizens to new ideas and movements, changing the established balance of power. As Andrew Gamble suggests:

> Crises expose points of weakness and force the recognition of new realities. They signal the rise of some sectors and some states and the decline of others. In the fog of a good crisis it sometimes takes a while for the long-term effects of what is happening to be understood, but in retrospect certain turning points can be recognized.
> (Gamble 2014: 186)

He offers a comprehensive analysis of such crises, making a crucial distinction between relatively short-term externally driven 'existential' crises, responding to emergency measures through the traditional policy channels of human agency; as opposed to 'deep structural crises' which often take decades to develop. These latter crises contain multiple levels of complexity and overlapping sources of causation and asymmetries of power, which can render almost any orthodox solution self-negating, so that resolving one or more issues simply exacerbates others.

From Gamble's perspective (and our own), the EU/Eurozone (EZ) and the UK remain in an underlying state of structural crisis – a crisis which threatens to define their future directions and (of particular relevance to this book) poses particularly serious questions for the UK as the leading dissenting member-state. Gamble also suggests that the structural impasse is currently masked by the fact that the immediate crisis appears to have been successfully contained without the fall of any liberal democratic regimes, or halt to wider globalising developments, which has allowed the forces of economic and political orthodoxy to maintain their credibility and pursue austerian policies with little effective opposition from the left or right. However:

> The current calm is deceptive... The 2008 crash was an existential crisis, created by a sudden emergency, a moment of danger, which required quick decisions and firm action. But it was also a symptom of a much deeper structural crisis... the neo-liberal order, like its predecessors [the classical liberal and Keynesian embedded liberalism] has become increasingly ungovernable and is an amalgam of unstable and unpredictable forces.
>
> (Gamble 2014: 6–7)

If he is correct, and there are many indications in our book that he is, the present underlying structural crisis will have profound implications for the future direction of the EU and the UK's place within, or outside, it.

In tandem with Gamble's political economy model, we see the Gramscian model of 'organic crises' as useful. An organic crisis is characterised by a loss of political hegemony by governing elites as many citizens cease to believe the rhetoric of their leaders and turn away from traditional governing parties to anti-regime alternatives. Furthermore, under conditions of deep uncertainty and popular challenge, ruling elites seek salvation in strong leaders, or self-proclaimed 'technocratic' solutions, centred on a depoliticised discourse (Bates 2002: 258–259). As a consequence it becomes difficult to map new movements and parties onto a traditional left/right spectrum – a situation we have witnessed across parts of the EU/EZ and in the UK with UKIP adopting both Conservative and Labour policies, and elsewhere in the EU, with movements such as Golden Dawn in Greece and Beppe Grillo's Five Star Movement in Italy.

This is significant because both the UK and the EU are undergoing interlinked political, economic and social crises. In the case of the UK, a slow drawn-out recovery has centred largely on the London region, fuelled by the value of the pound falling, bailing out of the banks via Quantitative Easing (QE) and ultra-low interest rates. This has resulted in asset speculation, a housing bubble in the South East, rising consumer borrowing, falling real wages for many and stagnant productivity. From early 2012 this created the paradox of the highest growth in the G7 economies, matched by the largest fall in living standards for the majority of UK citizens for over 100 years, with real wages falling by 10%. With low-wage, low-skill and often part-time or 'zero hours' contracts expanding from 1.9% of the workforce in 2006 to 8% in 2014, while often low-income low-skill self-employment has gone up by 2.5%.[1]

In October 2014, the Social Mobility and Child Poverty Commission stated that the UK was 'on the brink of becoming a nation permanently divided between rich and poor', predicting an absolute rise in poverty over the following decade for the first time since records began. Significantly the report linked this development to home ownership halving among young people in 20 years and 5 million workers trapped in low pay.[2]

At the same time the upper sections of British society have seen real incomes rising above low inflation, with tax rates falling and, for many, the value of their properties rocketing too. Meanwhile, the 'austerity' narrative continues to dominate orthodox politics, threatening at least a lost decade for many workers and their families and containing the potential to collapse the Coalition-promoted cheap money, debt-fuelled consumer 'recovery' and inflated housing market growth model, which could dangerously undermine the UK's already fragile social fabric.

This has reinforced an already widespread rejection of the major parties by an increasingly alienated electorate, exemplified by low voter participation and the rise of UKIP, which mixes traditional fear of immigrants with populist euroscepticism. This alienation from the London-based establishment was also seen in the 2014 Scottish referendum where a large minority (including a majority of younger Scots) voted to leave a union they saw as London-centric, undemocratic and against Scotland's communal values and interests. General public attitudes towards the EU continue, however, to be confused and confusing.

A poll from IPSOS/MORI conducted in October 2014 suggested that 56% of Britons would vote to stay in the EU in a referendum – the highest support since 1991, suggesting that the rise of UKIP has polarised the debate.[3] However, in a sign of the current volatility, this was followed a week later by a YouGov poll which showed 35% for staying in against 44% for leaving.[4]

The concurrent crisis of the EU/EZ in part mirrors the UK's crisis of austerity applied to the young, women, the un- and semi-skilled classes and former state employees, especially among the populations of the 'debtor states' – Portugal, Italy, Ireland, Greece and Spain (pejoratively labelled the 'PIIGS'). Lacking the levels of growth generated by the laxity of monetary policy evident in the UK and with an intransigent Germany refusing to sanction full QE spending, while trapped in a euro currency which prevents them from devaluing their currencies, several debtor states were showing signs of entering a deflationary 'death spiral' by late 2014. As a result, the social fabric of southern Europe has been stretched to the limit with up to a quarter of the population unemployed and drastic falls in living standards and social welfare provision for a majority of the population.

Meanwhile, wealthier citizens have taken their capital out of the debtor countries and invested in property in London and other safe asset classes abroad while avoiding national taxation. In addition, the EU/EZ authorities have acted in an openly elitist manner in seeking to solve the crisis, making decisions behind closed doors, appointing (or promoting) unelected technocrats to drive austerity and restructuring, forcing the sale of state assets and threatening expulsion from the EZ and economic collapse unless bail-out loans were accepted at onerous rates to pay off creditors and prop up their economies. Germany in particular has acted in a passively aggressive manner behind the scenes, ensuring that the crisis is viewed and solved entirely from the creditor nations' perspective and dictating terms for the future development of the EU/EZ based upon ordoliberal (statist neoliberal) principles of centralised macro-economic oversight promoting 'balanced budgets' and 'sound money'. Consequently, by late 2014 Italy was facing a possible triple-dip recession and Greece had several banks under severe market pressure, as market borrowing costs to service their debts rose once again towards penal levels.

Against this background, the orthodox political elites of some debtor states were under huge pressure from electorates close to political mutiny over seemingly endless and harsh austerity, with the main results being stagnation and deflation. If one were to implode under market pressures the breakup of the EZ could follow, undermining the still fragile UK and global recoveries. The fact that by 2014 the German economy was also weakening from a general loss of demand underlines the seriousness of the situation.

As if this were not sufficient potential destabilisation and uncertainty, a UK governed by the Conservative Party after the election in 2015 looked increasingly likely to campaign to withdraw from the EU in an in/out referendum, which would potentially cause turmoil in European and global markets and be capable of bringing down the still weakened EZ and global economic system once again (Wolf 2014: 318–353).

Britain and Europe in the new global environment

These different crises have been taking place against a backdrop of long-term tectonic shifts in the global order which affect and are affected by the dynamic at play within the EU. It is therefore necessary, we feel, to preface the inter-relationships of the UK and the EU which form the core of this book with an understanding of the global geopolitical context which has also affected this relationship. Two long-term inter-related trends have affected Britain's position in Europe and Europe's position in the world since 1991. The first is globalisation, understood as the dramatic rise in economic, financial and cultural flows between countries transforming the environment in which Britain and Europe operate, especially the emergence of competing new technological powers, mostly in Asia, alongside a raft of unanticipated environmental challenges. The second trend concerns the decline of the USA as the unchallenged hegemon and the emergence of new global powers and transnational threats, especially Islamist terrorism and a succession of so-called 'failed states'.

The relative decline of US power is one dimension of globalisation which directly impacts on the UK since the UK based its post-1945 foreign and security policy on its 'special relationship' with the USA (Cox 2001, Joffe 2009). The USA was the clear winner of the Cold War and emerged in 1989 as the sole remaining superpower, which at first sight confirmed the relevance of the original British choice. Yet hopes for a relatively stabilised, US-sponsored liberal order after the end of the Cold War proved short-lived as new conflicts and threats emerged, including on European soil with the break-up of Yugoslavia and the failure of Bush's neo-Conservative foreign policy after the attacks of 11 September 2001 (Quinn 2011, Rachman 2011). The invasions of Afghanistan and Iraq illustrated the USA's relative impotence in asymmetrical conflicts, highlighting the inadequacy of the objective of exporting US-style democracy by force (Cox 2007: 651).

Growing internal weaknesses and contradictions in the US political and economic system were exposed by the financial crisis of 2007, combining a huge budget deficit with levels of recession unheard of since the Great Depression. Moreover, trust in the capacity of the US system to rise to the challenge was undermined by gridlock between the Democratic presidency and Republican Congress, breaking the 'unwritten social contract among labor, business and government' necessary for a successful democratic society (Packer 2011). The 2000s also witnessed the relative decline of the USA in relation to China, while the so-called BRICS (Brazil, Russia, India, China, South Africa) also became global actors. Consequently, the idea that the world was experiencing a power transition – fraught with danger (Ikenberry 2008, Kagan 2008) – from an American to a 'post-American' multi-polar world became fashionable (Zakaria 2009) and seemed confirmed by Barack Obama's focus on disengaging the USA from both Iraq and Afghanistan.

This decline obviously needs to be qualified since the USA remains the primary global military power, spending as much on its military as does the rest of the world put together (Kagan 2008). Furthermore, the USA remains the locus of most high-tech innovation and research, while its soft cultural power still eclipses that of any emerging power (Joffe 2009). Nevertheless, the perception of decline, if not its truth, is acute and the 'unipolar' moment clearly past, turning the USA into *a primus inter pares* in a multi-polar world and causing a degree of unease and anxiety among its closest allies.

The declining strength, in relative terms, of the USA challenges both Europe and the UK. The USA's post-2007 economic difficulties meant sharp reductions in the number of US troops stationed in Europe and Europe shouldering more of the costs of its own security (US Department of Defense 2012: 2–3), whereas the reality has been a sharp reduction of defence spending almost throughout the EU, especially in Germany, the UK, France, Italy and Spain as a result of austerity measures (Youngs 2014: 34).

Europeans are also affected by the perception of their own decline (Grant 2009, Bozo 2012). The European population is ageing and expected to shrink in relative and possibly absolute terms (representing less than 5% of the global population). More importantly, the gap between Europe's economic potential and its weaknesses is becoming conspicuous. Europe experienced a relative decline in its share of world manufacturing from 26% in 1980 to 17% today and also in world trade, especially when compared with China which doubled its market share between 1995 and 2008, reaching 14% of world trade (Brown 2005, European Commission 2008, Van Ark et al. 2008). Europe also experienced persistently high levels of unemployment even before the 2007–2008 crisis (8.7% for the EU 25 in 2005), especially among workers over the age of 55.

As a political actor on the global stage, Europe's achievements are distinctly underwhelming. EU member-states do not always agree on foreign policy issues and disputes have prevented effective international action. Europe was also heavily dependent on US political and military intervention in Bosnia in 1995, in Kosovo in 1999 and in Libya in 2011. Anand Menon argues that its responses to crises and challenges in Asia and its own backyard, especially Ukraine, have been inadequate (2014). The nature of European power has been constructed as 'post-Westphalian', 'neo-medieval' (Zielonka 2006), 'post-modern' (Cooper 2000) or 'civilian' (Duchêne 1972, Smith 2005) but even Europe's soft power or 'power-by-attraction' has been dented by the extent of the economic crisis – the idea of a European model of economic and social prosperity and multilateral cooperation is harder to sustain in this new environment (Youngs 2014). As Menon noted, the crisis has also made European countries more 'inward-looking', with immediate priorities such as saving the euro making it difficult to face more global challenges effectively (Menon 2014).

In this new world, UK policy-makers have been faced with a dilemma: either overhaul completely the foundations of British foreign policy to adjust to a changing environment, or make a few small adjustments. John Major (1990–1997) rejected radical change in British foreign policy. At no point did he or the then foreign secretary Douglas Hurd question the main tenets of past British foreign policy, summed up by Churchill as the 'three circles' – the Empire/Commonwealth, the transatlantic partnership and Europe (Daddow and Gaskarth 2011: 13). In contrast, Tony Blair and Gordon Brown modernised British foreign policy discourse, insisting on new possibilities of globalisation, a phenomenon to be embraced, which offered a continued role for national governments, both domestically and at EU level (Schnapper 2011: 105). Globalisation was not just about the economy, rather it had important political aspects, defined through 'global interdependence'. Thus, since events in one country had consequences across the planet, traditional respect for abusive national sovereignty did not apply anymore and military intervention was legitimate, provided a number of conditions were met (Blair 1999). But Blair reverted to tradition when he simultaneously claimed to see Britain effective as a 'bridge' between Europe and the USA (Hill 2001: 348, Gamble 2003), convinced as he was that British 'leadership in Europe' would pave the way for more influence in Washington and vice versa (Blair 1998, Wallace 2005). British participation in the invasion of Iraq in 2003 confirmed the priority given to the special relationship with the USA and the traditional power politics approach embraced by the Blair government behind the rhetoric about moral values and interdependence.

Attempts to provide a new narrative about Britain in the EU under New Labour also proved unsuccessful. Blair genuinely believed that a modern Britain should be a leader in Europe (Wall 2008, Blair 2010) although apparently without the need to consult with his European partners. But by the time he left power in 2007 Blair was disillusioned with the EU capacity to embrace the correct (neoliberal and open regionalist) economic reforms (Baker et al. 2002: 413–415). Ultimately he failed to fulfil his ambitions for Europe, which were in any case not shared by his successor Gordon Brown.

The Conservative/Liberal Democrat coalition government which took power in May 2010 did not attempt any major strategic rethink of Britain's role in the world, following on New Labour's footsteps. The National Security Strategy (NSS) published in October 2010 talked about globalisation in equally positive terms. The network of alliances in which Britain was involved followed a seemingly immutable order. The Conservatives (who controlled foreign policy) were returning to a traditional view of the special relationship epitomised by Margaret Thatcher. Indeed, 'liberal Conservatism' (Cameron 2006, Hague 2009) was close to Blair's doctrine of the 'international community', although Cameron was more cautious in his definition of conditions under which military intervention for humanitarian purpose was legitimate:

> First that we should understand fully the threat we face. Second, that democracy cannot quickly be imposed from outside. Third, that our strategy needs to go far beyond military action. Fourth, that we need a new multilateralism to tackle the new global challenges we face. And fifth, that we must strive to act with moral authority.
> (Cameron 2006)

Nevertheless, there was now an identifiable reborn liberal interventionist tradition in British foreign policy that defined the parameters of what was acceptable and unacceptable in British foreign policy (Daddow and Schnapper 2013).

Crucially, there has been no redefinition of Britain's role in the EU as a response to the possible decline/withdrawal of the USA and the growth of emerging economies as international actors. This clearly has to do with the importance of the choices embraced after 1945, by which British governments offset the end of the empire with influence in Washington, a continuation of what Gamble called 'Anglo-America', not a prize any government would easily abandon:

> Anglo-America is a political space constituted by wider economic, political, ideological and cultural relationships... It is a military alliance, a model of capitalism, a form of government, a global ideology and a popular culture... and has most recently been the site of the discourses and projects of globalisation and of the new world order.
>
> (Gamble 2003: 86)

The world in 2015 is very different not only from what it was during the Cold War with its tense but relatively (at least in Europe) stable bipolar structure, but also from what it was in the 1990s, when the USA appeared the sole 'hyperpower'. Atlanticism was a strategic and rational decision after 1945 and probably also in the uncertain period right after the end of the Cold War. The question is whether this preference is as relevant today as it was 20 years ago. The USA remains in relative decline – though still a hegemon – and is less interested in Europe, while the EU is weaker but still potentially influential in world affairs, both on its own or in partnership with the USA. There is a strong strategic case for more British engagement to strengthen the EU which contradicts recent trends towards more wariness towards the EU among both the British public and large proportions of the Conservative political elite. However, as we shall see, British attitudes towards Europe are hardening and the Conservative Party appears quite capable of initiating and leading separation from the EU if elected to govern in 2015.

Notes on theory and methodology

This is not a work of high theory, and we do not intend to engage in the specific testing of particular theories, but we do wish to share the normative underpinning of our analysis and our methods with students who read the book for pedagogical purposes.

Our work combines a number of theoretical approaches which vary according to the nature of the subject matter at hand. Our basic method is normative (value based) and qualitative in the form of comparative historical and institutional analysis, while employing the findings of quantitative political science where appropriate. In terms of schools of thought we draw heavily on historical institutionalism and 'new' comparative and historical political economy models.

Intergovernmentalism and historical institutionalism

With regard to theories of European integration, including the UK's place within it, we adopt a critical intergovernmentalist approach, arguing that a great deal of the past construction and ongoing maintenance of the EU/EZ edifice is based upon the actions of the heads of government and Council of Ministers/European Council working towards special treaty gatherings, supported and encouraged by the unelected European Commission. This process is, we believe, propelled by horse-trading between state elites attempting to preserve their own state's advantage in return for giving up (or resisting the loss of) sovereignty. This process has traditionally required the creation of 'grand coalitions', the most successful of which has been the recently weakened 'Franco–German alliance'. In this sense, the UK's infamously defensive posture is a noisy version of other member-states engaged in intense jockeying for national advantage.

Moravcsik is, in our view, the key figure in this approach to studying European integration. He argues that the 1987 Single European Act (SEA – signed in 1986 ratified in 1987) represented a watershed in the evolution of the European Community (EC) with the replacement of neofunctionalism with intergovernmentalism, exemplified by inter-state horse trading between France, Germany and Britain, made possible by a fortuitous coincidence of perceived national interests.

From this perspective, member-states seek to protect national interests first and foremost, placing limits on the erosion of national sovereignty unless a considerable strategic or economic gain can be made by sacrificing it (as with German's relinquishing of the Deutschmark for the Euro). According to Moravcsik, this intergovernmentalist turn accounts for the continued strategic power of intergovernmental institutions such as the Council of Ministers (Moravcsik 1991, 1993, 1998, Moga 2009: 800–803).

We also rely upon historical institutionalist, neo-institutionalist and state-centric research which suggests that the executive branches of the state and powerful economic elites close to it enjoy a considerable degree of autonomy from societal scrutiny and pressure over policy-making in the areas of 'high politics' considered vital to the survival of the state (Macartney 2011, Schmidt and Thatcher 2013). Our institutionalist approach relies on a sociological view of institutions observing the manner in which they interact with and affect society, influencing human behaviour through rules and norms, and tracing how institutions emerge in a particular manner within a given socio-economic context (Berger and Luckmann 2011). However, we would qualify the elite autonomy model in respect to the EU's long-running 'permissive consensus', which allowed considerable elite institutional decision making autonomy over the past 40 years. This has clearly weakened since 2009 in the face of the elite-driven solutions to the sovereign debt crisis centred on austerity, sovereign debt repayment and the forced restructuring of debtor economies, causing mass unemployment and widening inequality, with growing public and media suspicion of elite-led decision making and an associated rise of 'dissensus' (Hayward and Rüdiger 2012: 1–13).

We tend towards a normative view of institutionalism, meaning that actors are constrained and obligated by institutional rules, as opposed to rational choice institutionalism where actors are seen as engaging in a series of calculated actions designed to maximise perceived benefits. However, rational choice institutionalism is, we feel, useful when dealing with issues of regulatory capture and private market rent seeking. Finally, we subscribe to the usefulness of 'constructivist' or 'discursive institutionalism' which seeks to understand the role of ideas and discourse in politics (Hay 2006: 56–74, Schmidt 2008: 303–326). This is particularly relevant in the British context, where eurosceptic ideology has proved a powerful ideological counter-narrative to the federal discourse long prevailing in other member-states.[5]

We also accept the premise of constructivist theorists that identities and ideational factors pay an important role alongside material and organisational structures, rejecting 'bounded rationalism' where policymakers make rational choices, under conditions of uncertainty, based on utilitarian calculations (Christiansen et al. 2001, Hooghe and Marks 2008). Thus individual actors and social groups are seen as bound and motivated by shared values, norms and identities, especially neoliberal ones in economic affairs (Schmidt and Thatcher: 2013, Leuffen et al. 2013: 85).

In short, we consider that real world politics, whether in the UK or at the level of the EU, are governed by ideas and norms, as well as institutions and political processes (Hay 2002: 201). Working within this constructivist paradigm, Blyth et al. have demonstrated that ideas can provide the ideological tools necessary to mount successful challenges on existing institutional structures, especially during periods of crisis and war (Blyth et al. 2007: 748, see also Mirowski 2013).

As historical institutionalists we view state actors in European integration as constrained by short-term domestic considerations – electoral cycles, nationally based economic interests, the nature and historical development of political parties, etc. Thus while we agree that many of the difficulties that have arisen between the UK and the EU have been due to the commercial and service sector (especially financial) interests of the UK, we suggest that British euroscepticism has become increasingly detached from national strategic interests through a long process of intensive political radicalisation centred around nationalist concepts of sovereignty and independence and a post-Thatcher financialised hyperglobalist utopianism (Moravcsik 1998, Baker et al. 2002). This approach dovetails with Paul Pierson's seminal historical institutionalist model of path dependency in European integration, with his idea that states, like the UK, are often impacted in unanticipated ways by EU-level policies they have agreed to for entirely different purposes (Pierson 1998: 29–30, see also Pierson 2000, 2004).

Linked to the study of institutions, and human interactions within them, are the related concepts of 'path dependency' and 'positive feedback' (Lipset and Rokkan 1967, Pierson 2004: 17–53) based upon the tendency of institutions, once 'embedded' in political and/or socio economic systems, to become self-reinforcing and difficult to radically alter, let alone reverse. The particular timing and sequencing of events are also viewed by us as significant factors, cruelly apparent in the tragic chronology of the EZ crisis (Pierson 2004: 10–14).

Comparative and historical political economy

In our study of economic issues we employ two related strands of political economy. The first, termed 'new political economy', is based upon interdisciplinary social science and the second draws upon a more narrowly focused historically oriented tradition.

Most political economists accept the restrictions of a normative (value based) analysis and impute greater weight to impersonal economic structures and ideologies over assumed rational human agency (as aggregated through impersonal markets) to explain economic phenomena. From this perspective the present global economic crisis is seen as caused by the build up of a nexus of interrelated structural and ideological forces, beyond individual or aggregated free market control, summed up on one level by Keynes as 'Animal Spirits' (Blyth 2013, Gamble 2014).

In respect of the EZ sovereign debt crises, we argue that while powerful nation state actors and interests were responsible for setting up the deeply flawed Single Market and European Monetary Union (EMU) financial institutions, they did so under the deforming weight of the historical, ideological and institutional inertia of pre-existing political economy structures – especially the rise of financialised global investment markets, EU free movement and competition rules, and a growing mainland European neoliberal and ordoliberal economic orthodoxy, centred on the 'efficient markets hypothesis' (Dymski 2010: Section 6).

Our macroeconomic perspective also emerges from the progressive 'new political economy' (NPE) tradition seeking to combine elements of the approach of the classical political economists with more recent forms of analysis, drawn from across the social sciences via 'a historically contingent comparative analysis of particular state/market relationships' (Clift 2014). In Andrew Gamble's words:

> This new political economy spans several disciplines and many different literatures. Four of its key components in contemporary political science have developed as critiques of established literatures – international political economy (ipe), state theory, comparative government-industry relations, and public choice... [It] is prepared to make use of both institutionalist and rational choice analysis to make sense of the profound changes in the global economy and the state system which are currently taking place. It is also comparative, policy-oriented, and not confined to the analysis of one level of the world system.
>
> (1995: 516–517; see also Payne 2006)

We also draw upon historical political economy which complements the NPE approach, and is best exemplified by the Harvard historical political economist Charles Maier who suggests that:

> Political economy, in sum, regards economic ideas and behaviour not as frameworks for analysis, but as beliefs and actions that must themselves be explained. They are contingent and problematic; that is, they might have been different and they must be explained within particular political and social contexts. Historical political economy applies this approach to the study of the past.
>
> (Maier 1987: 6)

We also accept that all macroeconomic theorising is at root normative with facts/evidence and values/beliefs inextricably intertwined with the chosen methods, models and theories, including our own, and that this requires an understanding of the history of states and markets as 'contingent and problematic'.[6]

Outline

This book looks at the interplay and complex dynamic between the UK and the EU's political, economic and social crises. It throws light on the paradox that Britain is moving away from the EU, under pressure from eurosceptic parties and the press, at a time when British political and economic policy preferences have never been as influential in Europe – intergovernmentalism on the one hand and ordo/neoliberalism on the other are the increasingly dominant features of post-recession EU debate and policies.

In Chapter 1, we outline the development of the economic crisis in the EZ, going back to its origins in the deregulation of finance, and show how it has fuelled hostility towards the EU in Britain and, especially, in the countries of Southern Europe which were directly hit by the austerity measures imposed by the 'troika'. The consequence of the crisis on the balance of power within the EU is also analysed, with Germany emerging as the dominant power, supported by some Northern European member-states, while France is severely weakened and the UK is gradually excluding itself from the core EU.

Chapter 2 explores the paradox that this is happening in contrast with the previous decades where, in spite of a persistently sceptical rhetoric in London, British governments successfully defended what they defined as their national interests in the successive treaty and budget negotiations. They were able to build ad hoc coalitions at an EU level to achieve their goals and pursued them pragmatically – even under Margaret Thatcher, whatever her Conservative and UKIP heirs claim today. Since 2010 this is no longer the case, with the coalition government unwilling or unable to find allies in Europe and its partners no longer ready to accommodate increasingly unreasonable demands from the British government.

Explaining this evolution requires an understanding of the eurosceptic phenomenon and its ramifications in the UK, which we do in Chapter 3. It shows that euroscepticism, which used to be a fringe phenomenon, has now become more entrenched and more mainstream in Britain while also spreading to many other member-states. We nevertheless underline the specific features of the British post-imperialist and hyperglobalist rejection of the European project and map the positions of the main parties as well as their divisions on the issue. The ambiguities of public attitudes towards European integration are also stressed in this chapter.

Chapter 4 relates euroscepticism to the wider crisis in the British political system, illustrated by voters' disaffection with the political elites and representative institutions. Various symptoms of this include low turnout, the fragmentation of the party system, demands for referendums, growing North-South divisions, Scottish nationalism and the emergence of new parties on the political scene, especially but not only UKIP. Populist euroscepticism has been the possibly dangerous response to this disillusion with the domestic political system, especially with regard to immigration issues. Indeed, we argue that in the background to this crisis lie fears about globalisation and economic change such as are briefly mentioned above in this introduction.

Chapter 5 extends this analysis to the political crisis in the whole EU, which we connect to the state of domestic politics. We discuss the 'democratic deficit' in Europe and the end of the 'permissive consensus' which had enabled integration to proceed away from public opinion in the early decades. The 'constraining dissensus' (Hooghes and Marks 2009) which has replaced it has been exacerbated by the financial and economic crisis, with populist parties across the EU making gains in the European Parliament and voters rejecting several European treaties by referendum. It looks at attempts to reduce this gap and politicise the European debates and explains why they have mostly failed.

Finally, Chapter 6 looks more closely at the way the economic crisis in the EU has increased europhobia in the UK. It looks at the way British elites have responded to the crisis and the shifts it has provoked within the EU, and then at the traditions of British exceptionalism and the increasing domination of the hyperglobalist discourse in the public debate. This explains the self-defeating aggressive attitude of the Cameron government in Brussels and ultimately the risk that Britain could leave the EU in the future.

1
The Political Economy of the Eurozone Crisis

We begin with the wider context of our study, the economic crisis of the EU, since many of the recently heightened political and institutional problems relating to the UK which we cover elsewhere in the book have been exacerbated by the EZ's economic crisis. We look at how it unfolded and how, in well under a decade, a Europe of growth and growing prosperity was replaced by one of insolvent banks, austerity, mass unemployment, street protests and sluggish or negative growth. Together this has encouraged the growth of negative attitudes towards the EU, expressed as political extremism, and (especially in the UK) euroscepticism and hostility towards federalism, as well as reigniting the 'German question' – how to curb the excessive influence of a state too powerful for its geopolitical context (Stevens 2014). Jean Monnet famously remarked that 'Europe will be forged in crises, and will be the sum of the solutions adopted for those crises', but it is doubtful that he envisaged such a traumatic and dangerous crisis, or such a Germanic solution (Bergsten and Kierkegaard 2012: 1).

The meltdown of the global economy in 2007–2008 sparked by the subprime lending disaster in the USA and transmitted globally by the seizing up of the interbank lending system was the product of a number of intersecting factors. These included the under regulation of increasingly globalised finance; lax credit facilities which encouraged high-risk 'smart' investments with associated excessive high-risk borrowing and lending; dangerous trade imbalances both within the EU and internationally; real-estate bubbles which European banks became major players in funding; and insufficient non-financial economic growth and questionable policy choices relating to government revenues and expenses.

The EZ's sovereign debt crisis, which began in 2010, represents the second stage of this global financial meltdown, bringing with it serious repercussions for the EZ and EU. This secondary crisis arose from the transfer of private debt into public debt on an enormous scale as all member-states, but especially the weaker EZ economies, sought to bail out their bankrupt banks and service rising interest payments on their pre-existing sovereign loans while interest rates rose to penal levels. Global hedge funds and investment banks responded to perverse incentives in financial markets by refusing to purchase the government bonds of the debtor states, in part to raise interest rate returns on future loans and in part to force sovereign defaults in order to claim Credit Default Swap insurance payments (Blyth 2013: 78–93). Thus, as one shrewd commentator ruefully observed of the EMU system, 'the euro's architecture makes bond markets master of national governments' (Palley 2013: 43).

This secondary impact of the wider global Great Recession also undermined the community solidarity of member-states, creating a 'beggar my neighbour' negotiating stance and, through harsh austerity measures, led to the geographically and socially selective impoverishment of millions of EU citizens, while capital flight protected and even enriched their wealthy fellows, ensuring that many definitely didn't feel that they were 'all in it together'. The huge costs of bailing out unrepentant banks and unappreciative debtor states also outraged Northern European taxpayers in particular. Meanwhile, in the debtor states fierce anger exploded onto the streets aimed against those foreigners and their local proxies who had forced their countries into bearing the burden of paying down sovereign debt, at the cost of haemorrhaging of jobs, housing and social provisions and selling off of state assets. Finally, the crisis accelerated economic migration across the EU, with the UK in the front line of this process, provoking widespread anger in local communities subject to competition for low-paid jobs, housing, education and social provision (Ford and Goodwin 2014: 141–182).

The initial response of the EU authorities was to continue to pump increased capital and liquidity to the insolvent national private banking systems, while enforcing ever deeper austerity on the debtor states imposed through the 'troika' (Commission, IMF and ECB) in exchange for bail-out loans (Krugman 2012, Blyth 2013, Fazi 2014). Austerity measures included state cutbacks, shedding labour to restructure the economy, selling off state assets and privatising the economy and reductions in pensions and state welfare entitlements. This led to unprecedented levels of unemployment in the debtor states, reducing tax takes, helping to further transform an insolvent private banking crisis to a sovereign debt crisis. The weaker EZ economies (Portugal, Ireland, Italy, Greece,

Spain, the so-called PIIGS, joined later by Cyprus) were unable to borrow by selling sovereign bonds in global markets to service their debts because of high interest rates with credit-rating agencies downgrading their ratings. PIIGS came close to default and were forced to seek loans from the emergency funds administered by the 'troika', the quid pro quo for which was further austerity measures, creating further mass unemployment, and further undermining social welfare provisions, so further reducing the tax take (Patomaki 2012: 28–56, Fazi 2014: 1–37).

At best the EU's response appeared sluggish, fragmented and fractious, based on improvisations agreed in closed and sometimes secret meetings, with leaders of the weaker economies reduced to pawns in an EZ game dictated by Germany and its proxy instrument, the 'troika'. The European Parliament (EP) was also sidelined with decisions made by unelected officials, finance ministers and heads of the most powerful states reinforcing long-running perceptions of a deepening democratic deficit, with remote officials running the EU/EZ, with Germany, 'the paymaster of Europe' calling the shots, whilst itself profiting the most from the EZ and single-market rules. The crisis had also awoken powerful forces in Germany pushing for a fully federalised core EZ to stabilise the fiscal and monetary systems, preventing a recurrence of this economic imbroglio and (they assumed) restoring the steady growth of prosperity on which the EU depended for legitimacy.

Crucially, as we develop in the following chapters, the crisis also opened up even greater economic and political distance between the EU and the UK, further emboldening British eurosceptics and silencing pro-EU sentiments, threatening to tip the UK into leaving the EU entirely, or at best drive it further towards the outer circle of semi-detached membership for decades to come (Baker and Schnapper 2012, Geddes 2013: 252–260, Marsh 2013: 102–107).

Anglo-American debt-led financialisation was, of course, deeply implicated in the EZ debt crisis, by creating what Warren Buffet referred to as 'financial instruments of mass destruction' which, along with excessive risk taking and easy rewards infected the European banking system to its core (Buffet 2002, Blyth 2013: 21–56). In the wake of the banking and sovereign debt crises the EU, along with the USA, was the most indebted economic bloc. In the first financial quarter of 2013, government debt in the 17 states in the EZ reached a record average of 92.2% of GDP despite large-scale austerity measures. Total debt stood at $11.4 trillion (8.75 trillion euro), rising from 8.34 trillion euro in 2012, a rise of 4.0% year-on-year (Eurostat 2013). And herein lay the roots of the present crisis.

The Eurozone: A crisis waiting to happen

The causes which underlie the crisis in the EU rest upon a number of political, ideological and institutional pillars, stretching back to the early 1980s with the 'Paris Consensus', which launched an insidious process of political and institutional path dependency which has propelled the EU/EZ into a long-term crisis from which they show little sign of emerging (Gamble 2014). The chief causes centre on a number of interlinked processes: the flawed institutional architecture of the euro system itself, creating monetary without fiscal union, and lacking a state lender in the last resort; the 'neoliberalisation' of the EU's economic integration process which ignored the increasing exposure of European banks to global market practices; and since the crisis a slavish adherence to an ordoliberal austerity solution and the amplification of the already adverse terms of trade between most of Europe and the neo-Mercantilist German economy.

High-risk speculative financialisation (casino capitalism) spread throughout the mainland European banks via an insidious mechanism in which the euro system reduced the weaker states' borrowing costs almost to German levels, encouraging reckless lending of surplus capital by northern European commercial banks via the purchase of high-risk sovereign debt bonds in the southern EZ states and funding their inflated private property markets, while cross-investing in high-risk subprime 'assets' and other 'innovative' financial assets (CDS, CEOs, etc.) through the 'Repo Markets' in London and New York. In short, risky secondary bank-to-bank borrowing on short contracts lent over longer periods at higher rates of interest (Blyth 2013: 78–86, Palley 2013: 33–41).

This led to the development of massively over-leveraged European banking conglomerates and regional banks, which became individually and collectively 'too big to bail' across the EZ, as Mark Blyth explains:

> The top two German banks had assets equal to 114 percent of German GDP. In 2011, these figures were 245 percent and 117 percent, respectively. Deutsche Bank alone had an asset footprint of over 80 percent of German GDP and runs an operational leverage of around 40 to 1... The top four UK banks have a combined asset footprint of 394 percent of UK GDP. The top three Italian banks constitute a mere 115 percent of GDP... In the periphery states the situation is no better. Local banks weren't going to miss out on the same trade, so they bought their own sovereign debt by the truckload... No sovereign,

even with its own printing press, can bail out a bank with exposures of this magnitude.

(Blyth 2013: 82–83)

In the immediate aftermath of the global crash this caused a huge rise in public debt as Germany refused to allow an EZ-wide funded bail-out, fearing 'moral hazard' would occur if individual states did not stand by their national banks. In the USA the fully federal system ensured that the weaker states like Wyoming were partly bailed out by the tax dollars of the strongest states, such as California and Texas. In contrast, weaker European states were forced to bail out their own banks by borrowing at rapidly rising rates to pay off their creditors, so transferring private debt into *national* public debt.

Contrary to the standard myth that the levels of EU-wide public (sovereign) debt were largely due to years of state mismanagement, corruption and excessive expenditure, much of the sovereign debt was actually the result of this necessary bailing out of the private banks. Thus, as Krugman and Layard suggest: 'the large government deficits we see today are a consequence of the crisis, not its cause' (Krugman and Layard 2012: 63). The one clear exception is Greece where state corruption and profligacy added greatly to rapidly rising private debt and bank malpractices (Blyth 2013: 62–73). The widespread political and electoral success of this false premise, which turns a manifest crisis of private debt into a simple trope of profligate state spending and management, was described by Mark Blyth as the 'greatest bait and switch [misdirection trick] in modern history' (2013: 73–74).

The fatally flawed architecture of the EMU created a European Central Bank (ECB) forbidden (through Germany's insistence) to act as a true lender of last resort. In addition, falling borrowing costs occurred across all the EZ states because they were now valued in line with the strength of the German economy, encouraged German and French commercial banks to lend to banks and investors in the increasingly less competitive southern EZ states. These states set about employing the funds to artificially inflate their economies, consuming German goods, building grand projects and, in the case of Ireland and Spain, stoking property booms. With interest rates across the EZ converging, investors and private individuals in PIIGS were able to borrow from northern commercial banks at low interest rates often to buy German goods and expertise. This in turn boosted the German export-led economy much more than a higher valued Deutschmark would have permitted. Finally, these fatally interwoven developments secured for Germany (whether it sought it or not) first economic supremacy and, after the global collapse of 2008, political hegemony over the EU and its future direction.

The EZ banking system is perceived by many EU leaders and officials as too big to bail-out a second time. Another banking collapse, whether precipitated by a state leaving the Euro or another external financial shock, could take the still indebted and overleveraged German and French banks and therefore the whole system down with it. Hence the huge pressures applied to PIIGS to rapidly put their houses in order and reduce their sovereign debt levels, through the strict application of 'Sado-Monetarist' solutions. They were informed that to default and leave the EZ would be catastrophic for their economic growth and social cohesion (Blyth 2013: Ch. 3, Marsh 2013: Ch. 6, Fazi 2014: Ch. 4).

As Heikki Patomäki has observed:

> The difficulties facing the European Monetary Union have been primarily caused by the asymmetries in the formation of overall demand in the European political economy as a whole, and also by the institutional arrangements and restrictions that were put in place by the Maastricht Treaty. Global financial markets have intensified these difficulties by first causing the 2008–09 financial crisis, and then by dramatically increasing the costs of debt of the worst-hit countries.
> (Patomäki 2013: 79)

Patomäki's reference to the impact of global financial markets refers to those hedge and other 'vulture funds' which engaged in speculative attacks on PIIGS, and cynically loaded up with their public debt in anticipation of debt failure, thereby collecting insurances they had taken out to protect against this, in the full knowledge that the insolvent countries couldn't escape by devaluing currencies inside the EZ. On top of this the deeply flawed EZ financial architecture institutionalised a situation in which the member-states remain locked into an uncomfortably high-value euro currency largely dictated by the powerful low wage, high productivity, high capital value, export-orientated German economy, so further reducing the competitiveness of their goods and services and increasing the costs of servicing their huge debts (Palley 2013: 42).

A potential economic 'death spiral' of stagnation and deflation has been reinforced by a series of 'rescue' bail-outs by the 'troika' made contingent upon the imposition of harsher and harsher levels of austerity, which has impoverished many vulnerable citizens and led to further capital flight and falling tax takes, weakening economies still further and leading to years of negative, or at best stagnant, growth (Patomäki 2012: 57–81, Blyth 2013: 82–93, Palley 2013: 33–45). The causes of this sorry turn of events have been succinctly summarised by Dyson:

> The result of this process...was an EMU project that Europeanized German monetary power on strict Ordoliberal conditions ... from the outset, the asymmetry between economic and monetary union added to the sense of a precarious imbalance at the heart of the project. It was vulnerable to asymmetric shocks, to cross-national banking crises, to fiscal indiscipline and to divergences in competitiveness [between its member-states]. Monetary union [also] lacked the supportive infrastructure of a political union.
> (Dyson 2012: 197)

The sense of interstate solidarity and shared European purpose was undermined by the creation of clear winners (creditor states) and losers (debtor states) while exacerbating differences within the Franco–German alliance (as France struggled to endorse German solutions which undermine its own free market economic position). It also revealed Germany's growing position as the unrivalled hegemon within the EZ/EU. As Paterson suggests, the crisis has 'made Germany much more of an awkward partner, much less able to operationalise the Franco–German relationship to deal with the Eurocrisis...Chancellor Merkel has increasingly stressed the Franco–German relationship, but this emphasis remains more at the level of presentation than substance' (Patterson in Hayward and Wurzel 2012: 247).

Equally damaging, Germany and other creditor states view the debtors as profligate, lazy, inefficient and hooked on support from the creditor's tax payers. In response, many in the debtor states see their former European partners as little more than self-interested dictators, profiteering from their misfortunes and allowing their own wealthy citizens to export their wealth abroad and buy up former state assets at ultra-low prices.

Solidarity has also been fractured within the debtor states, distancing themselves from Greece, as well as selectively from each other. Several states, Ireland in particular, vie to be the poster child for the success of austerity, claiming to have successfully restructured their economies and become 'competitive' again; while others, especially Greece, but also Italy and Spain, chafe against the destruction of their social solidarity under austerian measures, which they see as destroying their societies and threatening the future prosperity of all Europe. In July 2011,

Italian Finance Minister Giulio Tremonti observed that creditor states, by demanding unreasonable levels of austerity, were risking becoming first-class passengers on the Titanic (Dyson 2012: 193).

The Eurozone crisis: An analytical chronology

The EZ crisis developed in two overlapping periods. The first, although stretching back to the foundations of the EC, began in earnest with the signing of the Maastricht Treaty in 1992, formalising the 'road map to Monetary Union' and ended with the EU's initially sluggish response to the global economic meltdown of 2007–2008; the second phase began in 2009 with serious attention being paid to bailing out the European banking sector, and shifted up another gear in 2010 with the appearance of the sovereign debt crisis in the EZ. This second phase has been marked by a mixture of crisis management and austerity applied inside the EZ and wider moves in the EU to transfer to a still ongoing 'more Europe' solution.

Phase one: From Maastricht to Meltdown

A full currency union always represented the Holy Grail for committed European federalists, representing the last and arguably most significant building block in an ongoing teleological process designed to propel Europe towards a prosperous fully federal state and economic super power. Thus, Article 2 of the Treaty of Rome made explicit the long-term goal:

> The Community shall have as its task, by establishing a common market and progressively approximating the economic policies of member states'. [Privileging] the free movement of persons, services, goods and capital...The market being based on the principle of free competition, the Treaty prohibits restrictive agreements and state aids...whose objective is to prevent, restrict or distort competition.
> (Treaty of Rome 1957 non-consolidated version)

Thus, from the outset long-term economic principles privileging neoliberal market forces over the social market economy and neo-Keynesian 'embedded liberalism' of the original 'cooperative capitalist' Europe were deeply embedded in EC, EEC and EU rules and statutes.

In the quest to achieve a working currency union, a series of monetary systems, all unsuccessful, were put in place from the early 1970s by EEC and EU policy-makers, mainly 'currency snakes' superseded by 'currency snakes in tunnels'. The Franco-German alliance remained convinced throughout of the necessity for further economic and monetary integration and at the Bremen summit in 1978 a European Monetary System (EMS) and linked Exchange Rate Mechanism (ERM) with the European Currency Unit (Ecu) was devised and launched in 1979. This architecture was designed to achieve monetary stability and currency harmony in order to prepare for full-blown Economic and Monetary Union. A prophetic warning of the dangers for weaker economies in such a system was offered by the disastrous events of Black Wednesday (16 September 1992) when the pound sterling was forced from the ERM as the pound fell below its lower limit in the ERM, allowing currency speculator George Soros to make over £1 billion by short selling sterling and costing the Exchequer over £3 billion in a futile attempt to defend the pound (Tempest 2005).

Nevertheless a majority of member-states signed up for full EMU with a single currency in 1993 through the Maastricht Treaty, coordinating member-state economic policies and inter-regional exchanges. The need for a parallel fiscal (tax) union was raised, but because of issues relating to loss of sovereignty any action was postponed (a classic case of intergovernmentalist non-decision-making). The 'Euro' currency was born on 1 January 1999, with coinage and notes issued two years later (Stephens 1996, Geddes 2013: 178–180). Unsurprisingly the British (along with the Danes) opted out of the third currency merging stage of the EMU at Maastricht in 1993, the ramifications of which will be explored below (Geddes 2013: 73–76).

David Marsh suggests that the grand design of the euro brought together four related political and economic strategies. First, to promote greater harmony between the old rivals for EU supremacy, France and Germany. Second, to further free up the Single Market that had hitherto stymied cross-border trade and investment. Third, to create a strong and stable European currency that would challenge the dollar for global supremacy, ending the dollar's inbuilt economic advantage as the global reserve currency. Fourth, replacing the Bundesbank with the European Central Bank and dissolving the Deutschmark within the euro to curb once and for all the potentially overweening power of the German economy, harnessing its power to the general needs of the European Union (Marsh 2013: 14–17). This was carried out in parallel with further developments to the Single Market designed to reduce transfer costs and make cross-border trade largely 'frictionless' as in the US federal economy, so reinforcing the socio-economic homogeneity and efficiency of trade and commerce within the EU.

Angela Merkel famously asserted that the euro was always much more than just a matter of unifying Europe's currency and, in a classic neofunctionalist manoeuvre, 'the euro house was assembled from the roof downwards: intent on speedy completion, the builders planned to reinforce the foundations later on' (Marsh 2013: 15). But fundamental economic institutions are not so easily designed top down. As Michael Mann observed:

> The fundamental weakness is not economic but political, for the Union lacks a coherent political mechanism for implementing effective economic policy. There is a European Central Bank but there is no single Treasury to apply fiscal as well as monetary discipline and to make fiscal transfers to depressed areas, as nation-states can do. To develop a true Treasury would improve the ability of Europe to weather future crises, but this implies more federalism and the last two decades have revealed fierce popular opposition to deepening the Union.
> (Mann 2013: 353)

Phase two: The sovereign debt crisis

Once the sovereign debt crisis broke across the EZ in 2009–2010 the flawed design of the euro was starkly revealed, acting like a foreign currency outside the control of any component nation, or for that matter any supranational authority, including the ECB. Its ordoliberal advocates had described it as 'denationalised money' mandated to be free of government influence, deliberately modelled after the German Bundesbank. But whereas the Bundesbank was in charge of a powerful rule-bound, efficient, highly capitalised, high savings, low wage, export-orientated economy, the euro was spread across a variety of European capitalisms, none of which mirrored German capitalism and some of which were economically backwards and politically corrupt.

Once the crisis broke the ECB was unable to regulate levels of liquidity and interest rates on global capital markets by engaging in purchases of government bonds, thus applying 'quantitative easing' to take pressure off the struggling parts of the EZ economies and when the possibility of breaking such rules was raised, German ordoliberals overruled such moves (Marsh 2013: 31–33). One leading Spanish monetary official put it succinctly:

> Countries that join a monetary union lose more than one instrument of monetary policy. They also lose their capacity to issue debt in a

currency over which they have full control, so that they issue debt in a kind of foreign currency... For the Spanish government can no longer ask or force the Bank of Spain to buy government debt because it does not control that institution... Therefore, it suffers a liquidity crisis; that is, it cannot obtain funds to roll over its debt at reasonable interest rates.

(Marsh 2013: 34)

The EZ system acted like the early 20th century Gold Standard, where weaker member economies enjoy initial gains which are soon reversed by their inability to compete with the stronger economies in the system, suffering runs on their currencies while the system locks in austerity as the only 'cure' whilst inside the system (Blyth 2013: 180–185).

Marsh speaks of 'five mutually reinforcing miscalculations' in the construction of the EMU. First, the ECB's exclusive focus on achieving a 2% overall EZ inflation target ignored the instability of private European banks. Second, a belief that a 'one size fits all' monetary policy would avoid any asymmetrical distribution of winners and losers was fatally flawed. Third, uniting national economies with different levels of prices and productivity under one fixed exchange-rate currency system greatly exacerbated pre-existing differences in competitiveness, which increased to around 30% between Germany and the southern European economy's by 2009. Fourth, by allowing low-cost borrowing across Euro-based economies with a mixture of large current account surpluses and deficits (in effect accepting the neoliberal assumption that deficits and surpluses would be self-financing and self-regulating). The net result was to generate major surpluses for the already surplus countries, especially Germany, and after the collapse the burden of readjustment in the system was chiefly offloaded onto the deficit states. Fifth, the ECB was confined by its ordoliberal statutes to limiting public debt and budget deficits, ignoring the exponential growth in private sector debt with disastrous consequences (Marsh 2013: 39–40).

Prior to the advent of the euro, a trade deficit in the weaker states would have led to currency depreciation, making exports more competitive, while a surplus in the more powerful economies would have caused currency inflation, making their exports less competitive and imports from the less efficient economies cheaper, so helping to avoid continually rising or falling deficits and surpluses. But this safety valve disappeared under the EMU (Fazi 2014: 76).

The system also encouraged 'beggar-thy-neighbour' neo-Mercantilist responses, where an efficient country that trades heavily with other less competitive states in the currency system can achieve huge economic gains, if in so doing it deprives them of significant market shares in EU and/or global trade.

Thus, by creating monetary union without a proper fiscal and economic union to balance it, member-states were effectively pitted one against the other in a manner which naturally favoured Germany (Fazi 2014: 76–77). The euro also allowed Germany to experience a lower currency valuation than under the Deutschmark making its goods and services more competitive (and German industrial exports have the lowest price elasticities in the world), while the surpluses which accumulated in the German banking system as a result of this process were lent back to the less efficient southern states, some of which went to purchase desirable high-status German goods, or to speculate in bubble housing markets.

Most Germans were outraged at the debtor states profligacy, considering their country's relative success to be due to a mixture of prudent savings, high investment levels and sensible labour reforms (wage cuts and harder working conditions, for guaranteed jobs introduced by the Social Democrats in the early 2000s). However, Germany's export-led growth was equally reliant upon the relative lack of serious competitors in the euro system, plus German- and French-funded credit-fuelled booms of the debtor states, in conjunction with the usefully low (for the Germans) value of the euro under the EMU (Fazi 2014: 76–78, Blyth 2013: 75–78).

In the end the EZ survived the initial onslaught. Even Greece remained in the currency union. By the end of 2013, Wolfgang Schäuble, the powerful German Finance Minister, was in Europhoric mood: 'The world should rejoice at the positive economic signals the Eurozone is sending almost continuously these days. While the crisis continues to reverberate, the Eurozone is clearly on the mend both structurally and cyclically' (Schäuble 2013).

However, as Peet and La Guardia suggest, 'the euro's is a story of survival, not success'. Savage austerity has taken its toll and by the end of 2014 the EZ growth figures still showed only slow growth in some states and stagnation in others, while many banks remain relatively weak. Debt deflation and mass unemployment still haunt several of the debtor states and sovereign debt to GDP ratios have remained stubbornly high. The dangerous asymmetry of the crisis of the EU/EZ remains embedded in the system, dividing north from south in particular and the markets may yet call Mario Draghi's bluff on 'doing whatever it takes' to support the euro if the economic situation deteriorates in Italy or Greece.

Solutions become problems

Many critics of Europe's sluggish and piecemeal response to the crisis point to the role of ordoliberalism as the economic orthodoxy underpinning the monetary integration process since the late 1980s, set within the Anglo-American inspired process of Single Market neoliberalisation over the same period, including an uncritical acceptance of global financialisation.[1]

From this perspective, the foundations of the original global banking crisis and (after a brief flirtation with interventionist neo-Keynesianism) its subsequent attempted resolution have been conditioned by neoliberal/ordoliberal ideas, institutions and policy prescriptions. For instance, the halting pace of crisis management and rule-bound responses to the European sovereign debt crisis, combined with the application of rigid austerity to the debtor states, is closely associated with the orthodoxy of German ordoliberalism.

Until relatively recently the triumph of 'ordo' and 'neoliberal' economic ideas and policies over the European state-centred 'social market' model, which occurred from the 1970s onwards, was neglected by scholars, an omission fully corrected in studies by Huw Macartney (2011 and 2013) and Palley (2013), Mann (2013), Fazi (2014) and in edited volumes by Schmidt and Thatcher (2013) and van Apeldoorn et al. (2009).

Ironically, given the assumed hostility to Anglo-American neoliberalism in all its forms within the EU, much of the neoliberal momentum behind the EMU and the post-crisis austerity regime of the troika has been led by mainland European federalists from France, Italy and Belgium, with Germany leading the powerful Ordoliberal variant (Van Apeldoorn et al. 2009, Blyth 2012, Lapavitsas 2012, Macartney 2012, Zacune 2013, Fazi 2014).

The popular belief that French economic preferences naturally cluster around state planning (*dirigisme*) centred on control of key industries including transportation, energy and telecommunications, with state incentives to banks and private corporations to merge or undertake strategic projects, ignores the evidence that leading French politicians and officials played a vital role in the neoliberalisation of the EU and EZ (Schmidt 2008b, Clift 2006, *passim*). Mitterrand's Socialist administration, elected in 1981, began by attempting to regulate capital flows, along with sweeping statist economic reforms, but under pressure from global markets affected a U-turn from 1983 onwards with the *tournant de la rigueur* (austerity turn) in which the fight against inflation was prioritised, partly to remain competitive in the EMS and partly to appease speculators against the Franc. From 1985 onwards policies of financial deregulation were also brought forward including the liberalisation of most capital transactions (Abdelal 2007: 58–64).

In 1985, Jacques Delors, the Socialist economics and finance minister, became president of the European Commission, bringing his nascent 'third way' views on capital movements. An economist who occupied a series of posts with the Banque de France and as finance minister protected France's membership of the EMS by giving priority to monetary stability over state investment, Delors was a prime mover in the successful transfer of 'light-touch' (i.e. ineffective) capital controls to an EU level, making it a central component of the fledgling European Single Market project through his *Delors Report*. Thus, the British were not the main driving force behind market liberalisation, although they strongly supported Delors' efforts. Indeed, Margaret Thatcher reluctantly approved of Delors' appointment to head the Commission because she understood him to be neoliberal on economic affairs (Mudge 2007: 222).

Like Blair, at the domestic level Delors fostered the neoliberal financialised 'counter-revolution 'in the form of the 'Paris Consensus', laying down the basis of a highly neoliberalised European financial system (Fazi 2014: 24). As Abdelal puts it: 'This new definition of the European [was] itself the engine of free capital's spread on the world stage... Global financial markets are global primarily because the processes of European financial integration became open and uniformly liberal' (Abdelal 2007: 84–85). A number of other influential neoliberals were involved at the heart of the construction of the internal market and monetary union including Michel Camdessus, 'the uber-liberal' head of the Bank of France (1984–1987), who moved on to head the IMF (1987–2000), and Henri Chavranski, who chaired the OECD's Committee on Capital Movement and Invisible Transactions from 1982 to 1994 (Fazi 2014: 25).[2]

Macartney suggests that while elements of Anglo-American neoliberalism partly repelled German and French leaders by promoting shareholder value, welfare austerity, short termist foreign and finance-led investment and accumulation, nevertheless a strong current of market liberalisation ran through elites in both countries in the face of spreading globalised market opportunities and competition, plus the apparent success of the Anglo-American heartlands during the 1990s under globalisation encouraging the growth of powerful investment banking lobbies in both countries (Macartney 2012: 3–15).

Macartney refers to a 'common sense' neoliberal mindset which limits the parameters of investigation and debate surrounding global and EU financialisation, pervading the discourse of powerful politicians, EU bureaucrats, central bankers and finance market practitioners (Macartney 2011: 20–23). He also points to the 'embedded intellectual' capture of policy-making in the EU/EZ educated in the narrow, elite world of leading economists and business studies academics, exposed to welfare economics and the efficient markets hypothesis during periods spent in the world's leading university departments of economics and business studies, many of them located in the USA and the UK. This intellectual or 'epistemic' community of like-minded and closely networked experts and advisors holds to a variegated neoliberal causal model of finance capitalism and the superiority of free markets over state interventions, based upon a common set of (in Germany ordoliberal) beliefs and values (Macartney 2011: Ch. 6–7).

With regard to the exact forms of neoliberalism adopted by the EU/EZ, van Apeldoorn correctly suggests that:

> the neoliberalism that triumphed was not the orthodox neoliberalism that, at least as an ideological project, had become hegemonic in the Anglo-Saxon capitalist heartland, but rather a more continental European-style neoliberalism that became articulated with a 'modernised' social democratic discourse (as in the 'Third Way' discourse of the 1990s...) while also seeking to address the concerns of that part of European capital in need of a more pro-active, though not necessarily protectionist, role of the state.
>
> (Apeldoorn 2009: 24)

Ordoliberalism is the powerful legalistic neoclassical economic orthodoxy which has underpinned Germany's approach to the creation of the EMU and its reaction to the subsequent sovereign debt crisis. Literally, 'order-liberalism' or 'rule-liberalism' is carried out under *Ordnungspolitik* (literally regulatory politics or policy). Economic discourse in Germany is dominated by this approach, to the virtual exclusion of alternatives. However, as Dullien and Guérot (2012) argue, it represents more than a morbid obsession with 1920s hyperinflation, or a convenient excuse to bolster German national interests by profiting from its comparative neo-Mercantilist trading advantage inside the EZ. Instead it represents sincerely held beliefs stemming from an academic tradition dating back to the 1930s in the writings of economists and legal scholars from the 'Freiburg School', including Eucken, Böhm, Grossmann-Doerth and Miksch. Ptak has demonstrated that ordoliberalism also represents a German offshoot of neoliberalism, linked directly to the Mont Pèlerin Society (Ptak 2009: 124–125). Padgett defines ordoliberalism as follows:

> A central tenet of ordo-liberalism is a clearly defined division of labor in economic management, with specific responsibilities assigned to particular institutions. Monetary policy should be the responsibility of a central bank committed to monetary stability and low inflation, and insulated from political pressure by independent status. Fiscal policy – balancing tax revenue against government expenditure – is the domain of the government, whilst macro-economic policy is the preserve of employers and trade unions.
> (Padgett 2003: 126–127, see also Dyson 2001: 141)

The core of ordoliberalism as embodied in a belief that governments must regulate markets to ensure that they approximate to perfect competition – creating an ordered sphere in which the efficient market hypothesis becomes a reality, to be achieved through sound monetary policy and the outlawing of cartels and monopolies. In contrast, Anglophone neoliberalism is more or less unconcerned with cartels and monopolies due to blind faith in the automatic correction tendencies embodied in the efficient market hypothesis (Dullien and Guérot 2012: 2). This is a feature which makes their beliefs inconsistent with 19th and early 20th centuries neoclassical economics which was critical of monopoly tendencies in capitalism (Crouch 2009: 388–389).

Where ordoliberalism does coincide with mainstream neoliberalism is in its rigid preference for 'supply side' economics, as against state intervention to apply expansionary demand stimuli to markets. Output and employment are viewed as largely dictated by supply factors of production, capital, profit and investment. Both creeds also share a preference for driving down wages and conditions of work in order to achieve 'competitiveness', a holy grail of both ordo and neoliberalism. However, in the ordoliberal case this end is achieved through statutory enforced arbitration in the national interest (the law on collective bargaining in Germany is a paradigm example). Ordoliberals are cautious with regard to neoliberal financialisation, since strict monetary stability is traded away for speculative credit and debt-fuelled booms and busts, and investment channelled away from concrete productive capacity.

Ordoliberalism is subsumed within German neoclassical economics and consequently is seldom employed as a term in German academia; nevertheless its pervasive influence explains why recent German governments under Angela Merkel have reacted to the global banking collapse and subsequent sovereign debt crisis by appearing overcautious, uncompassionate, rigid, moralistic and legalistic, frustrating their EU partners and the USA too. One of Merkel's favourite dictums is 'step-by-step' (Peet and La Guardia 2014: 178). Many leading members of the German Finance ministry are lawyers rather than economists, adding to the rule-governed elements of ordoliberalism. In response to the moralising of German officials concerning the moral hazard of bailing out bankrupt states, Mario Monti is said to have quipped that in Germany 'economics is a branch of moral philosophy' (Peet and La Guardia 2014: 156).

It also explains Merkel's ruling out of the use of Eurobonds to stabilise the debtor nations borrowing costs and resisting calls for the ECB to become the lender of last resort, as with the Federal Reserve and the Bank of England. In both cases this was viewed as inviting moral hazard by letting the debtor nations off lightly and giving a blank bail-out cheque towards future profligacy by the debtor states. Merkel exemplifies the ordoliberal politician, 'analytical, cautious, mistrustful' but she also viewed the crisis through East German eyes having witnessed the collapse of the Soviet system (Kornelius 2013: 220 and 228).

Ordoliberal preferences were evident in the outcome of the crucial December 2011 European summit on long-term strategies for dealing with bank and sovereign debt crises. This ruled out the ECB as the last resort lender and Eurobonds, and a 'Fiscal Compact' was created which, once signed into national and EU law, compels all members of the EZ to impose a debt limit modelled upon the German *Schuldenbremse* system. Equally, the ECB was formally forbidden from using its funds to directly bolster the newly created European Financial Stability Facility (EFSF) and European Stability Mechanism (ESM). Finally it was stipulated that bail-out loans should only be offered at above market rates and subject to the harshest austerity measures in return. Subsequent manoeuvres by Mario Draghi, the new head of the ECB, have seen back-door methods for getting around these restrictions, such as the quasi-bond buying Securities Markets Programme (SMP) and, in February 2012, the larger round of ECB loans to European banks entitled the Long Term Refinancing Operation (LTRO), employed with some success. However, core legal and German political barriers still stand in the way of full-scale quantitative easing and debt burden sharing.

The German solution was also revealed in the speed and ferocity of the application of austerity measures to the insolvent PIIGS. Ordoliberal theory insists that *only* deep and painful cuts in public expenditure and the rapid elimination of low-productivity jobs and corruption can achieve the budget consolidation necessary to restore market equilibrium and growth (as applied under entirely different circumstances and with huge inward investment monies in East Germany after reunification). Any failure to achieve these necessary ends is viewed by many German politicians and officials in terms of weakness and lack of will on the part of local political elites. Similar ordoliberal supply-side arguments insist that if wages fall rapidly and sufficiently under austerity, 'competitiveness' will eventually be restored and growth resume, with no equivalent regard for falling tax takes, and loss of demand for goods and services (Dullien and Guérot 2012: 4–5).

As we suggested above, the ordo/neoliberalisation of the EU economic system began long before the sovereign debt crisis. The deeply flawed monetary and fiscal institutions and rules for the EMU created at Maastricht, and since, bear a powerful German stamp. For instance, the primary objective of the European Central Bank (Article 2 of the Statute of the ECB) is to maintain price stability within the EZ. Indeed, the 1991 'constitution of EMU' was founded on German ideas of 'sound' finances and money, based on the independence of the ECB remaining sacrosanct, along with the ruling out of bail-outs for insolvent memberstate governments. This process also entrenched the 'excessive deficit procedure lock', which operationalises the limits on budget deficits and public debts as formally enshrined in the Growth and Stability Pact. Thus, as Dyson observes: 'A clear and powerful cognitive script was institutionalized in the ECB and the wider Eurosystem and protected by the ECB-centric Maastricht Treaty. EMU was set on a track defined by the sound finance and money paradigm' (Dyson 2000: 186–187).

European integration: From embedded liberalism to variegated neoliberalism

The power of the neo/ordoliberal ideologies over European solutions to the sovereign debt crisis should come as no surprise to students of past integration processes in the EU. They long ago overcame neo-mercantilist business and social democratic welfare preoccupations which drove forward the early process of EU integration, promoted by the European trade union movement and many social democratic parties. Initially, the corporate and industrial sectors represented the neo-mercantilist elements, seeking protection for domestic EU markets and production and distribution systems. But with the industrial sectors either in relative decline by the 1990s, or increasingly centred in the global economy and undergoing financialisation, the corporate sector was increasingly neoliberal in preference (Holman and Van der Pijl 1996).

Neoliberalisation was vigorously promoted by the most globalised sectors of European capital, located in the financial and knowledge economy. Van Apeldoorn gives this synthesis of neoliberalism with earlier political economy formations the title of 'embedded neoliberalism':

> Thus, the 'embedded' component of embedded neoliberalism addresses the concerns of the former neo-mercantilists as well as those of the European labour movement and social-democratic political forces, but these concerns are in the end subordinated to what has become the overriding objective of 'competitiveness' defined in neoliberal terms of market liberalization and market disciplines.
> (Van Apeldoorn 2009: 26)

However, the advent of the economic crisis has seen the social democratic component of this uneasy partnership in decline with open neoliberal austerity warfare on welfare, wages and jobs in many EU states (Scharpf 1999, Scharpf 2002: 665, Holman 2004a, Van Apeldoorn 2009: 26).

As a result the EU has come to preference competitiveness over social cohesion such that, as Scharpf suggests, 'the only national options which remain freely available under European law are supply-side strategies involving lower tax burdens, further deregulation and flexibilization of employment conditions, increasing wage differentiation and welfare cut-backs' (2002: 649–650). Van der Pijl sees this as constructing, 'the EU along the lines of the Lockean heartland: a free space for capital, with separate state jurisdictions keeping political sovereignty and democracy away from the larger structure' (Van der Pijl 2006a: 266).

Huw Macartney offers an equally comprehensive parallel analysis of the role of neoliberalisation at the heart of the process of European integration. He starts from the linkages between German ordoliberalism, or Rhenish project: *'socio-liberal neoliberalism'* as he refers to it, French *'social neoliberalism'*, and the Anglo-American *'liberal neoliberalism'* favoured by UK elites, which he also refers to as the 'Atlantic Project'. Building on the works of Van Apeldoorn and Peck and Tickell, he demonstrates how powerful sections of globally oriented capital have made national versions of neoliberalism into the 'common sense' of their respective economic and political elites and leading EU officials (Peck and Tickell 2002, Van Apeldoorn 2002, Macartney 2011).

He correctly views neoliberalism as inherently *variegated* (marked by a diversity of forms) 'rather than the narrow "neoliberal = Anglo-Saxon" binary alternative'. Second, he highlights the 'strategic agency of transnationally oriented fractions of [national] capital' in promoting their version of neoliberalism, both at national and EU levels. Third, he suggests that the agent for transmission is represented by a body of ideas offering 'a nascent neoliberal common sense as socially constructed worldviews'. Thus financial expansion, at the heart of neoliberalisation, is clearly rooted in the amalgam of new classical, monetarist and rational expectations theorems; the hegemony of these ideas, coupled with the dominance of the Atlantic heartland, has contributed to the seemingly ubiquitous conception of neoliberalism as the only alternative (Macartney 2012: 5–6, 132; see also Hay and Watson 2003: 290).

In both France and Germany the private financial sector, influenced by, and in competition with, deregulated Anglo-American finance capitalism, saw 'innovative negotiable financial instruments becoming increasingly cost-effective sources of investment just as the downward spiral of liberalization fuelled the rise in foreign-owned shareholdings' (Macartney 2012: 34). This process of financialised neoliberalisation was, and continues to be, fiercely contested by the left and right in France, but has not been halted let alone reversed.

As early as the 1980s, German firms began to engage in European and global acquisitions, joint ventures and investments abroad, becoming transnationalised in Europe and globalised (Hodges and Woolcock 1993: 338). A classic indication of this process came when Deutsche Bank, the most powerful German bank, relocated its international banking operations to London in 1985. And in the same period Paris and Frankfurt, in both cases with state approval and assistance, began to challenge each other for second place to London as the EU's investment banking financial centres and in hopeful preparation for an eventual take over from London should the UK withdraw from the EU.

This was reflected at the EU level through the Single Market process, as well as the EMU project. Macartney notes how the Lamfalussy Process, Financial Services Action Plan and Lisbon Agenda were all based upon versions of neoliberal 'common sense' and were 'contingent upon the wider integration project and the immediate concerns of Economic and Monetary Union' (Macartney 2012: 39). This, he argues, encourages 'market-led' EU integration which dovetails with the preferences of finance capital (Van der Pijl 1984: 10). Here a leading German think-tank chair suggests that:

> The dominant view among economists of the German economy [for example]...is rather close to Thatcherism actually. They see the problems of the German economy...low growth rates and high unemployment, as being in the labour market and the need for reform is to loosen up the labour market, reduce the power of the unions, roll-back the welfare state... [So] the economics profession is dominated by the Anglo-Saxon tradition.
> (Macartney 2012: 125–126)

Combining the evidence assembled through the embedded and variegated neoliberalism models it is clear that by the time the EMU was under construction, a mixture of pessimistic rule-bound German ordoliberalism and an optimistic Atlanticist 'liberal neoliberal' efficient-market hypothesis thesis, laced with federalist top-down policy spillover idealism, created a monetary system riddled with dangerous internal contradictions and incapable of coping with any serious banking liquidity crisis. When faced with the contradictions through exposure to the global financial crisis and subsequent European sovereign debt crisis, and after a brief flirtation with neo-Keynesian bank bail-outs, the EU/EZ's elite has naturally returned to supply-side austerity solutions and is busy constructing a future preferencing the rule-governed and centralised ordoliberal route to a distinctly neoliberal Europe.

Conclusion: Winner takes all, but at what cost?

At the time of writing Europe has survived its particular version of the Great Recession, but at an exceptionally high cost. In Gamble's terms it has done little to address the deep underlying structural crisis, nor the organic crisis of legitimacy, by undermining the connection between Europe's citizens, and its politicians and policy-makers.

As a result the EZ system could further destabilise the EU, perhaps shrinking it to a rich 'northern' union, or lead to a further Japanese-style lost decade, and in the worst-case scenario disintegrate, tipping the global system back into recession. In the process the balance of power between member-states and between the various EU institutions has been decisively altered, tipping towards Germany and its northern and eastern satellites, and away from the weak Mediterranean bloc, as well as from the self-marginalised UK. It has also widened the EU's democratic deficit, side-lining the elected EP and even the Commission, in favour of the most powerful national governments acting through the European Council and across numerous crisis summits, led by Germany.

Finally, the crisis has also changed the terms of debate across the EU and within its component states, led by the growing populist eurosceptic movements across the continent, and in the UK by the powerful eurosceptic governing Conservative party and its rival UKIP offshoot (Hayward and Wurzel 2012, Lapavitsas 2012, Patomaki 2012, Soros 2012, Blyth 2013: Ch. 3, Palley 2013, Fazi 2014, Peet and La Guardia 2014).

When it comes to the immediate aftermath of the sovereign debt crisis and the future direction of the EU/EZ, all eyes naturally turn to Germany. In many ways Germany, after the initial shock of discovering that its own banks were insolvent, has enjoyed a good crisis. Monetary union has deepened and entrenched Germany's pre-existing comparative mercantile advantage and has also greatly enhanced Germany's position with regard to shaping the future direction of the EU. The narrow remit of the ECB, along with the impact of global financialisation and aggressive German export-led growth, has propelled Germany to a position of unparalleled ascendency in the EZ/EU. Against the electoral trend across most of the EU, Chancellor Merkel has been re-elected twice and remains popular, with most Germans experiencing little change in their financial situation, and unemployment levels the lowest in Europe and with GDP back up to pre-crisis levels.

Whilst pressurising deficit countries to reduce their debts as rapidly as possible, the Germans have protected their surpluses at all costs, leading to a widening trade divergence between Germany and the debtor states. If this process continues, as Brancaccio and Passarella suggest:

> The peripheral economies of the continent will be progressively integrated within the German system. The industries of the southern Europe in competition with German industries will be gradually excluded from the market; the ones that are bought up, or that operate within German supply chains, will survive. Capital will be gradually concentrated in Germany and in the core countries of the Union, while the countries of the periphery will be increasingly populated by minority shareholders and low-wage workers.
> (Brancaccio and Passarella 2012: 89–95, quoted by Fazi 2014: 148)

Germany has also benefited from a dramatic variation in bond spreads since the financial crisis, with wealthy investors bailing out of debt-laden states to the safe haven of Germany in some cases for negative interest rates – actually paying to invest their money there. By December 2011, Germany was estimated to have made in excess of €9 billion out of this movement, while the reduced interest rates enjoyed by Germany under monetary union had contributed an estimated €63 billion by the end of 2011 (Pop 2012, Fazi 2014: 147).

At the same time Germany insisted that the principles of the emergency Fiscal Compact should be transferred to the heart of any future Fiscal Union, so institutionalising a permanent automatic veto mechanism over national budgets, exercised by the Commission and European Council, with an embedded ordoliberal austerity agenda as the policy basis of the system including a 'competitiveness pact' in a future fiscal union (Fazi 2014: 156–157). Radice warns: 'These proposals, when fully implemented, will not only enforce a permanent regime of fiscal austerity, but also further remove macroeconomic policy from democratic control' (Radice 2013).

Thus, a currency union intended to further promote a 'European Germany' has, when impacted by a severe financial and sovereign debt crises, accelerated the creation of an increasingly 'German Europe' (Marsh 2010: 221). The Germans, understandably given their 20th century history, have been ambivalent with regard to the political implications of these developments, proving a highly reluctant hegemon (Patterson 2011, *passim*). In a telling observation, Helmut Schmidt suggested that Germany is 'an economic giant but political dwarf' adding acutely that 'the Germans on the whole prefer to stay pigmies' (quoted in Marsh 2013: 21).

Wealth and stability remain the chief economic aims of the Germans in Europe, rather than leadership and power. But the Germans also have an overriding self-interested priority to preserve and stabilise the EZ, since if the euro disintegrates, so could the German banking system with little prospect of being able to bail out German banks for a second time. At the time of writing the future Europe looks likely not only to be German and ordoliberal in fiscal and monetary terms, but also a more federalised and centralised entity with huge implications, as we shall see, for continued UK membership.

In 2012, Angela Merkel delivered a famous speech in which she observed 'we definitely need more and not less Europe', adding that a 'political union' was essential to complement the economic and monetary union. At the same time she also made the right sounding noises for British neoliberals, referring to 'sound finances' and 'sound budgeting', drastically reducing the 'huge national debts' and improving '[low levels of] competitiveness of some states' (Merkel 2012: 6). But to British eurosceptics these were the right ends, but the wrong means.

The post-crisis primacy of Germany confirms our belief that in spite of globalisation and the added levels of EU governance, intergovernmentalism and the nation state continue to exercise decisive influence over policy direction in the EU, especially during periods of crisis. As Michael Mann suggests:

> The countries of the European Union are unique in having developed a two-level state, though the move of some political functions to Brussels and Strasbourg has not greatly weakened the governments of the member countries, ... The EU remains more of a regulating than a redistributing state (though there is some redistribution toward agriculture and poorer regions). Nationally caged identities also remain more important than any common euro identity, except for a few elites.
>
> (Mann 2014: 419)

Since its inception the main driver of European integration has been the most powerful member-states and the economic crisis has reinforced that trend, while on key economic issues reducing it to Germany alone. The problem is that these 'solutions' to the sovereign debt crisis have also increased the democratic deficit at the heart of the EU system of governance. Fazi again:

> As we have seen, the top-down 'federal' solution currently being proposed and pursued by the EU establishment consists in a game-changing and unprecedented transfer of sovereignty from the national to the supranational level ... the problem is that this transfer of sovereignty is not being paralleled by an analogous and proportionate transfer of democratic legitimacy, accountability and participation from the national to the supranational level (that is, from national parliaments to the European Parliament). In other words the democratic procedure is not being elevated to the European level; it is simply being usurped from the national level ... in the words of Jurgen Habermas, 'to a post-democratic exercise of political authority'. As Protesilaos Stavrou writes, we are witnessing 'a rapid and forceful emergence of a technocratic sovereign state within the EU'.
>
> (Fazi 2014: 160)

Merkel's technocratic federalist response to the crisis has inevitably proven deeply unpalatable to the already alienated and hostile Tory eurosceptics and members of UKIP, further encouraging their push to fully repatriate UK national sovereignty, raised now to an urgent national crusade, another 'Battle of Britain'. This is also a crusade with special potency for alienated and disgruntled voters when coupled with the growing issue of economic migration to the UK from poorer East European member-states. But even British europhiles are concerned over the narrow legalistic thrust of German policy and the danger that the EZ will usurp most of the strategic power from the EU's wider institutions with the effective renationalisation of the EU's economic governance in Germany's favour.

Finally, in a deeply ironic twist, while the ordo/neoliberal direction of the EU has been accelerated by the economic crisis, the accompanying federalising institutional thrust has further distanced it from Europe's leading neoliberal state, the UK, currently under the leadership of Europe's historically most successful neoliberal Conservative Party. And in a double irony Merkel has achieved this by elevating intergovernmentalism and 'union method' over the traditional *acquis communautaire* system, stealing the states' rights governing formula sought by generations of British negotiators in Europe in order to achieve her essentially federalist ends (Peet and La Guardia 2014: 127–128).

As *Financial Times* economic commentator Martin Wolf puts it:

> As currently designed, management of the Eurozone eviscerates national economic sovereignty over almost all important areas of economic policy, but rejects notions of collective insurance, at least in principle. In essence, then, member countries are free to do precisely as they are told. The Eurozone has achieved an almost complete separation of responsibility for deciding policy from political accountability for its consequences. The tension between the desire of people for a say in how they are governed and the reality of how power is exercised in the Eurozone surely guarantees a huge political crisis at some point in the future.
>
> (Wolf: 2014: 338)

As things stand at the time of writing there is a danger of the UK threatening to leave the EU with destabilising results for the whole EU. Of course, given the recent dramatic events in Greece it could be that forces internal to the Eurozone will precipitate a crisis first.

2
British Preferences in the European Union: Unsung Success

The current debate about European integration in the UK places considerable emphasis on the fact that the EU is moving towards a seemingly unstoppable federal union, increasingly diverging from the UK's preference for intergovernmental, open regionalist trade-based cooperation in Europe. British eurosceptics often claim that their country was 'cheated' into signing up for much more than they originally desired, essentially a simple free-trade area, and that the momentum towards ever more integration since the Maastricht Treaty is alien to the British tradition of parliamentary sovereignty and its global outlook.

Yet a closer look at British 'national interests' and preferences successfully defended at the EU level over recent decades, especially when new treaties were being negotiated, offers a very different picture, in which UK governments have been able to achieve most of their aims while preventing the kind of entanglements that they most feared. The gap between a recurrent anti-EU rhetoric and the reality of gains obtained points to the ideological nature of eurosceptic views irrespective of the outcome of negotiations and compromises.

Our theoretical starting point here is that of liberal intergovernmentalism, as developed by Stanley Hoffmann and Andrew Moravscik (Hoffmann 1982, Moravscik 1993). It rests on the idea that negotiated outcomes are less the result of an automatic spillover from one dimension of integration to another than of the interaction between government preferences, assumed to be rational, and the strategic environment in which they find themselves. In this perspective, national governments rather than supranational institutions remain largely in charge of the integration process. State priorities defended at the EU level are themselves the result of interactions with civil society through the following processes:

The primary interest of governments is to maintain themselves in office; in democratic societies, this requires the support of a coalition of domestic voters, parties, interest groups and bureaucracies, whose views are transmitted, directly or indirectly, through domestic institutions and practices of political representation. Through this process emerges the set of nation interests or goals that states bring to international negotiations.

(Moravscik 1993: 483)

Pressure from civil society is higher on economic and social issues than on 'high politics' ones, where the discretion of individual leaders is often much greater. We would therefore qualify the liberal intergovernmentalist approach with the institutionalist view that domestic constraints as well as external events may modify the national governments' negotiating stances (Olsen 2001, Sverdrup 2001).

Starting with these premises, one can then see that over the last decades and certainly since the 1980s, British preferences within the EU have been broadly similar in spite of differences in tones adopted by the different governments. They have included:

- a choice for intergovernmental cooperation rather than supranational integration, especially in the field of social policy, foreign policy and home and justice affairs;
- a reluctance to negotiate and sign new treaties and a preference for practical policies;
- a reliance on NATO as the main provider of security in (Western) Europe;
- priority given to the completion of the Single Market and to free trade;
- a preference for reform of the EU budget;
- enlargement to central and eastern Europe as well as Turkey;
- flexibility within the EU, allowing the UK to at least opt in or out of as many policies as possible if not total *à la carte*.

These preferences have, of course, not been shared by all member-states at all times, and have sometimes been opposed by some other big players, nevertheless there were countries which did share at least some of these goals, whether it be intergovernmentalism (France) or economic liberalism (Germany, the Netherlands, and later Scandinavian countries). Prior to 2010, London was often able to advance its position via *ad hoc* bilateral or multilateral coalitions. Even domestic political constraints, in particular the strength of euroscepticism and the lack of flexibility this entailed, were used by UK governments to obtain what they originally intended from EU negotiations, which was most of the time simply a lowest common denominator position – ever the paradoxical achievement of 'recalcitrant states' when unanimity is required to modify treaties (Moravscik 1993: 501). This was clearly the case with the Maastricht Treaty, for example, where John Major obtained an opt out from the EMU and the Social Charter as well as intergovernmental cooperation for the common foreign and security policy and Justice and Home Affairs, which a jubilant British official claimed to represent 'game, set and match for Britain' (Major 2000: 288).

While it is unnecessary to engage in yet another history of the UK in Europe since 1945, a theme well covered in the literature (see for example George 1998, Young 1998, Gowland and Turner 2000, Gifford 2008), we will explore the often overlooked success of British governments since at least the 1980s in achieving their objectives, in almost complete contradiction with a domestic political discourse of 'battles', 'encroachments', 'sovereignty', 'red lines' and 'protection' which have become ubiquitous throughout British political engagement. The first section will briefly recall that the UK was late to join the EC and therefore unable to influence the framing of the original EC institutions and policies. In contrast, sections two (on the 1979–1997 period) and three (on New Labour) will demonstrate that, once inside the EU, British governments, both Conservative and Labour, were able, to a considerable extent, to shape and influence the course of European integration, whether through treaty negotiations or day-to-day policy-making. In the last section we will assess the extent of the break introduced by the coalition government after 2010, which has willingly relinquished any meaningful influence in the EU largely to gain domestic political advantage.

Consequences of a late entry, 1945–1979

The short-term reasons why successive governments chose not to join the first steps towards European integration in the 1950s – the European Coal and Steel Community (ECSC), European Defence Community (EDC) in 1950 and the European Economic Community (EEC) in 1957 – choosing instead to support the process from the outside while encouraging cooperation in the field of security (with the Treaty of Brussels) are well known. A combination of domestic and international factors coalesced to make membership appear unnecessary to both Conservative and Labour elites. Until the Suez debacle of 1956 at least, the UK still saw itself as a great international power which had defeated the Axis powers, almost equal to the USA and the Soviet Union – the two true superpowers emerging from the Second World War. Unlike its European neighbours the UK was neither occupied nor defeated during the conflict, and although much weakened economically, the British could still rely on the pound as an international currency albeit with US sponsorship. The UK was still a major imperial power, even if its empire was starting to unravel a geopolitical position, which gave access to resources and encouraged a global outlook, especially in trade. Products from the empire/Commonwealth countries had preferential access to the British market, an economic link which was also a symbol of their geopolitical bonds. This self-perception contrasted with the vision of the continent as economically and politically in tatters, where cooperation between weak states made sense in order to rebuild and to prevent the danger of future wars.

Domestically, the issue of sovereignty and control of one's own political and economic systems were salient in the political debate. The British political system had survived the war intact and enhanced, unlike those of its neighbours, and there was no pressing reason to undermine it or subsume it under a supranational organisation. A European army would be particularly unacceptable in that respect. As for coal and steel, the idea of pooling production clashed with the recent nationalisations decided by Clement Attlee's Labour government, making it politically impossible to relinquish control of these two crucial resources to a European body. Herbert Morrison famously summed up the difficulty by saying 'We cannot do it: the Durham miners won't wear it.' Nor did Churchill or Eden – self-proclaimed 'Europeans' who had criticised the Labour government while in opposition – overturn this policy when in power after 1951 (Young 1998: 219).

Yet while, from a British perspective, there were good reasons in the 1950s to turn down the French and German offers to join the ECSC, EDC and EEC, nevertheless these decisions had significant long-term consequences, especially when the UK joined in 1973. First, the EEC was by then politically dominated by France, which did not share the UK's economic interests and model of capitalism, especially as far as agriculture was concerned. As a result, once in power General de Gaulle was able to block British entry for a decade after 1958. Second, British governments did not have any influence on the way the EEC was designed, whether in regard to its legal and institutional architecture or to its policy preferences. For example, European law was founded much more on the continental Roman tradition than was British common law. The influence of the French *haute administration* was also felt in the setting up of the Community institutions such as the Commission. The budget, based on levies and taxes on imports into the Community, was also chosen without taking account of the interests of the UK, which imported more foodstuffs than other member-states. The common agricultural policy, established in 1962, protected European farmers in a way which was hardly compatible with the UK's preference for free trade. As Hugo Young put it, 'Britain, a free-trading nation with a low-tariff tradition sustained by its worldwide Commonwealth, faced a Europe largely shaped by France, a protectionist nation, jealous of Britain, determined to protect the agriculture Britain wanted to leave out,' (Young 1998: 116). Yet not all EC developments in the 1960s were detrimental to the UK: the 'empty chair' crisis prompted by De Gaulle in 1966 reinforced the intergovernmental nature of European integration, with the 'Luxembourg Compromise' safeguarding member-states' ultimate national interests and giving them a veto right when these interests were deemed to be threatened.

By the time it joined the EC in 1973, the UK was therefore not in a position to take full advantage of membership in the way that France and Germany had done. Europe helped to modernise the French economy and provided France with political leadership, while giving Germany at least partial sovereignty and security. By contrast this architecture was largely alien to British political traditions and economic priorities. It is of course impossible to speculate about what would have happened to the EC and to the UK's attitude towards it if the UK had joined from the outset, but it is useful to bear in mind the failures of successive British governments to grasp the importance of the organisation they eventually joined. The severe economic crisis which followed the 1973 oil shock also played a part in limiting any benefits the British economy could have enjoyed from membership.

The period that followed, from the mid-1970s to the mid-1990s, showed that in spite of their ambivalence towards the whole project, British governments were able, if not to steer it positively, at least to negatively protect British 'national interests' within the EC/EU. In the 1970s, the UK earned its reputation as an 'awkward partner' (George 1994), first because membership of the EC was only fully completed in 1975 after Harold Wilson had promised a renegotiation of the terms of entry while in opposition. Having secured cosmetic changes from his European partners, he then delivered an in/out referendum in 1975, in which he campaigned for a 'yes' vote, supported by most of the

Conservatives, the Liberals and part of the Labour Party as well as most business groups and the bulk of the media, achieving victory by a substantial majority of two-thirds.

The second reason for this reputation was the fact that the Labour governments of Wilson (1974–1976) and Callaghan (1976–1979) were lukewarm towards the two main projects being discussed in the Community at the time – the direct election of members of the EP and the creation of an EMS. The issue of the sovereignty of Westminster made the prospect of a supranational and democratically elected EP unpalatable to many British MPs, although the bill instituting the European election was eventually passed in 1978. The then German Chancellor, Helmut Schmidt, and the French President Valéry Giscard d'Estaing were the main promoters of the EMS, but Labour's Roy Jenkins, then president of the European Commission, played an important part in setting up the project, a fact often overlooked in UK domestic discourse (Young 1998: 300). Moreover as early as 1972, before the UK had officially become a member, Edward Heath had signed up to the Werner report, which included plans for a currency union by 1980 (Peet and La Guardia 2014: 10). The Callaghan government, though, declined to take part in the resulting system, which allowed the currencies to fluctuate within a narrow band. Callaghan's main arguments justifying his decision centred on issues of economic sovereignty and the fact that sterling was still an international currency, therefore the stability of currencies would be better achieved using the dollar and other non-European currencies.

Conservative governments, 1979–1997

Hugo Young summed up perceptively the ambiguities of the Thatcher years (1979–1990) as far as the British commitment to Europe was concerned:

> For the first six years of British membership of the European Community, Britain was led by people who were otherwise engaged. Ted Heath, preoccupied with domestic survival, did not begin to make an impression. Harold Wilson and Jim Callaghan, though compelled to give the matter some attention, were always trying to fend it off. Their successor was the first in the line to see Europe as a subject not for apologetic reticence but for triumphal prominence. For eleven of the first seventeen years, the tone was set and the policy made by someone who, at important moments, gave Europe the loudest place on her agenda (...) In her time she took Britain further into Europe

than anyone except Heath. Institutions and markets and laws became far more deeply imbued with the Europe effect (...) Mrs Thatcher, at every stage, was part of it. Yet simultaneously all her political energy was directed against what she herself was doing. Even as she took Britain further in, she stoked the fire of those who opposed this every step of the way.

(Young 1998: 306)

Thatcher's influence on developments in the EC was two-fold. First, the budget issue, which dominated the period between 1979 and 1984, put her at the forefront of the EC, albeit in a defensive manner. She was determined to 'get her money back' and reform a system which made her country one of the main contributors to the EC budget. She was unhappy with the first three-year deal that was agreed in 1980 (Wall 2008: 7). Tensions remained high with her partners, especially as she threatened to use the British veto on agricultural price negotiations, until eventually an agreement was reached at the 1984 Fontainebleau European Council on a permanent rebate mechanism for the UK, which greatly reduced the gap between its relative contribution and that of its partners.

Throughout this period, the Thatcher government was confronted with proposals for further political and monetary integration in Europe, such as the Genscher-Colombo plan for political union in 1982, the Spinelli draft treaty in 1984, the Dooge committee and the drive for intergovernmental conferences in 1984 and 1990. Though the prime minister was wary of these plans, she always remained engaged and defended what she considered as British interests from the inside. The British contribution to the European debate never faltered during that period. Indeed, she wrote later that '[she] considered [herself] a European idealist, even if [her] ideals differed somewhat from those expressed with varying degrees of sincerity by other European heads of government' (Thatcher 1993: 536–537). Even her 1988 Bruges speech, widely interpreted at the time as strongly anti-European, can be seen in hindsight as a contribution to the debate, as a call for cooperation in an intergovernmental Europe, not a case for disengagement.

This was particularly true of the Single European Act signed in 1985: although Jacques Delors, then president of the European Commission, was the main driver to establish the free circulation of goods, capital, services and people in the EU, the British government was strongly committed to the plan which chimed perfectly with its free-trade neoliberalism. The paper it produced, *Europe-The Future*, presented a set of constructive principles for future developments in the EC, including further cooperation in a number of new fields such as the environment and defence and even supported the principle of 'an ever closer union' (Wall 2008: 42). The British commissioner at the time, Arthur Cockfield, played a crucial role in this respect, producing a white paper identifying imperfections in the Single Market (Young 1998: 329). Although Thatcher did not approve of the principle of a new treaty to secure the free market or the increase in qualified majority voting (QMV), the powers of the EP and the principle of economic and monetary union which other countries supported, she calculated the price worth paying to secure her key objective, the signing of the Single European Act (Thatcher 1993: 551–553).

Once this objective had been achieved, relations deteriorated with her European partners as the end of the Cold War was followed by a push towards political union (strongly supported by Germany) and economic and monetary union (which France hoped would weaken its dependency on the Bundesbank). The Bruges speech of September 1988 was an attempt to apply the brake to both initiatives, sticking to a Community based principally on the Single Market and political cooperation. By then even the Single European Act was no longer seen as a positive achievement. As Young put it:

> After a few years, many Conservatives were singing a different song about the Single Act. They came to regard it, not as a lynchpin of the liberalised market, but as an instrument through which the ever closer union of Europe made its way forward. They saw it, increasingly, as a moment of serious defeat, possibly of treachery against the nation: a treachery, even, for which they themselves might be somewhat responsible, and might therefore have a duty to make condign repentance by reneging on their own handiwork.
> (Young 1998: 335)

Yet by the time she left power in November 1990, Thatcher had yielded to her Cabinet and allowed the pound to join the exchange rate mechanism of the EMS, albeit at an unsustainable rate. More generally, even if the last years of her premiership were marked by increasing bad temper and bitterness about developments in the EU, Thatcher was on the whole much more pragmatic and ready to compromise with her partners in order to secure important goals than the caricature of her now conveyed by her hard eurosceptic supporters in the UK.

John Major, who succeeded Thatcher, was a euro-pragmatist aware of the need to change the harsh diplomatic style which had reduced the UK's already relatively weak influence in Europe. He was also keenly aware of the need to find allies in Europe, describing his attitude at that time in these terms:

> I believed it was in our economic interests to be a member. I welcomed sensible cooperation. I had no hang-ups about Germany. I accepted that being one of a community of fifteen meant that sometimes we had to reach a consensus that was not entirely to our taste. I was keen to rebuild shattered fences, to prevent Britain from being seen forever as the odd man out to be excluded from the private consultations that so often foreshadowed new policy in Europe.
> (Major 2000: 265)

In this spirit, even though he was not keen on the principle of an intergovernmental conference, he negotiated in the intergovernmental conference (IGC) which led to the future Maastricht Treaty so as to secure key British objectives – an opt-out from the EMU and social policy, and a purely intergovernmental political union which would prevent the Western European Union (WEU) created in 1948 from entering the remit of the EU. In particular, thanks to support from France, the British government secured a victory on the 'temple' structure for the new treaty, which kept the EC totally separate from both the new Common Foreign and Security Policy (CFSP, the so-called second pillar) and Home and Justice Affairs (HJA, third pillar), both strictly intergovernmental. This represented a major British 'victory' over the 1991 Dutch draft treaty which had contemplated a traditional 'tree' structure where all policies would remain under the control of Community institutions. Major was also able to achieve two other goals he cherished, the inclusion of the principle of subsidiarity, by which decisions would be taken at the EU level only when they could not be taken effectively at the national level, as well as the removal of the reference to a 'federal vocation'.

On economic and monetary union, Major was particularly concerned about the lack of convergence between the British and continental economies and the need therefore to avoid any entanglement in a single currency, though he was careful to leave the door open for a possible change in the future if the economic reasons to join became compelling (Major 2000: 271–272). In the end he did obtain an opt-out from the EMU and the Social Chapter was a protocol added to the treaty, not included in it, something gained by arguing that he would not get the support of his parliament otherwise (Major 2000: 286). On defence, Major's priority was to preserve at all costs the primacy of NATO in protecting the security of the continent. A common foreign policy was to remain ruled by unanimity and a common defence relegated to a possible distant future. This, as we have seen, was a vital part of the UK's preference for Atlanticism when it came to foreign and defence matters (Gamble 2003: 83–102).

The Maastricht Treaty was therefore, on the whole, another considerable success for British diplomacy. Although both Thatcher and Major were not in favour of economic and monetary union and were unable to prevent it from happening, they secured what were for them primary British interests, that is the freedom to join or not to join the single currency in the future. Similarly, although they could not prevent political union from being established, they made sure the common foreign policy would not be a substitute to national policies and NATO remained the main provider of security in Europe.

The next stage in the institution-building process of the EU was the Amsterdam Treaty, which was negotiated under Major but signed by Blair. An IGC had been written in the Maastricht Treaty in 1991. Coming shortly after the Maastricht Treaty came into force (because of the delay in ratification) the IGC had only limited ambitions, which suited the Major government well. It was intended simply to adjust EU institutions to the prospect of enlargement to several ex-communist Central and Eastern Europe states, especially the increase in the size of the Commission and EP as well as the reweighting of votes in the European Council (Bache et al. 2011: 174). A strengthening of CFSP and HJA would also be on the agenda, as well as moves to reduce the 'democratic deficit' in Europe (see Chapter 5).

The British government's approach to the IGC under John Major was clearly negative and defensive. As a result David Davis, the UK Europe Minister and representative on the Reflection Group which was convened in 1995, often found himself in a minority of one (Laursen 2002: 5). Stephen Wall, then UK Representative in Brussels, expresses this vividly:

> As the UK representative on the negotiating group, I was on a very tight rein. Every week, before each negotiating session, I would receive pages of minute instructions from the Foreign Office, personally authorised by David Davis. The Foreign Office could have saved themselves a lot of trouble by sending a one-line instruction: 'Just say no'. There was virtually nothing on the agenda that was palatable to the government.
>
> (Wall 2010: 157)

The government was totally opposed to any further power being transferred to the EP (in the co-decision procedure) and to any extension of QMV. They had not changed their minds about the WEU being incorporated into the EU, as France and Germany desired, nor were they prepared to talk about EU employment policy. Finally, the control of British borders was to be maintained at the national level at all costs. These stances reflected long-held views across the political spectrum in the UK and the specific political constraints upon John Major, as his majority in parliament dwindled and his MPs became more rebellious (Baker et al. 1993). A powerful group of Conservative eurosceptics applied considerable pressure to Major against conceding any concessions, as they had during the IGC in the run-up to the Maastricht Treaty (Forster 1998) and as a result no deal could be reached before the general election of May 1997 which saw the victory of New Labour, led by Tony Blair.

The New Labour years

The continuity in British preferences in EU policy was soon made clear under Blair, in spite of a much more positive rhetoric about ending British isolation in Europe and taking on a leadership role. He was ready to sign the Social Chapter, a significant difference with his Conservative predecessors, and supported the principle of the UK joining the single currency in the future, but only if the proper conditions were met and a referendum endorsed it. Moreover he kept the same 'red lines' as his predecessors, rejecting 'federalism' and was keen to maintain the unanimity rule in foreign policy, budget, taxation and social security. He also demanded a reform of the common agricultural policy (CAP), another traditional British theme in European negotiations. Other priorities also remained unchanged, including the control of frontiers and the refusal to have the EU absorb the WEU – Blair was still very cautious about defence at this early stage, in contrast with what happened subsequently. The change of government nevertheless made negotiations on the future Amsterdam Treaty easier.

One issue on which the British government was able to achieve most of its goals was flexibility. In 1994, John Major had already advocated a variable majority, which gave maximum freedom to individual memberstates, while opposing the 'hard-core' model which had been suggested by Karl Lamers and Wolfgang Schaüble, where pioneer countries are then followed by other member-states. Major's view of flexibility was closer to a *Europe à la carte,* whereby ideally the UK would be able to pick and choose among the Community policies. But he was also aware of the risks of exclusion for the UK if the EU became too flexible. The issue was once again on the table in the 1996 IGC. 'Enhanced cooperation' was adopted as a way for a majority of member-states to move forward in some areas of JHA without being impeded by others, but always subjected to unanimity. The compromise found on the use of veto over flexible arrangement in the second pillar was that QMV would be used but a veto would also be possible 'for important... reasons of national policy' (Stubbs 2002: 100). Other caveats limited the extent to which flexibility could be used, which also satisfied London. Indeed, one could argue that the UK's greatest success at Amsterdam, and in the years that followed, was to establish the principle of flexibility as central to the EU.

At first sight, it might seem that London 'lost' on the extension of co-decision procedures to the EP, which it rejected originally. But this extension of powers was to the detriment of the Commission, with which the procedure is shared, not the European Council, which also suited the British (Moravcsik and Nicolaidis 1998: 21).

The British government's success in Amsterdam was most conspicuous in the second and third pillar. A High Representative for CFSP was set up who also acted as vice-president of the Commission. While introducing QMV had been considered for CFSP in the IGC, the outcome confirmed that foreign policy would remain strictly intergovernmental. QMV would be used to implement measures but any member-state could exercise a veto. The only change introduced concerned 'constructive abstention', which would allow a form of strengthened cooperation by some member-states without others embarking on actions likely to impede EU action, and the creation of 'common strategies' to be defined unanimously. More important for London, the WEU was not absorbed by the EU – a protocol added to the treaty only mentioned that the EU might recommend actions to the WEU. The only significant step, to which London did not object because it did not overlap with what NATO did, was to include the 'Petersberg tasks' (especially humanitarian intervention) in the remit of the CFSP.

On HJA, the UK and Ireland insisted on their geographical specificity, which made it easier to control borders while reducing the need for identity cards inside their countries. They therefore opposed a communitarisation of these policies. The solution that was found, again to the benefit of the UK, was to integrate the Schengen agreement into the treaty and to move the third pillar into the first one (though keeping unanimity, with QMV possible after five years) but to give the UK, Ireland and Denmark a protocol allowing them to opt in or out of the policies involved. Variable geometry was therefore entrenched in the treaty. Stephen Wall recalls:

> Britain...retained her frontiers and, with it, the right to determine her own migration arrangements. But Britain also secured the right to opt into the individual frontier and migration measures which the other member states would make among themselves. At the time, it looked like the best of both worlds.
>
> (Wall 2010: 167)

Finally, agreement on the reweighting of votes in the Council before enlargement, meant to prevent QMV from being reduced to 48% of the EU population after enlargement, could not be reached at Amsterdam and was postponed to a future new IGC.

Once the Amsterdam Treaty was signed, Blair was able to try to claim a leadership role in Europe. This was done through bilateral relationships with other European leaders and, especially, with his unexpected initiative on defence. In December 1998, he and Jacques Chirac signed a declaration calling for an autonomous European defence capacity, which was then endorsed by the EU as a whole in 1999. Without Blair's sponsorship, the European defence and security policy, whatever its flaws and limitations, would not have become reality.

Nevertheless, continuity with the previous government was also clear in the actual choice, if not the rhetoric, concerning the single currency. Whereas Blair had shown cautious support for the euro and the creation of an organisation, 'Britain in Europe', which was meant to campaign for adopting the single currency, no decision was taken and no referendum organised in the UK during his premiership, for two main reasons. First Gordon Brown's leadership on economic issues meant that he was effectively in charge of policy in this area and in October 1997 he announced in the House of Commons that five economic tests would need to be met before joining the euro (on the convergence of the European economies, flexibility, consequences on investment, the City, growth and employment). The Treasury's view was that they were not met in that year, or in 2003, when they conducted a new assessment (Riddell 2005). The second reason was political: opinion polls showed widespread opposition to the euro and Blair was not ready to risk his leadership on an unpopular low salience measure. He valued the support of the eurosceptic press, especially Rupert Murdoch's *Sun*, and consequently never attempted whole-heartedly to change public opinion on that issue.

Meanwhile, a new intergovernmental conference was in the pipeline in 2000 to clear up the issues left unresolved in Amsterdam. Council voting, the number of Commissioners and members of the EP needed to be agreed on before the candidate states became new members in 2004. The treaty, finally concluded after a marathon of three days and nights' negotiations in Nice, has often been criticised, along with the badly organised French presidency of the EU (Bourlanges 2001). Yet these flaws should not obscure the fact that, once again, a consensus was found that the British government could comfortably live with.

The British were less isolated in the intergovernmental negotiations than in Amsterdam, especially on the issue of Council votes which pitted large member-states, including the UK, against smaller member-states. In a speech in Warsaw on 8 October 2000, Tony Blair supported strengthening the European Council, 'streamlining' the Commission and limiting the changes in the existing procedures for flexibility in CFSP and HJA in order to prevent a 'hard core' from emerging in the EU (Blair 2000).

The deal agreed raised the threshold for a qualified majority to over 73% of votes, reinforcing the intergovernmental nature of the Union. This was reinforced by the rule that qualified majority should also represent a majority of at least 62% of the European population. Co-decision was not extended. It was also agreed that big member-states would lose their second Commissioner, that new member-states would have one, but that the total size of the Commission would be limited to 27 members.

The British government was satisfied with the French proposal for the reweighting of votes, which maintained Germany's voting weight at the same level as the other big states in spite of its increased size following reunification (though the number of German MEPs was increased). But the double majority, that is of a majority of countries as well as a majority of votes, effectively gave Germany extra weight due to its population. The agreement generally increased the strength of larger member-states in the coming enlargement, since the five bigger countries (Germany, France, the UK, Italy and Spain) would represent 60% of the votes instead of 55% previously (Lequesne 2001: 6). This, together with the increase in the threshold for QMV, was again seen as a success for the UK and its allies, though not for European integration (Bourlanges 2001: 596, Larsen 2006: 313).

The extension of QMV to 27 new areas, which may appear radical, was actually limited to uncontroversial small areas such as the free circulation of citizens or the status of MEPs. Issues like taxation or social security, which had been presented as British 'red lines' by the government, were kept under the unanimity rule (Lequesne 2001). Enhanced cooperation was extended to CFSP but not to defence, as London had wished, and the treaty removed the veto right on the creation of such cooperation except on foreign policy. Finally the Charter of Fundamental Rights was adopted, but only as a declaration at that point, again because of British objections. The balance sheet of this limited treaty was therefore highly positive for the UK.

The Convention and the constitutional treaty

The idea of having a Convention established to examine a possible constitution for the EU was adopted at the Laeken European Council in December 2001, only a year after the Nice summit. Once again, the British government was not at first enthusiastic about another bout of what Gordon Brown would describe as 'institutional navel-gazing'. This position had changed by 2002, when Blair described his view of a European constitution:

> we do need a proper Constitution for Europe, one which makes it clear that the driving ideology is indeed a union of nations not a super state subsuming national sovereignty and national identity. This should be spelt out in simple language. A new Constitution for Europe can bring a new stability to the shape of Europe – not a finality which would prevent any future evolution, but a settlement to last a generation or more.
>
> (Blair 2002)

The domestic political context, though still favourable in electoral terms, was less comfortable for the Blair government. The prime minister's popularity was on the wane following the Iraq war and the eurosceptic press, as well as the Conservative party, were strongly opposed to the idea of a European constitution. From early 2003 onwards, the tabloid press launched scathing attacks against the supposed threat to British freedoms that the negotiations entailed and the *Daily Telegraph* started campaigning for a referendum on any future treaty (Menon 2003: 975). As a consequence, from then on the government was under close scrutiny from the British press. Menon showed that this pressure led to a hardening of the government's tone in the Convention, though this does not mean that the British government was any less successful in the negotiations. The domestic constraints became obvious when Tony Blair announced during the course of the following IGC, in April 2004, that a future constitutional treaty would need to be ratified by referendum in the UK – much to the chagrin of his partners, including President Chirac of France who soon felt compelled to make the same dangerous promise to his own electorate. This was an unexpected U-turn, which he presented as a way to confront and defeat the 'partially, at least, successful [eurosceptic] campaign to persuade the UK that Europe is a conspiracy aimed at us rather than a partnership designed for us and others to pursue our national interest properly in a modern, interdependent world' (quoted in Norman 2005: 302). Once again, the promise had an effect in the 'two-level game' being played out in Brussels, with the British delegation pressing for more concessions on the ground, arguing that it could not otherwise convince British voters to ratify it (Norman 2005: 303).

British representatives in Brussels were particularly skilful throughout the lengthy process leading to the constitutional treaty in 2004. The Laeken declaration adopted in 2001 already owed a lot to the influence of David Miliband, then a backbencher who had been appointed to the Laeken group (Menon 2003: 964). In the Convention itself, Peter Hain, the Europe Minister representing the British government, and Gisela Stuart, the Labour MP representing the British Parliament, were particularly active and influential in 2002–2003 (Menon 2003, Norman 2005: 41). This was all the more remarkable as the discussions took place against the backdrop of the crisis over Iraq, where the UK found itself at odds with several key partners. Indeed, tensions were very high between the UK on one side and France and Germany on the other – since in their eyes Blair's instinctive Atlanticism exposed the real limits of his engagement in the EU. In 2005, Franco-British tensions erupted again, this time about the EU budget for agriculture in the period 2007–2013, which Blair wanted to reduce, with Chirac retaliating by seeking to decrease the British rebate.

In the negotiations on the constitutional treaty, the British government had several objectives, already expressed in Blair's Warsaw speech in 2000 and repeated in Cardiff in 2002: to strengthen the European Council by appointing a permanent president, to strengthen the Commission in its executive role and to increase the role of national parliaments in European decision-making (Blair 2002). As domestic hostility to the treaty grew, the UK government dropped its insistence on a strengthened Commission and focused on the intergovernmental body, the European Council (Menon 2004: 11). The British government was also extremely wary of a number of plans put forward by other members.

They included a Charter of Fundamental Rights to be incorporated in the treaty, a new European foreign minister accountable to the Commission, a European public prosecutor and the so-called *passerelle* clause which would allow decisions in the European Council to be taken by QMV rather than unanimity (Menon 2004: 21).

The draft treaty which was submitted by the Convention to the intergovernmental conference in June 2003 satisfied the government to a large extent – 'eighty or ninety percent of it' according to Peter Hain (Menon 2004: 19). This was a result of British diplomacy and of the Convention president's effort to keep the UK satisfied (Norman 2005: 300). The reference to federalism or 'ever closer union' had been dropped on Blair's insistence. The CFSP remained purely intergovernmental although at that point a European foreign minister was still contemplated. There were also a number of 'red lines' that the UK government was going to defend in the IGC, especially on taxation, border police and defence.

The government was equally successful in the course of the IGC itself. By the end of it in June 2004, QMV had not been extended to taxation, social policy, the supervision of European banks by the ECB, or the budget rebate. The *passerelle* clause had been limited in that a single national parliament could block it. A stable president of the European Council had been approved. The UK had accepted that the Charter of Human Rights should be legally binding at that point; having obtained safeguards that it would not undermine national law, as well as the European prosecutor and foreign minister. So in contrast to the Conservative rhetoric, Blair insisted in the foreword to the government white paper on the constitution that the text 'represented a good result for Britain and for Europe. We can be proud of the strong part we played in shaping the Treaty – a role widely recognised across the EU,' (Foreign Office 2004). He repeated in Parliament that the treaty should be seen as a British success:

> This treaty makes it plain, again for the first time in a European treaty, that the European Union has only the competences conferred on it by member states, and it states expressly, also for the first time, that member states can withdraw from Europe should they want to. This treaty makes clear where the European Union can and cannot act. It provides for qualified majority voting where we need it, for the single market, for reform of the common agricultural policy and for action against international crime and terrorism. It keeps unanimity for the most important decisions and, at our insistence, in

particular for tax, social security, foreign policy, defence and decisions on the financing of the Union affecting the British budget contribution. It keeps our ability to opt out of measures affecting our laws on asylum and immigration, and extends that so that we cannot be obliged to co-operate on criminal law procedures where we do not want to do so.[1]

London was not alone in wanting to conclude quickly the negotiations and ratify the treaty by parliamentary means wherever possible. The UK's European partners had no intention to encroach on Blair's 'red lines', which had been aired mostly for domestic consumption anyway, and easily gave way to the government on opt-outs from police and judicial cooperation as well as the constitutional symbols (Nugent and Phinnemore 2010: 80–81). The draft agreed on in September 2007 (under Gordon Brown, who had taken over as prime minister) stipulated that the Charter on Fundamental Rights would be separate from the treaty and not encroach on UK law. The new rules about votes in the European Council (55% of member-states representing 65% of the population needed to reach a qualified majority) benefitted large member-states once again, including the UK. The post of foreign minister was downgraded to High Representative for Foreign Affairs and Security Policy, which was an improvement in British eyes from the constitutional treaty. Finally, the UK's opt-in/out in HJA was strengthened to cover policies extended under the Lisbon treaty.

While the British were once more able to achieve their aims in EU negotiations, the government language at home had become increasingly defensive in response to eurosceptic pressure (Nugent and Phinnemore 2010: 86). Although, as we have seen above, this domestic constraint could be turned into an asset in Brussels, it nevertheless represented a difficulty for the government (Riddell 2005: 375). 'Britain in Europe' organised some rallies and published pamphlets explaining the constitutional treaty, but the anti-constitution campaign, led by the Conservative Party and UKIP and supported by a majority of national newspapers, was much more vocal and successful. For them, the result of the constitution would mean the end of the UK as an independent state. Reacting to the government's publication of a white paper supporting the constitution in September, Michael Ancram, the shadow foreign secretary, asserted that: 'The fact is that the constitution will take huge powers away from Britain and give them to Brussels. It forms the basis of a federal European state... it's a gateway to a country called Europe.'[2] This campaign was successful in that opinion polls in the UK showed widespread ignorance of the content of the treaty as well as opposition to it.[3] The anti-campaign abated after the French and Dutch referendum rejections, but resumed under the new Conservative leader, David Cameron, in Spring 2007. The party relentlessly demanded a referendum on the new Lisbon Treaty and waged a doomed battle in Parliament during the ratification process in early 2008.[4]

Conclusion

Two conclusions can be drawn from this analysis. The first one confirms the gap between the British political discourse on Europe and the reality of an EU increasingly moving towards a 'British' model, with an enlarged and more flexible Union, a reinforced Council and a weakened Commission, as well as the crucial Single Market framed largely along British neoliberal lines. All British governments resort to militaristic language of 'red lines' and of 'battles' fought and won, when the reality is that, until 2010 at least, the UK's European partners were usually ready to accommodate British demands during the different treaty negotiations which dominated the 1990s and early 2000s. In particular, opt-outs to the single currency, the Social Chapter, the Schengen agreements gave the UK a satisfactory deal and a uniquely privileged status within the EU. Yet even Blair's New Labour accepted the rhetoric of euroscepticism, which as we will see in the next chapter has become hegemonic, giving spurious legitimacy to vociferous accusations of *not* having defended British interests.

The second conclusion, which will be developed in the following chapters, is that this gap between discourse and reality has been in a way filled by the coalition government elected in 2010. David Cameron has been equally negative and aggressive about the EU in London *and* in Brussels and seemed to give up any attempt to create alliances and compromise with his partners in order to achieve favourable deals for his country. As a result, he antagonised most of his partners by his government's obstructionist manner. This was particularly clear during two of the most symbolic episodes of the coalition's European policy – the December 2011 'veto' over the fiscal compact and Cameron's June 2014 attempt to block the appointment of Jean-Claude Juncker as president of the European Commission, both ultimately unsuccessful, leaving the UK more isolated in Europe.[5]

3
Euroscepticism in Britain: Cause or Symptom of the European Crisis?

Euroscepticism used to be a largely British[1] phenomenon, at least in terms of mainstream political parties and political and opinion-forming elites. Indeed, the word was coined in the 1980s to describe Margaret Thatcher's policies and attitude towards the EC at a time when she was reasserting British sovereignty against Brussels' plans for political and monetary union (Leconte 2010: 3). It was later applied to the anti-European wing of the Conservative Party when it battled against the ratification of the Maastricht Treaty in 1992–1993 (Baker et al. 1993a, 1993b, 1994, Alexandre-Collier 2002, Forster 2002). At that time, Britain was considered as the 'awkward' or 'reluctant' partner, exceptional in the EC for the ambivalence of its political class and general public towards a project it had joined belatedly (George 1998, Young 1998, Gowland and Turner 2000). Party divisions and a general reluctance towards integration imposed constraints on policy-making, made brutally clear under John Major and more subtly under Tony Blair, who in spite of his own preference refrained from organising a referendum on adopting the European single currency when faced with strong media and political opposition.

Twenty years after euroscepticism emerged as a central feature of the public discourse in Britain, the picture has evolved in two ways. On the one hand, euroscepticism has not been undermined by changes in the international environment identified in the Introduction, such as the relative decline of the US and the rise of China and other emerging economies, rather it has become more entrenched within a large section of the British political elite and the wider public for reasons we shall develop here. On the other hand, although rooted in different beliefs from the British branch, varieties of euroscepticism are now much more common in the other EU countries than they were in the early 1990s, both in party systems and amongst the general public. Indeed, euroscepticism is now a near universal feature of the party systems of the EU countries, even if its electoral impact varies (Szscerbiak and Taggart 2002: 21). Europe is no longer a significant cleavage in the UK only, but also in the other EU countries. Thus, as Leconte suggests: 'what was considered a eurosceptic discourse in the Thatcher era has now become common parlance in relation to the EU' (2010: 12). Concerns about economic or political sovereignty and threats to national cultures have become common in the EU in general, especially since the onset of the EZ crisis in 2010 although, as we will see, British euroscepticism remains distinctive in its post-imperialist and hyperglobalist outlook.

In order to explore these issues further, we will first define British euroscepticism, question its exceptionalism in relation to other EU countries and review the explanations for it found in the academic literature. We will also briefly recall the history of euroscepticism in Britain between 1945 and 1997. The second section will focus on the ambiguities of New Labour towards the EU when it was in power (1997–2010) and also since. The third section will examine the consolidation of an increasingly hard-line euroscepticism in the Conservative Party in opposition during the same period and in the present coalition government. In the final section, we judge to what extent party positions reflect public opinion and more generally compare the UK's eurosceptic political culture with that of other member-states.

British euroscepticism

In the last decade considerable in-depth research has been done on euroscepticism in general and British euroscepticism in particular, enabling us to build on a conceptualisation of the phenomenon which was hitherto lacking. The starting point is our assertion that the term is partly misleading. 'Scepticism' in itself suggests a healthy detached and critical frame of mind about European integration, with openness with regard to the conclusion of such an analysis. It describes a positive critical attitude which refuses to take for granted the inherent benefits of integration *per se* or of specific policies. In practice though, euroscepticism has tended to be more negative about the EU than the term suggests and is associated with different degrees of ideological europhobia, that is a complete rejection of the European project, or of its recent incarnations, for reasons which can range from the political and constitutional to the economic/social and symbolic. There has also been a wide range of arguments, from an equally wide variety of actors drawn from the right and left of the political spectrum, employed to justify eurosceptic attitudes.

Anthony Forster identified two broad forms of Euroscepticism, one associated with views on sovereignty and the other formed from innately ideological impulses. Sovereignty-based eurosceptics believe passionately that the nation-state is the only basis of political legitimacy and should therefore control its own destiny, a belief that cuts across the left/right spectrum, while more ideologically motivated eurosceptics are ideologically sceptical of the nature of European integration – rejecting federal political union and state-centred forms of public administration and drawn largely from the right of the political spectrum (Forster 2000).[2]

Euroscepticism has therefore been used to describe very different combinations of attitudes, adding to a general analytical confusion. Thus, as Sørensen suggests:

> The lack of definitional clarity has not hindered the flourishing of many conclusions with regard to the public attitudes towards the EU. One frequent conclusion has been that Denmark and Britain are Eurosceptic countries. A statement like this is misleading for the simple reason that there can never be one and only one public attitude. It is not possible to label 50 percent of a population 'sceptical' – the situation, of course, is highly nuanced. The simple, though critical conclusion is that not only will public attitudes towards the EU be somewhere in between scepticism and pro-integration attitudes (degree); they are also likely to be directed against different types of integration (type).
>
> (Sørensen 2004)

Szscerbiak and Taggart's ideal-typical distinction between 'hard' and 'soft' euroscepticism has proved useful in clarifying the concept (2008). Hard euroscepticism in their analysis refers to a fundamental rejection of the European project from its inception or of its later developments leading to a demand for a withdrawal from the EU. In Britain, UKIP and British National Party (BNP) have followed this line consistently, while the Labour Party and the Green Party supported it at some point in their history. Szscerbiak and Taggart add usefully that hard eurosceptics tend to judge Europe according to a pre-existing set of values or ideology. The EU is therefore opposed because it embodies a separately identified enemy, whether it is socialism (for Conservatives), neoliberalism (for socialists), bureaucracy (for populists) or culture and race (for extreme nationalists).

Narratives and tropes centred upon a defence of the nation and national community have become more prevalent in post-Maastricht eurosceptic discourse, as the EU has started encroaching on core national sovereignty issues such as taxation, currency and foreign policy rather than extending the common market (Hooghe and Marks 2007: 121). Indeed, in the British case, parliamentary sovereignty has been repeatedly used by opponents of membership of the EC/EU, from Tony Benn and Enoch Powell to John Redwood and Bill Cash, who depict sovereignty as a zero-sum game where any 'gain' for supranationalism is a 'loss' for Britain (Gifford 2010). This was fuelled by a view that British parliamentary sovereignty was so central to its constitution and national identity that it could not be limited without undermining the foundations of the nation itself (see for example Enoch Powell 1972).

In contrast, soft euroscepticism is defined not by a fundamental principled objection to the EU, but by 'concerns on one or a number of policy areas [which] lead to the expression of qualified opposition to the European Union or a sense that "national interest" is currently at odds with the EU's trajectory' (Szscerbiak and Taggart 2008: 8). Soft eurosceptics tend to adopt a pragmatic case-by-case approach, whereby they emphasise the gap between their perceived interests and specific EU policies and insist on changes to these policies in order to make membership of the EU compatible with perceived national interests (Szscerbiak and Taggart 2002: 7). Both the main governing parties have experienced periods of soft euroscepticism – Labour first in the 1960s and 1970s, and the Conservative Party in the early 1990s.

We argue, however, that the soft/hard distinction may have become insufficient to describe the many varieties of euroscepticism that can currently be mapped onto British political discourse. At least one new form of euroscepticism has emerged, especially within the Conservative Party, between 'fundamentalist' supporters of withdrawal and the 'pragmatic' eurosceptics represented by the present leadership. They represent what we term 'radical renegotiators', an increasingly vocal group in the present parliamentary party, who although they do not wish to leave the EU altogether support a radical transformation of Britain's position in the EU with the repatriation of some powers to the national level and a two-speed Europe. With his Bloomberg speech of January 2013, Cameron signalled that he was moving to this relatively new position. One may argue that this is *de facto* fundamentalist euroscepticism in the sense that such demands are unlikely to be agreed by other member-states, which could lead radical renegotiators to support full withdrawal as looks possible for Cameron; nevertheless their position does differ from 'fundamentalist' eurosceptics who want nothing less than immediate and total withdrawal via a referendum. (Szscerbiak and Taggart 2002: 7).

The academic literature provides several explanations for British euroscepticism. Historians have highlighted the underlying lack of commitment towards European integration amongst governing British political elites following the Second World War, based on perceived discrepancies between British and continental interests (Baker and Seawright 1998, George 1998, Young 1998). Analysis of the renewal in British euroscepticism in the late 1980s and early 1990s understandably focused on intra-party divisions, especially in the Conservative Party (Baker et al. 1994, Alexandre-Collier 2002, Forster 2002). Nevertheless recently a third type of explanation has focused on the influence of the British political system on the debates about Europe and the positioning of eurosceptics within parties (Wilks 1996, Usherwood 2001, Aspinwall 2004).

Aspinwall highlights the significance of the UK's first-past-the-post (FPTP) electoral system, which eliminates small parties from parliamentary representation and forces large ones to encompass a variety of views. This means that eurosceptic views, instead of being marginalised and pushed to the fringes of the political system, have to be accommodated within the 'broad church' of mainstream parties, particularly the Labour and the Conservative parties. As a result these views become more influential and constrain governing parties. But this analysis, convincing as it is, fails to explain *why* these eurosceptic views were so important in the first place in Britain.

A fourth explanation attempts to fill this vacuum, with two further variations. One focuses on the history of the British political economy, showing how Britain chose to develop an economic model based on free trade, alongside the unequal partnership with the USA and lately in support of Anglophone globalisation. These aims are perceived to be at odds with the wider European project, especially the deepening of political and economic union (Rosamond 2002, Gamble 2003, Gifford 2010). The other approach focuses on deep-seated attitudes linked to the construction of British cultural 'identity' (Colley 1992, Schnapper 2010). Linda Colley has shown how, in the course of the 18th and 19th centuries, 'Britishness' was constructed in opposition to Catholicism and absolutism on the European continent, correlated with the colonial enterprise. This made it difficult for many Britons to accept a European future after 1945, since Europe continued to be perceived as alien and contradictory to an 'open seas' post-colonial identity, a view which overlaps with the previous model. Europe, as a cluster of identity issues, cuts across traditional party cleavages, explaining the depth of party divisions in the UK since the European project emerged at the end of the Second World War, to which we turn now.

Divisions about Europe, 1945–1988

Baker et al. have identified four different periods in the history of British euroscepticism since 1945, according to when it proved more or less powerful, and never entirely disappearing (2008). In the first phase, between 1945 and 1972, euroscepticism was the 'conventional wisdom' among British elites, who felt that the European project made sense for politically and economically weakened continental countries, but not for a 'great power' with global interests like the UK. Supporters of British participation in the project were relatively few in number and scattered across all three main political parties. The economic rationale which led Macmillan and then Wilson to apply for membership in the 1960s did not really impact on this powerful euroscepticism which was also fuelled by the 'dangerous' for British democracy loss of sovereignty which membership would entail for the self-styled 'mother of parliaments', a position dating back to Walter Bagehot's 19th-century constitutional triumphalism (King 2007).

The second, much shorter, phase was between 1972 and 1975, when membership of the EEC had been achieved. British eurosceptics found themselves in a minority fighting a rearguard action in the referendum campaign where they faced a powerful alliance of leading politicians, the media and business groups who favoured staying in the Community out of perceived economic self-interest – namely access to European markets. In the third phase, between 1975 and 1988, euroscepticism did not disappear but was 'latent' in spite of being adopted by the weakened Labour Party in opposition. It had a low salience in the public debate of the period, which focused on domestic policy issues – especially the economy – and therefore the issue of Europe did not impose heavy constraints on governments.

However, in the fourth phase since 1988, euroscepticism has once again become central in the political debate, spreading in the Conservative Party and other right-wing parties, leading to the creation of James Goldsmith's Referendum Party, then UKIP and to a lesser extent permeating Labour and the Liberal Democrats. In all this Margaret Thatcher played a pivotal role in establishing a discursive pattern on Europe based on the defence of 'British interests', 'red lines', 'battles' to be fought, adopted by her followers including Tony Blair, who adopted a pragmatically positive approach to the EU, but included many traditionally sceptical elements.

Although UK-wide euroscepticism evolved in various forms across the decades after the Second World War, one thing remained constant – internal party divisions over Europe, the exception being the Liberals. Pro-Europeans were originally a minority within both Conservative and Labour parties. Between 1970 and 1974 as the Conservative Party elite moved towards a more positive, if pragmatic, vision of Britain in the EEC, under the UK's only strongly pro-European prime minister, Edward Heath, a sizeable majority within the party, especially on the back benches, remained strongly opposed to it. The most famous figure in this Tory cultural ultra-nationalist movement was Enoch Powell, who campaigned vigorously against membership from 1969 onwards and resigned over the issue in 1974, creating tensions in the party and weakening Heath's leadership. The core ultra-nationalist party of the era, the National Front, was also strongly anti-European on cultural, nationalist and racist grounds, in contrast to Mosley's earlier Union Movement which had been for European alliances based on the existence of a common Anglo-Saxon 'European race-culture'.[3]

During the same decade and the following one, the Labour Party opposed membership, even when it was led by a moderate like Hugh Gaitskell who, in the Bagehot tradition, famously talked in 1962 about the end of 'Britain as an independent state, the end of a 1000 years of history' should the UK join the EEC. Tony Benn became the most vocal senior left-wing opponent to membership of the EC in the party. Like Powell, he appealed to the British people to defend the nation, bypassing the usual party loyalty (Gifford 2008: 10) in a move which we would describe today as populist – an example that Conservative eurosceptics followed in the 1990s. In an address to the Labour Cabinet discussing Britain joining the EU he said:

> The real case for entry has never been spelled out, which is that there should be a fully federal Europe in which we become a province...We are at the moment on a federal escalator, moving as we talk, going towards a federal objective we do not wish to reach. In practice, Britain will be governed by a European coalition government that we cannot change, dedicated to a capitalist or market economy theology. I believe that we want independence and

democratic self-government, and I hope the Cabinet in due course will think again.

(Benn 1975: 347)

Nevertheless important figures, including Roy Jenkins and George Brown, favoured entry on pragmatic grounds and took the party with them, but without silencing the eurosceptics in the party. Evidence of this can be seen in 1971 when 69 Labour MPs defied a three-line whip and voted in favour of accession (Baker and Seawright 1998: 58). As for Harold Wilson, having campaigned on an anti-EC platform in 1964, he applied for membership in 1967 (again on pragmatic grounds), later criticising the terms of entry Heath had secured in 1971, before campaigning in the 1975 referendum in favour of staying in the EC. Confusion remained after the referendum, as the Labour governments of 1975–1979, having secured British membership, subsequently earned Britain its 'awkward partner' reputation through their opposition to the EMS and direct elections to the EP. After the 1979 defeat, Labour under Michael Foot became increasingly opposed to the EC on 'socialism in one country' grounds, accusing it of being a 'capitalist club'. In 1979 the Party Conference passed a resolution advocating outright withdrawal, although this held little sway with sections of the Labour leadership which remained divided on the issue. The 1983 election was unique in British post-1945 history in having a mainstream party advocating withdrawal from the EEC, following a split in 1981 which saw the pro-European right wing of the party depart to create the Social Democrat Party (SDP).

Meanwhile, the Conservative Party now saw itself as *the* pro-European party – Margaret Thatcher, its leader after 1975, had voted yes in the referendum and was by 1979 a pragmatic though not uncritical – as we saw in the previous chapter – European. Stephen Wall quotes a foreword she wrote to the programme for a dinner organised by the Conservative Group for Europe in January 1983: 'We Conservatives must not allow ourselves to be deflected into an arid debate about the past and away from our purpose, which is to build a strong and enduring Community and to improve Britain's position within it' (Wall 2008: 18). The economic benefits of belonging to a single free market were seen as superior to the risks of isolation from the UK's main trading partners, whatever reservations the Conservatives had over specific issues such as the common agricultural policy or the size of Britain's contribution to the annual EC budget. Thatcher therefore signed the Single European

Act (SEA) in spite of the advances in majority voting at the European Council that went with it, raising questions of her understanding of the deal she had struck (Thatcher 1993: 554–555 and 1995: 473, Wall 2010: 50–51).

Conflicting views about the EC were nevertheless expressed within the Cabinet, for example between the economic 'wets', who tended to be more pro-European, and the Thatcherite neoliberal 'dries' (Alexandre-Collier 2002: 53). The first cracks appeared in 1986, when the government was split over the offered alternatives of a US or European future for the Westland helicopter company at Yeovil in Somerset, leading to the furious resignation of Michael Heseltine who favoured a European link up against the US-led Sikorsky one. Intra-party tensions had therefore risen even before the Maastricht Treaty was negotiated, when Franco-German plans for the EMU and political union took on a Eurocentric reality that Thatcher had under-estimated. Henceforth, for Thatcher and her followers, UK economic sovereignty was at stake, with, amongst other things, the threat of monetary domination by a European central bank located in, or at least dominated by, Germany.

In addition, NATO and the UK's independent foreign policies (ignoring the UK's and NATO's subordination to the USA) would also be undermined by possible integrated European foreign and defence policies. Thatcher's response was to suggest a vision of Europe centred entirely upon cooperation between sovereign nation-states, a view launched in her infamous Bruges speech of September 1988. It was highly controversial in the party, with several senior party members, including Edward Heath, Geoffrey Howe – then foreign secretary – and Nigel Lawson strongly disapproving of it. Resignations followed and Europe was partly responsible for Thatcher's downfall in November 1990 (Baker et al. 1993a and b).

John Major subsequently obtained a significant and face-saving opt-out from the single currency and signed the Maastricht Treaty, but monetary union provided the main focus for contestation of the EU project in the years that followed. Conservative euroscepticism, inspired by Thatcher, crystallised under John Major's troubled premiership following the rejection of the Maastricht Treaty by Danish voters in a referendum in May 1992 and the currency crisis leading to the humiliating exit of the pound from the Exchange Rate Mechanism (which it had entered under Thatcher in October 1990) on Black Monday in September 1992. In the long term, this disaster strengthened opposition to the single currency well beyond the hard core of Conservative eurosceptics. John Major described what happened in his memoirs:

> Black Wednesday turned a quarter of a century of unease into a flat rejection of any wider involvement in Europe. Many Conservatives threw logic to one side; emotional rivers burst their banks. For a few of my parliamentary colleagues, Black Wednesday awoke the instincts that turn a profound love of one's own country into a nationalism or insularity that encompasses a distaste for any other.
> (Major 1999: 352)

Opposition to the treaty grew amongst what was still a small minority of Conservative MPs made powerful by the government's very narrow majority in Parliament following the April 1992 general election. This is when euroscepticism 'came of age' (Forster 2002: 83), with a well-organised campaign both in and outside Parliament, supported by an increasingly strident anti-European press (Alexandre-Collier 2002). Following a parliamentary battle lasting over a year (Baker et al. 1993, 1994), John Major managed to get the treaty ratified but this was a pyrrhic victory as Tory eurosceptics had been emboldened and his own credibility fatally undermined. Under pressure from 'the bastards' in his own Cabinet, Major adopted an increasingly hostile stance in EU, giving up his hitherto limited engagement in Europe and eventually leading a policy of non-negotiation over the BSE 'mad cow' disease crisis in the dying days of his premiership.

Meanwhile, official Labour policy – as so often with British parties in opposition (since they no longer need to defend growing European integration to a sceptical populist media and their voters) – had followed an opposite trajectory, gradually embracing a pro-European stance (George and Haythorn 1996, Daniels 1998). This positioning was also partly in reaction to Thatcher's increasing euroscepticism and the result of a growing appreciation of the benefits that the EC/EU could bring in terms of social policy and workers' protection, severely weakened at home by successive neoliberal Conservative governments. Jacques Delors's influence as president of the European Commission was also a significant factor in this conversion of the party and the trade unions towards a more mainstream European social-democratic party. A degree of euroscepticism remained within the party, but it was now subdued and the leadership of Neil Kinnock and then John Smith was instrumental in bridging most of the divisions over Europe that the party had experienced in the previous decades. In their survey of Labour

Parliamentarians published in 1996, Baker et al. showed the extent of the shift, with an overall majority of Labour MP respondents supporting membership of the EU, especially in the threatening neoliberal context of globalisation, with a majority in favour of adopting the single currency, although a sizeable minority opposed it. Nevertheless, 20% of Labour MPs agreed with the idea that 'the establishment of a single EU currency would signal the end of the UK as a sovereign nation' while 75% disagreed. They also found a cohort effect, by which MPs elected after 1983 tended to be much more pro-European than their predecessors (Baker et al. 1996: 368), a trend which in the Conservative Party ran in the opposite direction with each successive intake since 1992 becoming progressively more anti-European (Cowley 2000, Norris and Lovenduski 2004).

By the mid-1990s therefore, the Labour Party had become less divided than ever before on the European issue and appeared broadly in favour of 'constructive engagement' as the 1997 general election manifesto put it, albeit in an EU devoted to open-market regionalism (Baker et al. 2002: 413–415), while Conservative Party divisions were more conspicuous than ever between euro-fundamentalists like Peter Lilley, Bill Cash and Michael Portillo, radical re-negotiators like John Major himself and europhiles led by Kenneth Clarke and Michael Heseltine. Sovereignty remained at the forefront of the debate on the EU, this time focusing on the EMU.

Blair and New Labour: An end to divisions?

The quasi-extinction of Labour euroscepticism as a potent political force was confirmed under Tony Blair's leadership. There is no doubt about his personal commitment to British engagement in the EU, which has been well documented (Blair 1996, 1998, 2005, Rawnsley 2010: 190). Blair also managed to keep his party united on the issue, which at the time could be seen as a remarkable achievement. His oft-repeated mantra was that, breaking with a sorry past, Britain should be a 'leader in Europe': 'The argument is simple. We are part of Europe. It affects us directly and deeply. Therefore we should exercise leadership in order to change Europe in the direction we want' (Blair 2001). But the limits of his engagement, which was often more defensive than positive, were made clear during his ten years in office. The mixed feelings towards the EU of some Cabinet members, including Chancellor Gordon Brown and Foreign Secretary Jack Straw, were obvious. Divisions within the party, limited as they were, remained latent and a form of soft euroscepticism, prompted in part by the aftermath of the financial and economic crisis of 2007–2008, reappeared under the premiership of Gordon Brown and again under Ed Miliband.

The New Labour discourse about Europe was grounded on the idea that the main determining factor of policy should be the shift in the economic paradigm summed up by 'globalisation' (Baker et al. 2002). These developments were viewed as inevitable and impossible to undo and should therefore be embraced, including making national adjustments, especially in the labour market, to meet global demands (Blair 1999, Hay and Rosamond 2002). European integration could be viewed as strategically useful to social democrats under globalisation summed up as 'open regionalism', which suggested that 'the development of new forms of regionalism in several parts of the world does not run counter to globalisation, but is rather an important step which helps promote it'. Regional organisations provide:

> forms of governance and regulation of the global economy. They remain open to world trade and subject to its rules. Yet, at the same time, they facilitate the creation of a new political space, a process which has gone furthest in Europe, which allows the discussion of common concerns, and the elaboration of new forms of governance.
> (Baker et al. 2002)

This avowedly 'Third Way' view of the EU represented it as a useful opportunity for Britain to modernise and adapt to the changes induced by globalisation – a view which came to be accepted by the party in general. In the 1997 manifesto, New Labour expressed the desire to be a 'leader' in Europe and cautiously endorsed the principle of adopting the single currency if the existing 'formidable' obstacles could be overcome (Labour Party 1997). The rhetoric was relatively low key, but the end of the UK's isolation within and hostility towards the EU were clear when the new government signed the Social Chapter of the Maastricht Treaty along with the Amsterdam and Nice treaties and incorporated the European Convention on Human Rights into national law. It was also conspicuous in the active part played by the government in the adoption of the Lisbon strategy of 2000, the championing of enlargement and the re-launch of plans for an autonomous European defence capacity following the Franco-British summit of Saint-Malo in December 1998. Blair's first administration was therefore marked by a break with the previous Conservative governments, accumulating a number of perceived achievements on the European scene, with the distinct possibility that the European single currency would be adopted by the UK during a second term.

Things changed markedly in the second term, however, when the New Labour government became much less proactive and engaged in Europe (Smith 2005: 704), with the sole exception of the negotiations on the constitutional treaty (Menon 2004). There were three main reasons, two internal and one external, explaining Blair's limited ambitions in Europe. The first was his growing divisions within the Cabinet with Brown. While Robin Cook had been perceived before 1997 as a more lukewarm European than Blair and Brown (Smith 2005: 708), it was the Chancellor who turned out to be the main obstacle to Blair's European policy. Brown took control of the policy on the single currency as early as the Autumn of 1997, on the grounds that it should be a purely economic decision and subsequently blocked Blair's attempt to put forward the case for the euro and organise a referendum (Mandelson 2010: 237–238, Powell 2010: 253, Rawnsley 2010: 191–193, Wall 2010: 170). The 2003 assessment of the famous 'five economic tests' which Brown had devised in October 1997 put the final nail on the coffin, as the Treasury concluded that only one of them had been met (on the impact of the euro on the City), leaving no choice to Blair but to withdraw his proposals. In his memoirs Blair claimed that purely economic conditions had dictated the fact that he hadn't 'gone for it', whereas his chief of staff, Jonathan Powell, was much more blunt about the disagreements with Brown (Blair 2010: 537, Powell 2010: 253–255). Rawnsley describes in detail the extraordinarily tense meeting which took place in 10 Downing Street on 1 April 2003 between Blair and Brown over the assessment of the five tests to join the euro (2010: 194–195).

But the disagreements within the Cabinet went beyond the Blair/Brown confrontation. Jack Straw, then foreign secretary, along with other senior figures including John Prescott and David Blunkett, agreed with Brown that no referendum should be held. Charles Clarke and Peter Mandelson supported Blair, but that was not sufficient to win the argument. Perhaps this was also partly due to Blair's style of leadership since, as Jonathan Powell put it, 'one of the strange things is that Tony never thought about building coalitions in his Cabinet' (Rawnsley 2010: 196).

By insisting on the primacy of the case of economics, Blair successfully downplayed another crucial domestic factor, namely the hostile attitude of most of the press, especially the Murdoch papers he had been busy courting to support New Labour, feeding public hostility in general. As Powell noticed, 'the Prime Minister of the UK suffers one major disadvantage by comparison with all other European leaders, one that massively complicates his negotiating hand at European Councils, and that is the British press' (Powell 2010: 253).

Two press barons in particular, Conrad Black (*Daily Telegraph*) and Rupert Murdoch (*The Times, The Sun, News of the World*), neither of them born British, came to share Thatcher's hyperglobalist anti-European views in the late 1980s and subsequently encouraged a radical and sometimes rabid anti-Europeanism in their newspapers (Anderson and Weymouth 1999). No academic work has been able to assess precisely the level of political impact produced by the press on its readers (Curtice 1999, Norris 2000) and if there is one, it may be limited (Carey and Burton 2004). But it is generally accepted that this hostility towards Europe has influenced successive prime ministers in their negotiations with the EU (Powell 2010). In a country where a majority of the population still read dailies, politicians certainly *think* newspapers are influential and act accordingly. Blair was clearly not ready to confront a eurosceptic press which represented a majority of newspapers, both in number and even more so in circulation size (with the *Daily Mail* and *Daily Express* added to those already mentioned).

Having promised a referendum, Blair was bound to have his decision affected by hostility from the press and crucial sections of the electorate. As a result, whatever his claimed europhilia, he never really made the case for Europe in his own country (Riddell 2005: 381). He made little attempt to engage the British public on Europe, nor did he launch any campaign in favour of the EU or the single currency, as illustrated by the ill-fated 'Britain in Europe' organisation, launched in 1999 without Blair attending and which he never properly supported or sustained. In short, Blair's wish to win the next election and therefore to appease eurosceptics always proved stronger than his commitment to Europe – indeed the short space devoted to the EU in his memoirs speaks volumes about where his real priorities lay.

The third factor which made his second term less successful in terms of influence in the EU was the war in Iraq and the tensions it created among member-states, especially between the British and French governments. Not only was the feasibility of a future common foreign and security policy undermined by this serious rift over a major international crisis, it also contributed to changing Blair's foreign policy priorities. The idea of the UK acting as a 'bridge' between Europe and the USA, which had been extensively developed by Blair prior to this, was more or less abandoned for a more traditional stress on the 'special relationship' with the USA (Gamble 2003). By 2005, with the dispute over the EU budget and reform of the CAP under way, Blair had effectively turned his back on Europe, which he saw as incapable of reforming itself in the way he wished as an open regionalist neoliberal body. The speech he gave in the EP shortly after the 'no' votes in the referenda on the constitutional treaty in France and the Netherlands summed up his disillusionment:

> If Europe defaulted to Euroscepticism, or if European nations, faced with this immense challenge, decide to huddle together, hoping we can avoid globalisation, shrink away from confronting the changes around us, take refuge in the present policies of Europe as if by constantly repeating them we would by the very act of repetition make them more relevant, then we risk failure. Failure on a grand, strategic, scale. This is not a time to accuse those who want Europe to change of betraying Europe. It is a time to recognise that only by change will Europe recover its strength, its relevance, its idealism and therefore its support amongst the people.
>
> (Blair 2005)

The continuity in rhetoric and policy towards Europe between Thatcher, Major and Blair is starkly revealed in this speech and has since been well researched (Wall 2010, Daddow 2013). Differences between Blair and his predecessors were often more about tactics than objectives. His choice to engage with his EU partners was essentially a defensive one – in order to prevent Europe from moving in a direction that did not suit British interests and to protect perceived British national interests. Significantly, priorities for Europe, such as the deregulation of services and energy, the protection of the City and Britain's considerable offshore banking interests, a European defence strengthening NATO, the control of national borders, 'red lines' on federalism, social legislation and taxation were shared by all British governments since the 1980s.

Gordon Brown, who became prime minister in 2007, was rightly seen as less euro-enthusiastic than his predecessor. Like many British politicians of the period, he had been traumatised by the 'Black Wednesday' debacle in 1992 and had no intention of taking any chances, as he saw it, with the British economy by taking it in the EZ. The Treasury in general, traditionally but especially under Brown, was considered eurosceptic, with the added influence of Brown's main adviser, Ed Balls (Rawnsley 2010: 191–192).

EU finance ministers had been used to the British Chancellor lecturing them in Councils of Ministers about the need to reform Europe and adopt the British model of economic stewardship, or skipping meetings altogether. As Seldon and Lodge cogently remark, 'speaking rather than listening, and suspicion rather than friendship, were the hallmarks of his attitude as Chancellor towards Europe' (2010: 66). In contrast with Blair's early years, Brown showed little interest in the EU in general and seemingly lacked any overall vision for Europe, except on a few global issues like climate change, or the fight against poverty, where he saw how useful the EU could be as a force for good in the world. For ten years Brown's outlook had been mostly economic, by inclination and necessity, and he found the EU wanting in this respect. A pamphlet published in 2005 summed up his thinking: for him Europe was failing to adjust to the pressures of globalisation and was too 'inward-looking', preoccupied with internal institutional issues (the constitutional treaty at the time) rather than adopting the right reforms:

> In the old trade bloc Europe, the emphasis was, understandably, on internal integration: breaking down barriers to the movement of capital, labour, goods and services within Europe. The focus was, understandably, inward-looking not outward-looking. The assumption was that a common market would become a single market, and then that single market would engender a single currency, and perhaps even a federal fiscal policy with tax harmonisation and then move to a supra-national state. But the shifting balance of global economic activity – with the rise of China, India and other rapidly growing emerging economies founded on the global sourcing of goods and global flows of capital – now creates challenges that Europe's founders could never have foreseen. Although some Member States are performing relatively well, Europe as a whole is losing ground to competitors in five key areas: growth, labour market performance, skills, innovation and enterprise.
>
> (Brown 2005a: 1)

This economic speech in some respects parallels the neoconservative views of 'Old Europe' based on military power. The term was first employed by US Secretary of Defence Donald Rumsfeld in January 2003 referring to European countries that failed to support the 2003 invasion of Iraq, specifically France and Germany.[4] In Brown's hyperglobalist view, Europe should simply follow the British model of neoliberalisation and deregulation (in part it already had) which he claimed had produced a costless period of uninterrupted growth since 1997. He made this clear in his Mansion House speech in the City of London that same year:

'In the last eight years, here in Britain, we have had to make and continue to make hard, long term choices to achieve stability, growth and flexibility. Now to be globally competitive, the European Union must make these long term choices too' (Brown 2005b). Nor did he believe in political union either, considering that the negative referendum results in France and the Netherlands showed that voters' identities were rooted in nations, not Europe. His conclusion was:

> Our position should be one of pro-European realism. Pro-European because we recognise the economic benefits of cooperation and a pooling of sovereignty to secure an enlarged single market of 450 million consumers. And pro-European because we know that – as trade shows – there must be a European dimension to how we respond to the challenges of globalisation. But pro-European realism, because we know that Europe can only succeed if it recognises and faces up to the scale of the long term changes that need to be made to meet today's global realities. And pro-European realism because we understand that it is by intergovernmental cooperation – recognising national values – that we build the long term political will and sense of purpose to implement these changes.
>
> (Brown 2005b)

This is a speech that a Conservative prime minister could equally have made. Brown's soft eurosceptic reputation was also fuelled by the way he avoided signing the Lisbon Treaty with the other EU leaders in December 2007 so as, it was claimed, to avoid appearing on the official photograph. This was part of his 'realist' pro-Europeanism or what Ed Balls called 'hard-headed' pro-Europeanism and therefore could be defined as softly eurosceptic (Balls 2007).

On the other hand, he appointed a pro-European, David Miliband, as foreign secretary and resisted the pressure from the Conservatives and the Eurosceptic press to organise a referendum on the treaty, which clearly qualifies his euroscepticism. Indeed, there was a minority in the Labour Party which was more eurosceptic than the government. Among the dissident voices were Gisela Stuart, who had represented the UK at the European Convention, and the veteran Scottish MP Ian Davidson.[5]

By the time the treaty had been ratified in Parliament in 2008, the government and opposition's attention had decisively shifted away from the EU towards the financial crisis and the debate about the budget deficit in the UK. Brown and Balls' regular claims that Britain's economy had performed much better than the continental ones (completely ignoring German's powerful global export-based economy and Britain's propensity to live off rentier capitalism, debt and property bubbles) was finally and fatally challenged by the outbreak of the financial crisis, which was widely blamed on the US and UK neoliberal drive towards deregulation of finance since the 1980s.

Yet when the financial crisis broke out in 2007–2008, Brown's instinct, in keeping with his previous views on globalisation and Europe, was to look for a global agreement on banking reform within the G20, especially when the UK chaired it in 2009. This, in addition to measures taken nationally (nationalisation of banks, bank bail-outs, etc.), was more successful in his view than seeking an EU-wide solution, although the UK's position outside the EZ also made its position peripheral in such a crisis. He considered that EU leaders were slow to understand the crisis in September 2008, although he got his bank recapitalisation scheme endorsed by the EU at a meeting in Paris (Seldon and Lodge 2010: 164). There were also disagreements with Germany and France about the fiscal stimulus that he envisaged (Rawnsley 2010: 593, 623–626).

By the time Labour left power in 2010, the overall party discourse remained much more positive about Europe than that of the Conservatives, but a form of limited euroscepticism had crept back within the leadership and a minority of backbench MPs had also become deeply unsatisfied with recent EU developments including, on the left, its Germanic-dominated neoliberalisation. In the 2010 manifesto a number of changes were sought, including more competitiveness for the EU economies, in line with Brown's own views, and a reform of the CAP (Labour Party 2010).

In a move suggesting a degree of continuity, two close allies of Gordon Brown, Ed Miliband as leader and Douglas Alexander as shadow foreign secretary, took charge of European policy after the general election defeat in the backdrop of the EZ debt crisis and Brown's retirement. Meanwhile, the Conservative Party's continued move to the extreme of euroscepticism and the constraints that coalition government put on the Liberal Democrats left Labour as the only pro-European party in Parliament. Indeed, party spokespersons criticised the government's at best lukewarm attitude towards the EU, particularly in the wake of the December 2011 European Council meeting.

Yet Labour rhetoric concerning the EZ became almost equally critical to that of the Conservatives as the crisis deepened in Greece and later Spain and Italy. In June 2011 Jack Straw asserted in Parliament that the end of the single currency was nigh: 'since the euro, in its current form, is going to collapse is it not better that this happens quickly rather than a slow death?'[6] Douglas Alexander also delivered a fairly critical speech on the EU and its economy, where the only positive aspects of membership of the EU mentioned were the old cherries of the Single Market and international trade. While criticising the government's 'complacency' about prospects for a two-speed Europe, his priority was typically defensive – to secure British interests: 'A better way forward would be to engage now with the reality that Germany is seeking treaty changes that enforce greater discipline within the EZ and seize this opportunity to safeguards the rights of non-euro members' (Alexander 2011). However, Ed Balls and Peter Mandelson signed a rare joint article in which they criticised the government's disengagement and called for reforms of the EZ with a strengthening of its political institutions.[7]

So euroscepticism in the party, which had been dominant in the 1980s then totally subdued in the 1990s and early 2000s, reappeared as a result of both pressure from public opinion and the economic crisis which has strengthened the voices of opponents to the single currency. This euroscepticism remains muted, however, when compared with the evolution undergone by the Conservatives.

The Conservative Party after 1997: The drift towards hard euroscepticism

By the time the Conservative Party lost the 1997 general election, it was once again in disarray over Europe. Major had failed to impose his own moderately eurosceptic line and two antagonistic views could be heard, one pro-European view led by Kenneth Clarke, Michael Heseltine and Chris Patten, and one minority but growing eurosceptic line intent on ruling out any opt-in to the single currency. In opposition this minority grew in size and influence, as illustrated by the choice of leaders, William Hague (1997–2001) and especially Iain Duncan Smith (2001–2003) and Michael Howard (2003–2005), two prominent quasi-rebels under Major. Conservative MPs and party members also became increasingly eurosceptic according to polls and surveys, with many local constituency selection committees making it almost impossible to be selected as a candidate without possessing strong eurosceptic credentials (Bale 2006).

Hague successfully managed to paper over the divisions in the party by getting his policy of opposition to the single currency for at least two Parliaments approved in an internal referendum in October 1998. He attempted to use the voters' perceived anti-European feelings against

New Labour in the 2001 general election by focusing his campaign on the 'threat' to British identity represented by plans to introduce the euro. The manifesto talked about 'being in Europe, not run by Europe' and was clear in that respect:

> The European Union has, with the prospect of enlargement, reached a fork in the road. Down one route lies a fully integrated superstate with nation-states and the national veto disappearing. The Government is taking us down this route. The alternative is a Europe of nations coming together in different combinations for different purposes and to differing extents.
> (Conservative Party 2001)

This deliberately echoed Thatcher's Bruges speech and anticipated a vision that now dominates the Conservative Party's pragmatic eurosceptic branch, that is the idea of a two- or multi-speed Europe, where the UK could cherry-pick the European policies that suited its national interest ('different combinations'). Yet this strategy failed to translate into any electoral gain in the 2001 election as Hague overestimated the saliency of the issue to voters. His followers, Duncan Smith and Howard, both entrenched this hardening euroscepticism by ruling out the single currency, toying with the idea of leaving the centre-right European People's Party (EPP) in the EP, and reducing the overall salience of the issue. Europe did not feature to any extent in the 2005 election (although the theme of 'bringing back powers from Brussels' emerged at this point), both because the Conservatives feared UKIP's potential electoral impact, as we will see below, and because New Labour had promised a referendum on the EU constitution that was being discussed at the time (Conservative Party 2005, Bale 2006).

By the time David Cameron was elected as leader in 2005, Conservative euroscepticism had clearly hardened and even though the leadership didn't wish to withdraw from the EU, an increasing number of MPs and influential party members did. The old europhile wing of the party had either been marginalised, or had retired, leaving Kenneth Clarke as a lonely, if respected, leading pro-European figure. Cameron proved to be little concerned with European issues (partly because of the danger the issue posed to party unity) and quickly promised during the leadership campaign to withdraw Tory MEPs from the moderate conservative EPP group to attract eurosceptic votes. Cameron's rhetoric on Europe as opposition leader focused on demanding a referendum on the Lisbon Treaty, accusing the EU of increasing centralisation in Brussels, as indicated by the failed constitutional treaty (Hague 2009, Lynch 2009: 190).[8] This enabled him both to attack the Labour government's failure to live up to its promise of defending Britain's 'interests' and above all to maintain party unity. When the treaty was ratified, he vowed 'not to let matters rest' and, once in government, to introduce a bill compelling any UK government to hold a referendum if any more power was transferred to Brussels. The 2010 election manifesto duly promised a referendum bill as well as the repatriation of some policies, especially social legislation and criminal law, from Brussels (Conservative Party 2010).

To implement this he required a majority Conservative government which did not emerge from the May 2010 election. The coalition government established after the election combined two parties with supposedly contradictory views on Europe, the Liberal Democrats having been consistently positive – though pragmatic – about the EU (Baker and Seawright 1998, Schnapper 2011). The agreement hammered out saw the Lib Dems agree to the referendum bill while the Conservatives dropped their demands for repatriation of powers (Schnapper 2012). In practice, the Liberal Democrats' input on EU policy has been limited: both the foreign secretary and Europe minister have been Conservatives (William Hague then Philip Hammond and David Lidington) and radical renegotiator eurosceptics. Nick Clegg was thus powerless to prevent David Cameron from vetoing the Fiscal Compact proposed to solve the early stages of the EZ crisis, led by the French and German governments at the December 2011 European Council.[9]

The European Union Bill, introduced in Parliament in the autumn of 2010, was insufficient to placate Conservative hard eurosceptics. Unrelenting pressure was put on the government throughout 2011 inside and outside Parliament, echoed by a supportive Conservative press. Cameron experienced a lull when he dramatically vetoed the fiscal compact in the December 2011 EU Council, with buoyant eurosceptic MPs hailing him as a hero and saviour of Britain. But the 25 EU members went ahead with the treaty and Cameron was forced to let them proceed using EU institutions, and strident eurosceptic criticisms were renewed. The EU Scrutiny Committee, chaired by the veteran eurosceptic Bill Cash, issued a critical report on the government policy, while MEP Daniel Hannan resumed his criticism of the government.[10] There were also rumblings about the supposed Liberal Democrat influence on EU policy, deemed too accommodating, fuelled by Clegg's attempt to rebuild bridges with the UK's partners and qualify Britain's veto.[11] The issue of an in/out referendum to be held before or after the

2015 general election also came to the fore again in 2011–2012, leading to Cameron's Bloomberg speech in January 2013.

The eurosceptic evolution of the Conservative Party can be explained in terms of a combination of ideological and electoral factors. On the ideological front, the late 1990s and early 2000s witnessed a crystallisation of the eurosceptic discourse around what Baker et al. called a 'hyperglobalist' view of the world, in which the EU bureaucracy was seen as not just threatening British political and monetary sovereignty – always an anathema to Conservative fundamentalists – but also as an obstacle to Britain enjoying the fruits of globalisation and free trade by imposing regulatory restrictions and protectionist policies (Lynch 1999, Baker et al. 2002, Gifford 2008). Unlike economic hyperglobalists, for whom the nation-state is necessarily hollowed out by the forces of globalisation, the Conservatives combine their analysis of globalisation with a strong attachment to the nation-state:

> The European Union is viewed as a long-term Franco-German project designed ultimately to create a federal super-state which would impose unacceptably high levels of taxation, spending and regulation on all its component parts, making the UK economy uncompetitive in global markets outside the EU. If successful it would undo the hard-won market disciplines created during the Thatcher era in the 1980s as an expression of the democratic preferences of the majority of British people.
>
> (Baker et al. 2002: 410)

This discourse, which draws on the 19th century imperial tradition of open seas and free trade as well as the more recent influence of Thatcherite neoliberalism, took hold of an increasing number of Conservative MPs and MEPs following post-Maastricht developments in the EU, as shown in Baker et al.'s survey of Conservative parliamentarians in 1994 and 1998.

The sovereign debt crisis in the EZ witnessed a resurgence of the argument among Tory eurosceptic organisations such as the Fresh Start Group.[12] Tensions over the sovereign debts in the EZ proved, from this perspective, that the single currency was not viable in the first place without full economic and political union and that the UK had therefore been right to stay outside to preserve its superior sovereignty of the people and economic way of life.

The electoral factor itself includes two developments. One is the change in party recruitment at grass roots level, where the older generation has been replaced by an increasingly eurosceptic younger one. The trend started in the 2000s and became apparent in the 2010 general election, when only fundamentalist eurosceptic candidates stood a chance in many constituencies of being selected as candidates.[13] The other is the external threat, real or perceived, posed by the Referendum Party (RP) to safe Conservative constituencies (in the 1997 election) and since then by UKIP. Created by James Goldsmith to demand a referendum on membership of the EU, the RP fielded candidates in all constituencies where the Conservative candidate didn't support their (hard) eurosceptic stance. Although it won no seats, the party got 800,000 or 3.1% of the votes and worried Conservative Party strategists because in 19 constituencies the RP share of the vote was above the winning candidates' majority over the Conservatives – although not all Referendum Party voters had switched from the Conservative Party (Curtice and Steed 1997: 306, Heath et al. 1998). In the event, the RP didn't survive the death of Goldsmith, but UKIP, founded in 1993 in the wake of the Maastricht saga, became the new single-issue party attracting fundamentalist eurosceptics campaigning for withdrawal from the EU and gaining an electoral base in many Conservative constituencies.

The party did particularly well in the European elections of 1999, 2004, 2009 and especially 2014 (held under proportional representation), winning respectively 3, 12, 13 and 24 seats. Although the party failed to gain any seat in the FPTP general elections (with 2.1% of the votes in 2001, 2.8% in 2005, 3.2% in 2010), its popularity has been rising, with almost a million votes in 2010 and opinion polls suggesting it might win 19% of the votes in 2015. It is a clear threat to the Conservatives, of which it is in effect a breakaway faction (as with the Tea and Republican parties in the USA) with UKIP activists sharing hardline law and order, ultra-nationalist and economically hyperglobalist liberal views. The party has tended to do better in rural constituencies and among older voters, who form the traditional Conservative base (Curtice and Steed 2001: 325). Evidence has shown that in constituencies where they have done relatively well the Conservative share of the votes has decreased (Curtice et al. 2005: 246). Ideological and electoral factors have therefore combined, once again, to fuel the Conservative Party's obsession with Europe.[14]

As a result, the intra-party dynamic has changed, with a general shift towards harder, more fundamentalist forms of euroscepticism. Tory europhiles have all but disappeared, and two broad groups within the parliamentary party can be discerned. The first is made up of fundamentalist eurosceptics, which includes prominent voices such as Bill

Cash and John Redwood, but also younger MPs like Mark Pritchard, Douglas Carswell or Jacob Rees-Mogg who, against government wishes, engineered a vote on an in/out referendum in the House of Commons on 24 October 2011 where in spite of a three-line whip against them, 81 Conservative MPs supported their motion.[15] Again in June 2012 a group of almost 100 Conservative MPs signed a letter drafted by John Baron to David Cameron asking for a referendum 'on the nature of our relationship with the European Union'.[16] Cameron produced a holding response, keeping the option open for one in the future, once the destiny of the EU and of Britain within it had been clarified:

> I will continue to work for a different, more flexible and less onerous position for Britain within the EU. How do we take the British people with us on this difficult and complicated journey? How do we avoid the wrong paths of either accepting the status quo meekly or giving up altogether and preparing to leave? It will undoubtedly be hard, but taking the right path in politics often is. As we get closer to the end point, we will need to consider how best to get the full-hearted support of the British people whether it is in a general election or in a referendum. As I have said, for me the two words 'Europe' and 'referendum' can go together, particularly if we really are proposing a change in how our country is governed, but let us get the people a real choice first.[17]

The second group of MPs is closer to the government's pragmatic renegotiating position and is led by George Eustice and members of the Open Europe organisation. We would refer to them as 'radical renegotiators', since they support a fundamental renegotiation of the UK position in the EU in the supposedly favourable context of the EZ crisis and the repatriation of some powers to the national level. They are comfortable with the idea of a multi-speed Europe where the UK would exclude itself from the inner core but enjoy the benefits of the Single Market – therefore remain in the EU but with fewer constraints (Open Europe 2012). They do not appear to harbour any doubts that Britain's partners would agree to such a renegotiation, at least in their rhetoric.

The distinction between these two groups can sometimes be blurred. Hence Liam Fox, former defence secretary and supposedly belonging to the second group, caused a stir by writing in an article that Britain should not fear leaving the EU if it did not get what it wanted through renegotiation.[18] As for Conservative Party members, a poll published by Conservative Home and Channel Four on 29 May 2012 had 80% of respondents supporting a simple in/out referendum and 70% supporting withdrawal, a complete reversal from a not-so-distant past. The government position has therefore moved from a pragmatic euroscepticism, where no more transfer of power to Brussels is acceptable but Britain should remain active in the EU, to rhetoric closer to the radical renegotiators, while resisting pressure from the fundamentalists who want to unilaterally withdraw from the EU.

In the event, intra-party management of the European issue has become almost as complicated and dangerous for David Cameron as it used to be for John Major. But the centre of gravity in the ideological debate about Europe within the party has clearly shifted in a more radically eurosceptic direction since Maastricht, paralleled by a shift in UK public opinion to which we now turn.

Public opinion since the late 1990s

British public opinion has traditionally been more eurosceptic than average European opinion. Eurobarometer polls conducted since 1973 showed this trend consistently, with the British public always less happy with membership of the EC/EU than other member-states, even though there was a clear 'yes' majority in the 1975 referendum on whether to remain in the EC.

Within the overall statistics there are some interesting sub-divisions, for instance Gabel's work highlights an educational/skills bias in European-wide attitudes towards EU integration since trade and commerce liberalisation benefits mainly the highly educated, who generally register more positive attitudes towards the EU, especially those located in professional or executive positions (Gabel 1998). In addition, there appears to be an interest/knowledge deficit over EU affairs amongst UK citizens. A 2002 survey suggested that 'in the UK...1% of the population felt they knew a great deal about the EU with 11% claiming they knew quite a lot about it. In contrast, 87% of the UK and 88% of Scottish respondents admitted they either knew little or nothing at all about the EU...[and o]nly 13% of UK citizens felt they were involved in EU affairs, compared with 26% across the EU.' Commenting on these findings Mahendran and McIver suggest that:

> It is worth not losing sight of the fact that half the respondents in the UK did not want any more information. This lack of understanding and apparent lack of concern about getting more information among over half of all respondents could be key in explaining the perceived

democratic deficit that some people suggest exists within the EU. The argument here is that if people do not understand, nor want to understand how the EU operates, they are in a poor position to influence decisions which may ultimately affect them or their business.

(2007: 16)

Attitudes towards Europe have followed a clear trend in the overall lack of enthusiasm in UK public opinion (see figure 3.1). The percentage of respondents considering EC membership as positive for Britain was below that of negative responses for most of the 1970s (except 1975–1976) and early 1980s, then again in 1993 (at the time of the debate over the Maastricht Treaty and the UK's eviction from the ERM), in 1998–2001, in 2004 and since the start of the financial crisis in 2008. The only sustained period of time when the EC was relatively popular in Britain was between 1985 and 1992, at the time of the Single European Act and the end of the Cold War. The available Eurobarometer data show clearly that British opinion was always (with the exception of 1989) less positive than the EU average, whether it was EC-12, EC-15, EU-25 or EU-27. In the early years the difference was over 30%, since the 1980s it has been between 10% and 20%. The New Labour years had no effect on this gap which has if anything widened with the crisis (23% in 2009 and 2010).

Finally, a Chatham House survey published in July 2012 found that 57% of respondents thought the government should commit to a

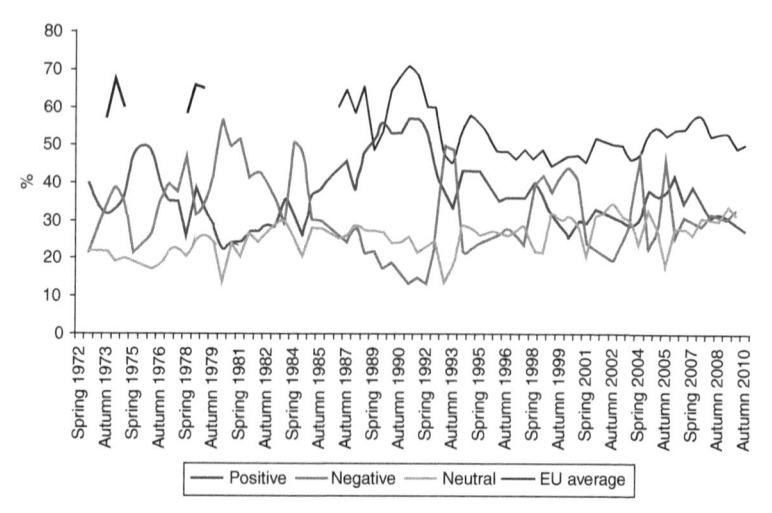

Figure 3.1 UK public opinion on the EC/EU, 1972–2010
Source: Fitzgibbon (2011).

referendum on membership of the EU (71% of Conservative voters, 50% of Labour voters and 40% of Liberal Democrat voters) against 26%. Some 49% of voters then responded that they would vote in favour of withdrawal against only 30% who would wish to vote yes. Labour and especially Liberal Democrat voters were more positive (40% and 64% respectively) which points to a polarised attitude along party lines (Chatham House 2012). These results are consistent with previous Angus Reid opinion polls conducted in 2010 and 2011 showing 48–49% of respondents supporting withdrawal from the EU.[19] Yet by October 2014, opinion had proved again volatile, with support for membership of the EU in case of a referendum on the rise according to an IPSOS/MORI poll.[20]

How does British popular euroscepticism compare with other EU member countries? For several decades, the UK was something of an exception among EC/EU member-states in having mainstream parties opposing European integration at different times in their history, whereas mainstream parties tended to be pro-European in other member-states, leaving opposition to Europe to parties in opposition and/or fringe or extremist parties of the right and left (Marks, Hooghe and Wilson 2000, Szscerbiak and Taggart 2002, Lynch 2009: 188). Following the 1995 and 2004 rounds of enlargement, including Scandinavian then Central and Eastern European countries, Britain has lost some of its specificity in having mainstream eurosceptic parties. Poland's PiS and the Czech Republic's ODS parties, for instance, share the Conservative Party's views on Europe and joined it to form a new group in the EP, the European Conservatives and Reformists (ECR) in 2009. Their shared scepticism towards the EU is combined, like that of the British Conservative Party, with a strong nationalism, authoritarian views on law and order and a neoliberal approach to economic policy with a strong suspicion of centralised bureaucratic government. Nevertheless there are still important distinctions as Sørensen suggests:

> British popular euroscepticism seems closely tied to its perceived role as an independent actor on the world stage as well as to the impression of not forming part of the Continent of Europe. Scepticism, thus, appears directed both towards the wording 'European' and 'Union' in the European Union.
>
> (2004, see also Hanley 2002)

Another difference between the UK and its neighbours was that little elite/public difference existed in attitudes towards Europe. As we have seen, a relative and fluctuating euroscepticism (hard/soft –

fundamentalist/pragmatic) permeated UK parties as well as public opinion from the 1960s, in contrast with founding member-states where enthusiasm about European integration was greater within the political elites than among the public, which was hardly consulted until the early 1990s, forming the 'permissive consensus' mentioned above. This was in part due to the British self-perception of being among the winners of the Second World War shared by both elites and the general public. Euroscepticism developed from Maastricht onwards in the Conservative Party in parallel with the shift in public attitudes – although whether the party followed or led the public in this respect is difficult to assess.

Although euroscepticism is an older phenomenon in Britain than in the rest of the EU, the UK is no longer unique in Europe. Two developments point to the rise of both pragmatic and fundamentalist eurosceptic movements and attitudes in *all* member-states, including the traditionally strongly pro-EU countries. Populist/eurosceptic parties, both right-wing and left-wing (unlike in the UK), have flourished throughout the EU, strengthened by the EZ crisis which has discredited pro-integration government parties. This has occurred in Poland and the Czech Republic, as we saw, but also in Denmark (People's Party), Finland (True Finns), the Netherlands (Geert Wilders), Italy (Northern League), Greece (Golden Dawn, Syriza), France (Front National, Front de Gauche), Hungary (Jobbik and even Fidesz), etc. All strongly criticise the EU although not all advocate withdrawal. Some of them have entered government in coalition with mainstream parties and exercised eurosceptic pressure upon them, apparent for example in the Dutch and Finnish governments' reluctance to bail out Greece after 2010.

The other development illustrating the rise of activist and populist, mainstream and fringe euroscepticism in the EU as a whole is the negative outcomes in referendums organised in Ireland (2000, 2008), Sweden (2003), Denmark (1992, 2000), France (2005) and the Netherlands (2005) to ratify different EU treaties or adopting the single currency, marking the end of the 'permissive consensus'. And it should be noted that these referendums mostly predate the aftershocks of the 2007 economic collapse and subsequent EZ crisis embodied in the harsh and often unpopular austerity policies supported by the EU.

As Leconte notes, the increasing use of referendums is in itself evidence of the growing influence of eurosceptics on the EU's agenda (2010: 20). With the EZ crisis, positive opinions about the EU have declined even in countries where they had traditionally been high. On average, negative perceptions of the EU rose from 14% to 30% in the two years between 2007 and 2009, under the impact of the financial crisis and its ramifications for weaker states (Fraile and Di Mauro 2010). Eurobarometer data show a drop of 9% in positive attitudes towards the EU on average between 2007 and 2010, from 58% to 49%, before rising slightly again to 52% in 2011 (Debomy 2012). Britain remains an exception, especially amongst old member-states, in having an exceptionally low level of positive opinion towards the EU, but the economic crisis has led to a general lowering of satisfaction towards the EU similar to that of the 1992–1997 periods.

Conclusion

We have sought to define British euroscepticism as a multi-layered phenomenon, and in the process have underlined aspects of its continuing exceptionalism in relation to other EU countries. British Euroscepticism, certainly in its leading *English* incarnation, offers a unique form of mainstream party political dissent from the European project which long predates the present economic and political difficulties in the EZ countries. It is centred on a mixture of assumed constitutional superiority, post-Second World War triumphalism and a post-colonialist hyperglobalist/open regionalist economic perspective, which (at the elite level at least) views the UK's interests in global financial services and service sector industries freed from bureaucratic interference from Brussels.

The history of euroscepticism in Britain that we have traced here confirms all these factors and explains the ambiguities and defensiveness of even the 'modernising' and normalising (in European terms) force of New Labour towards the EU, both when in power and since. So too does the increasingly hard-line radical euroscepticism in the Conservative Party since the 1980s. These, at best, ambiguous sentiments towards Europe as reflected in the two main parties' positions, have both reflected and led to a hardening eurosceptic public opinion lying within a generally more eurosceptic political culture when compared to most other member-states.

The eurosceptic landscape has clearly evolved and broadened in the last two decades across the EU as a whole, with an overall rise in distrust towards Europe in public opinion, partly translated into electoral advantage for some parties. We argue that the picture is both similar and different in the UK, where euroscepticism has always been important in public opinion and party politics, with the exception of the late 1980s.

Arguably the most significant development in Britain in this respect has been the radicalisation of the Conservative Party, with a majority of MPs coming to embrace forms of hard/soft fundamentalist/radical-renegotiation euroscepticism, and – partly as a result of this – a significant minority of UK citizens now wish to leave the EU immediately with a clear majority amongst Conservative voters.

It remains difficult to accurately assess whether Conservative elites lead or follow eurosceptic public opinion, but their views are reflected and reinforced in much of the written press, both tabloid and quality. Labour and the Liberal Democrats do continue to defend more positive views about the EU, but as we have shown they are not immune to the siren voices which blame the EU, or the EZ, for British domestic problems – especially for the Liberal Democrat leadership since 2011, as the coalition's economic policies have ploughed into the sand and Cameron and Osborne have repeatedly blamed the EZ crisis for holding back the UK's recovery.

More vocal, if still indirectly influential, parties support radical eurosceptic views in mainland Europe than in the past and public opinion trusts the EU less in most member-states. It is clear across the EU that the global economic crisis has underpinned and reinforced this trend, as British eurosceptics have plausibly claimed that their opposition to the single currency has been vindicated by the woes of the EZ. Also since the crisis and under the impact of domestic austerity measures, UKIP has managed to intertwine the other causes of British euroscepticism with a potent identification of Europe with an influx of (supposedly) 'benefits tourists' and cheap 'foreign' labour which has drawn a deep response from both Conservative and Labour working-class heartlands (Ford and Goodwin 2014).

The UK's particular form of deeply entrenched elite and popular euroscepticism is no longer completely unique, but it does remain embedded in a unique political culture steeped in a triumphalist view of national history in relation to Europe, depicted as *the* key-stone of modern parliamentary democracy; as the key European liberator of Europe in the Second World War; and equally as a central part of the 'manifest destiny' mission of the USA, expressed through the soft power of neoliberal global finance and hard military power under US leadership. That the UK's coalition government seems to wish to take the country increasingly away from hard-core Europe at a time when it appears to be less isolated than in the past in its euroscepticism, at first sight may appear perverse, until one recognises that such isolationism is a badge of honour for many, perhaps a majority, in the UK today.

4
The Crisis of Democracy in the United Kingdom

It has become commonplace to describe Western countries, especially in Europe, as experiencing a crisis of democracy. Crozier et al. first used the term to describe advanced Western democracies in the mid-1970s (1975). Others have talked of 'disaffected democracies' (Pharr and Putnam 2000) or of 'democratic challenges' (Dalton 2004) attributed to a decline in 'civic culture' (Kavanagh 1989 in the case of Britain) or to the rise of post-materialist values (Inglehart 1990). One of the main aspects of this crisis, especially in Europe, has been voters' disconnection from politics and the lack of trust towards the political elites expressed, among other outlets, by a rise in populist parties.

There are two possible levels of dissatisfaction among voters – with individuals in government, Parliament or the administration, or with the political regime as a whole, involving institutions and norms. The crisis becomes acute when the rejection of specific people extends to a delegitimation of the political system as a whole.

In the early 21th century the UK has experienced a crisis of confidence and trust not so much in the political system as a whole, as in the domestic political elites which embody it in the eyes of the wider population. As Philip Goggan suggests, there is little wonder that such sentiments are on the rise:

> Democracy seems to be failing to live up to one of its main attractions: the ability to deliver higher living standards for the ordinary person. Instead, it seems to be rigged in favour of a few groups that receive preferential treatment from the government, such as the banks or multinational corporations. Those groups fund the political

parties and, in some cases, take a direct place in government. Each citizen may have an equal vote; few believe that each citizen has equal influence.

(Coggan 2013: 1–2)

This has been acknowledged by the political class, with New Labour introducing constitutional reforms after 1997 and much concern about reconnecting voters and politics aired in the 2010 general election, especially by Nick Clegg (Kavanagh and Cowley 2010: 333). Yet no traditional party leader appears capable of responding to it in a way which would stabilise and improve the legitimacy of the political system. Rather than an abrupt crisis which calls for an immediate answer or leads to the collapse of the whole system, this is a crisis which threatens to gradually undermine its foundations.

British euroscepticism has risen not simply as a reaction to a European entity challenging a preferred national model, but in parallel with a domestic political crisis which has been unfolding since the 1970s. Indeed, it appears that this crisis, which is itself one element of a broader identity crisis, has reinforced rather than diminished euroscepticism. The crisis in the legitimacy of the wider European project echoes that of the legitimacy of the UK political system, each reinforcing rather than qualifying the other. Disillusion at the domestic level has spread beyond the borders, while fears prompted by European integration and globalisation have weakened the sense that the domestic political system can protect its citizens, a feeling reinforced in the UK by a reduction in spending and public sector job cuts. For mainstream politicians (particularly on the right) populist euroscepticism has been an easy and possibly dangerous response to this disaffection with the domestic political system, especially with regard to immigration issues.

The UK combines elements of a crisis of legitimacy that can be found in other Western democracies with specific features linked to its multinational character, the legacy of its national history and the question of its future as a union-state. These developments have become particularly conspicuous since the early 1990s, which is also a period when the popularity of the EU started to wane across the continent. We argue that the domestic crisis may be related to the increasingly difficult relations between the UK and the EU, embedded in a growing lack of trust towards national institutions across Europe, as this mistrust often goes hand in hand with growing scepticism towards the EU (Eurobarometer 2012). Our hypothesis is that inward-looking anxiety over the failures of the British polity may actually reinforce rather than quieten distrust towards the EU, especially when set in the wider context of a renewed and necessary questioning of Britain's place in a globalised world.

Disillusionment and the strains in the political system

There is a vast amount of literature on the crisis in British democracy showing the decline of the political system which had been described in Almond and Verba's *Civic Culture* in 1963 and Butler and Stokes' *Political Change in Britain* in 1971. Examining British society in the 1950s and 1960s, they had identified a successful civic culture in the UK which featured high levels of satisfaction among voters, reflected in a high turnout in elections and a stable two-party system with the Conservative and Labour parties alternating in power, together receiving between 80% and 90% of the votes. Party identification was very strong at the time with class the main factor explaining voting in the UK, a relative majority of the working class voting Labour and a majority of the middle class voting Conservative, along the lines of one of the cleavages described by Lipset and Rokkan (1967). Almond and Verba therefore defined Britain as a model civic culture, 'a pluralistic culture based on communication and persuasion, a culture of consensus and diversity, a culture that permitted change but moderated it' (1963: 6).

This description was rightly criticised at the time for being excessively rosy (Kavanagh 1989), but its basic features were not seriously challenged. Instead, what the subsequent academic literature describes is the erosion and decline of this pattern since the 1970s as a result of several related developments (Saerlvik and Crewe 1983, Rose and McAllister 1990, Denver 1994).

First, turnout in general elections, traditionally higher than in local and especially European elections, decreased steadily from more than 80% in 1951 to its nadir of 59.4% in 2001 (Norris 2001). Although it rebounded to 61% in 2005 and 65% in 2010, this is a dramatic drop even from the 1979 general election, when it was 76%. The greatest drop occurred mostly after 1992 and in particular between 1997 and 2001. The fall in turnout has been larger in safe seats than in marginal ones, raising the issue of the adequacy of an electoral system which creates such safe seats in the first place, to which we will return below (Whiteley et al. 2001: 777, Curtice 2005: 780).

In itself a low turnout may not be considered as a symptom of a crisis – some countries like the USA have a long tradition of low turnout – but its evolution combined with other factors reflects an overall level of apathy and disillusionment which is troubling, especially since young and less educated people are much less likely to vote than older and more educated people (only 43% of the 18–25 years olds voted in 2005, against 83% among voters aged 56 and above). This phenomenon, it is suggested, has tempted the coalition government to offer many sweeteners to pensioners in the form of pension and tax allowances, while largely ignoring the needs and interests of young citizens. This reveals a generational, geographical and social divide which detaches a section of the population from mainstream politics, leaving them with a sense of powerlessness. The fact that other countries in Europe have experienced similar evolutions, especially France (Bréchon 2009), Italy and the Netherlands, points to common though not universal trends in Europe in that respect (Stoker 2006, Delwitt 2011, Mair 2013).

The second major development affecting the British polity has been 'dealignment' since the early 1970s and the erosion of the two-party system – where there are multiple parties, but only two parties (Conservative and Labour) really 'count' in the formation of government since most of the time they are able to gain an absolute majority to govern alone. Since dealignment set in, a plurality of parties are represented in Parliament, while others are blocked from gaining seats by the FPTP electoral system although attracting significant numbers of votes. The third major party, the Liberals (now Liberal Democrats), who traditionally attracted around 10% of the votes between 1945 and 1970 but only one or two seats in the House of Commons, has experienced a revival since the early 1970s. It received 19% and 18% respectively in the two 1974 general elections, although still gaining only two seats. In 1983, following the Labour split and the creation of the alliance with the new SDP, it received 25% of the votes, but still only four seats. It then experienced a dip with around 17% between 1992 and 2001, before increasing again, thanks to a change in strategy and a focus on 'winnable' seats, to 22% in 2005 and 23% in 2010. By then its share of seats had risen to 62 and 57, making it a significant party (Webb 2005). The distorting effect of the FPTP electoral system on third parties was less obvious than in previous decades thanks to tactical voting from Labour voters and a regionally concentrated vote, however the Liberals/Liberal Democrats remained the main victim of the majoritarian system throughout the period and consequently argued strongly in favour of proportional representation.

Beyond the parties that 'count' in Westminster, regional, nationalist and other small parties also improved their share of votes from the 1970s onwards, increasing the number of parties represented in Westminster from 6 in 1950 to 10 in 1992 in spite of the unfavourable electoral system (Norris 1997: 48) and becoming major players in the devolved assemblies after 1999. The Scottish National Party (SNP) and Plaid Cymru in Wales have had three waves of revival in the mid-1960s, early 1970s and since the mid-1980s. The SNP increased its representation in the House of Commons to 6 MPs in 2010 and became the majority party in the Scottish Parliament after 2007, while in 2010 Plaid Cymru won 3 seats in the House of Commons and in 2011 obtained 11 seats in the National Assembly of Wales. The Green Party, which has no such regional or territorial base, at last managed to get its first seat in the House of Commons in 2010. Unionist parties in Northern Ireland split in the late 1960s and the SDLP was created in 1970, increasing the number of Northern Irish parties represented in Westminster. UKIP, with 900,000 votes (3.2%), failed to win a single seat, like the BNP with 1.9% of the votes. Overall, support for parties other than the three main ones plus the SNP and Plaid Cymru rose to 7.5% in 2010 though they gained only two seats (Denver 2011: 79).

Fragmentation and polarisation

With a party political landscape much more fragmented than it used to be, the flaws of the FPTP electoral system in representing a variety of opinions were clearly exposed and the two-party system challenged. The traditional argument in favour of FPTP, that it led to strong governments with stable majorities in Parliament, did not hold up to scrutiny with many of those supposedly strong governments seeing their policies blown off course by events, or failing due to internal contradictions.

In addition, no overall majority emerged from the 2010 general election, leading several commentators to argue that there was good reason to believe that the Conservative/Liberal Democrat coalition which resulted from the election was likely to be the culmination of a long-term trend in social change and electoral behaviour, rather than an aberration, and that there could be more coalitions in the future (Kavanagh and Cowley 2010: 347, Bogdanor 2011, Cowley 2011: 11). The net result has been a weakening of the prestige of the two-party FPTP Westminster model of power and accountability (Norris 1997: 5).

Another effect of the fragmentation of traditional party politics is that parties in government over recent years have been elected on an ever narrower base, which makes their claim to represent the country weaker and damages their legitimacy in the eyes of voters, especially in those regions that voted heavily against the incumbent party/parties. With a very low turnout in 2001, Labour's second landslide was based on 40% of the votes, less than Thatcher and Major's winning shares, while the

Conservative Party only attracted 36% of the votes in 2010, its lowest tally amongst the 24 elections since 1922 (Kavanagh and Cowley 2010: 386).

The geographical dichotomy in party voting is of equal concern. Although the Conservative Party was traditionally stronger in the South and Labour in the North, between 1945 and 1966 the Conservatives attracted about 40% of the votes in Scotland and swings between the two main parties were relatively equal throughout England (Norris 1997: 23). Margaret Thatcher's success was in part due to the Conservative Party managing to attract aspiring working-class votes in the North. Similarly, New Labour ensured electoral victory in 1997 by attracting middle-class votes, including in Southern England. Parties in government could therefore claim to represent the whole of the country. This started to unravel when fewer and fewer Conservative MPs were elected in Scotland in the 1980s and 1990s, prompting Scottish nationalists to claim that the Conservative government in London was not legitimate to rule Scotland. Since then, regional differences have increased inside England too. In the 2010 general election, the Conservative Party failed to win any seat in most big cities in the North of England, while Labour struggled to keep even a handful of seats in the South outside London (Bogdanor 2011: 3). The electoral system reinforces such trends and many voters can feel discouraged from voting, especially Labour voters in the South and Conservatives in the North. At a national level, a side effect of this polarisation is that whole regions or generations (particularly youths) are at risk of being ignored by national governments, while differences between England and Scotland/Wales or between cities and countryside are exacerbated (Bogdanor 2011: 43). Campaigning by the Countryside Alliance against the ban on fox hunting in the early 2000s was an example of the kind of tensions that this could lead to.

Can low turnout and voter apathy be explained by the gap between voting intentions and what potential voters anticipate will be the actual distribution of seats? The failure of the attempt to reform the electoral system in the 2011 referendum on Alternative Vote (AV) suggests that the answer needs to be qualified. Only 32% of the voters supported the change on a very low turnout of 42% (much less than the 1975 referendum on membership of the EEC), the low vote itself offering a graphic image of the apathy that reigns in the UK political system. It is also clear that other factors came into play in the vote, such as the unpopularity of the Liberal Democrats in power with the Tories, who strongly supported the change, plus the division of Labour on the subject of electoral reform, as well as the perceived cost of switching to AV (Curtice 2011,

Whiteley et al. 2012). Nevertheless the result and the polls carried out during the campaign showed a woeful lack of interest for and knowledge of electoral reform, suggesting that there was no strong demand for it as a way to improve the fairness of parliamentary representation, which was confirmed by Curtice and Seyd's findings (2012). There was no decline either in the level of interest for politics in general, already relatively low in the UK, with 36% of respondents saying they were interested in politics in 2012 (Lee and Young 2013).

It is therefore not against the political system as such that voters apparently react – although polls show some demand for reforms such as electing the House of Lords (Whiteley et al. 2012) – as against the political process, parties and politicians, or what Stoker calls 'anti-politics', that is alienation from mainstream politics (Stoker 2011). Lack of interest for or engagement in politics in Britain is not new, as Almond and Verba found in the 1960s, but it has become more entrenched. Lack of trust towards politicians, in particular, had increased even before the MPs expenses scandal of 2009. Whereas 46% of IPSOS/MORI respondents agreed that 'most MPs make a lot of money by using public office improperly' (an already high percentage) in 1985, the figure had jumped to 68% in 2009 (quoted in Stoker: 155). The *British Social Attitudes* surveys found that whereas only 12% of respondents 'never trusted' politicians in 1986, 40% did not trust them in 2009 – although the figure decreased to 31% in 2011 and 32% in 2012, which points to a short-term impact of the expenses scandal (Curtice and Seyd 2012, Lee and Young 2013). This was confirmed by the Hansard Society *Audit of Political Engagement* in 2005 which found that a majority of participants in focus groups thought that politicians were liars and hypocrites and failed to represent their constituents' interests (Ram 2006). This trend went back to the early 1990s – around the time when popular support for European integration, such as it was, started to decline sharply in the UK (Bromley et al. 2004).

Although pride in national identity remains relatively high in the UK, Pippa Norris's extensive comparative survey has shown that in the EU, Britain is the country where the drop in trust towards government, Parliament and parties has been the most dramatic. Between 1997 and 2009 trust was down from 48% to only 22% for governments; from 49% to only 19% for the national Parliament; and from the already very low 20% trust in political parties in 1997 to only 12% in 2009 (Norris 2011: 71–75). This is exceptional in Europe, even if other countries (but not all) have experienced various levels of decline in trust for governments, parliaments and parties.

The lack of trust in politicians mirrors the widespread feeling that governments fail to deliver on important policy areas. The *Continuous Monitoring Survey* of the British Election Survey has shown that between 2004 and 2010 a majority of the population thought the government's performance had become worse in the fields of crime, health, terrorism and especially immigration (quoted in Whiteley 2012: 31).

This is particularly interesting as immigration had by then become the focus of eurosceptic rhetoric within the Conservative Party and UKIP. One of Nigel Farage's recurring claims is that British mainstream politicians are unable to stop immigration to the UK and that the only way to do so would be to leave the EU. Another difference with the 1950s lies in the percentage of voters feeling that they can influence national decisions – only one in ten today, against six out of ten in Almond and Verba's survey (Stoker 2011: 156). This points towards the growing influence of globalisation, to which we will return below.

Attachment to parties (party identification), in parallel with party membership, has also been in long-term decline, with only 2% of the population now belonging to a party in the UK and electoral volatility also on the rise, partly as a consequence. Whereas 46% of the electorate identified strongly with a party in 1987, only 36% did so in 2010 (Lee and Young 2013). Lower partisanship also explains lower party/government loyalty from MPs in parliamentary votes. Cowley has demonstrated a clear rise in the number of backbench rebellions since the 1990s, reaching almost 40% of the votes between 2010 and 2012 amongst Conservative Party backbenchers (Cowley and Stuart 2012). Party discipline is also on the wane and with less control over their rank-and-file representatives and party activists, governments are under strong pressure. This particularly affects policy on Europe, with a series of soft eurosceptic and pragmatic governments being pushed by a hard eurosceptic rank and file, vociferously supported by the majority of the press.

Are traditional forms of political participation, though declining, being replaced by new forms of civic engagement in the public sphere such as social movements and protest politics, which signal a 'new politics' (Byrne 1997)? This is what Rosanvallon calls 'counter democracy' (*contre-démocratie*), the result of a distrustful society which controls its rulers through protest or litigation (Rosanvallon 2006). Protest politics (defined by a number of actions such as petitioning, demonstrating, occupying or boycotting) has risen in recent decades in many countries, including the UK (Norris 1002: 200–201). New technologies, especially the internet, allow users to spread information, call for action and address political elites in an example of e-democracy, contributing to a widening of political participation which in Britain has been actively promoted by the Hansard Society (Williamson 2010). Online social media have played an important role in the mobilisation of grass-roots movements against established elites and policies in the UK, for example in the Occupy movement in 2011, UK Uncut and student protests in 2010 (Avril 2015).

Yet surveys show that mostly educated citizens engage in virtual protest politics, which suggests that this new form of politics will not bridge the growing disconnection between working-class voters and politics (Parkin 1968, Byrne 1997). Protest politics is also, by definition, reactive and one-dimensional, it is no substitute to policy and the defence of the collective interest, which traditional politics is supposed to provide. The debate about whether the internet actually enhances the democratic debate is still very much open (for a summary, see Coleman and Blumler 2009). All this suggests that new forms of direct political engagement, however positive in themselves, will not necessarily offset the effects of disengagement from traditional forms of political participation, which therefore require more understanding.

The effect of national and global trends

Disillusionment with politics, in the many different guises described above, affects many Western industrialised countries, although to a different extent according to their national experiences. A combination of factors, some national, some global, can explain this evolution. Changing social structures in the UK, particularly the decline of the highly unionised working class, are often mentioned in explaining dealignment, with today's greater social mobility and lack of community sentiments and solidarities going hand in hand with volatility and a decline in party loyalty. It has also been noted that although overall levels of social capital have remained high in the UK, they are in decline among the younger population. Levels of civic engagement and political participation are lower among these 'disconnected' youths (Hall 2002). Another explanation, compatible with these, is the rise of 'post-materialist' values in a time of relative prosperity which are not adequately represented by traditional left/right party lines and therefore can lead to voter disengagement or issue voting (Inglehart 1977). Finally, voters also express a feeling of powerlessness, unsatisfied that they are only asked to vote nationally once every 5 years – a trend perhaps exacerbated by the 24/7 news cycle and access to information technology, including social networking sites which breed cynicism of traditional party politics. Media, especially the popular press, are sometimes accused of encouraging distrust and cynicism by focusing on negative reports about politicians, although there is actually little evidence that exposure to the media reinforces political disengagement (Norris 2002). What seems a fact is that citizens are now both more demanding of politicians and less deferential (Stoker 2011).

Those exogenous factors which encourage such trends mostly cluster around the end of the Cold War and the process of globalisation, including issues of global climate change. The end of the Cold War meant that communism was discredited. Marxism, which had influenced left-wing parties in Europe, including Labour's left, no longer shaped the cleavages in the political debate. Economic neoliberalism was hegemonic in Britain to the extent that the party embraced it in order to become electable again (Hay 2001). As a result, differences between the main parties' economic and social policies have become blurred in the eyes of many voters, possibly explaining volatility and lower turnout (Curtice 2005). The convergence of voters on traditionally right/left issue provides for a rise in 'valence issues' which voters agree on, although in the British case this does not include the European issue. Voters' party choices depend more on the perceived competence of leaders or their charisma than on their ideology (Stokes 1963, Clarke et al. 2004, Green 2007).

These ideological shifts are also a result of globalisation, which has embedded the idea in the British political debate that 'there is no alternative', as Margaret Thatcher said, to neoliberal economic policies, free trade and flexible labour markets (Hay 1999). Yet globalisation can have another effect as well, which is to convince voters that national governments are powerless in the face of transnational forces and global markets, making voting for them pointless. Anxieties over the effects of globalisation on the welfare state in the UK have been underestimated by hyperglobalist political elites who are equally convinced of its benefits. These fears, which affect most of Europe (see the next chapter), have surfaced through antagonistic attitudes towards migrants from Central Europe and the attractiveness of populist parties.

The same can be said of the climate change debate, in which huge ecological forces beyond the control of any one nation-state, or even groupings of them such as the EU, are seemingly unable to prevent the looming crisis threatening to engulf the planet. This can lead to a turning inwards and away from standard political engagement towards apathy, or, for a small percentage on the ground, to direct action activism (Byrne 1997).

The rise of populist parties

Dissatisfaction with mainstream politics in the UK has led, as in other EU member states, to a rise in populist and extreme parties. We define a populist party here as one which appeals to 'the people' against a supposedly corrupt or incompetent 'elite', challenging an establishment which is described as having betrayed 'the people' while looking after its own and its supporters interests:

> Populists see themselves as true democrats, voicing popular grievances and opinions systematically ignored by governments, mainstream parties and the media. Many of them favour 'direct democracy' – political decision making by referendum and popular initiative. Their professed aim is to cash in democracy's promise of power to the people.
> (Canovan 1999: 2)

Taggart argues that rather than 'the people' in general, populists actually refer to a 'heartland', which is a 'construction of an ideal world', ethnically and culturally homogeneous, which has been lost and which needs to be retrieved (Taggart 2004). Canovan speaks of 'our people', also an exclusive, not universal, definition (Canovan 1999: 5).

Leadership in populist parties is often highly personalised and charismatic, the leader using straightforward and direct language offering simple and quick-fix solutions to often highly complex problems. Populism does not rise in a political vacuum but rather as the consequence of a pre-existing crisis. As Taggart puts it:

> populism is a reaction to a sense of extreme crisis. Populism is not the politics of the stable, ordered polity but comes as an accompaniment to change, crisis and challenge. This crisis may well stem from a sense of moral decay but it always spills over into a critique of politics and into the sense that politics as usual cannot deal with the unusual conditions of crisis.
> (Taggart 2004: 275)

Three populist parties have become significant forces in the last two decades in the UK – principally in England, as Scotland and Wales are, so far, less affected by them: the BNP on the far right, the Respect Party on the far left and above all UKIP. All have acted as 'channels of discontent' towards political elites, conveying ideas that mainstream parties did not share or dare to express (Copus et al. 2009). These populist parties are 'relevant', in Sartori's sense: first they are not or hardly represented in Parliament (UKIP won two seats in the Autumn of 2014), but nevertheless can achieve significant results locally and in the single-issue European elections conducted under proportional representation, institutionally weakening the hold of the major parties (Sartori 1976). Second, they can have an impact on the behaviour of the three main parties by taking second place to the strongest party, splitting their vote and so awarding the win to the second party. They are therefore able to become agenda-setters, forcing issues to be debated and challenging the status quo, even leading to policy changes in fields such as immigration and law and order where they are often on their firmest ground in reflecting wider voter resentment with 'old guard' party elites.

The BNP is a far-right party, the heir of a long tradition of right-wing extremism with its three classical dimensions of authoritarianism, ethnic nationalism and xenophobia (Mudde 2000). It campaigns on an anti-immigration, anti-Islam and anti-EU platform. It is populist in that it opposes the dominant 'liberal' ideologies of liberalism and multiculturalism as well as membership of the EU. It rejects liberal democracy in Britain as a fraud (Ford 2010). Respect, originally a single-issue party created in 2003 to protest against the war in Iraq, has since developed a radical-left electoral programme of nationalisations and higher taxes on corporations. Both parties target working-class voters and, in the latter case, ethnic minorities. They share a limited relevance in terms of national votes and seats – their biggest respective success was to gain one seat in the general election of 2005 (George Galloway for Respect) and two seats in the EP in 2009 (for the BNP, with 6.2% of the vote). Respect won 16 council seats and the BNP won 32 in the 2006 local elections, increasing this further to 40 in 2009. Since then the BNP has experienced financial difficulties and internal squabbling, eventually losing most of its council seats in 2013 and its two MEPs in 2014, many of its voters having switched to the more respectable UKIP.

Yet although lacking adequate parliamentary representation, both Respect and the BNP have proved disruptive for the main parties. In the 2005 general election, Respect presented a challenge to the Labour Party in constituencies with a large Muslim minority. Labour lost on average 10% of the votes in those constituencies, although it didn't lose many seats overall (Schnapper 2005). The BNP attracted votes from sections of the white working class, also a traditional Labour constituency. Beyond purely electoral considerations, both populist parties managed to turn the political debate towards grievances which their voters felt were not addressed by traditional parties – Iraq in the case of Respect and immigration and multiculturalism in the case of the BNP. These issues were put to the fore, forcing reluctant mainstream parties to respond to them.

This phenomenon is even truer of UKIP, already mentioned in the previous chapter, which presents a much more respectable face than the BNP while raising similar issues, in particular the need to stop immigration and to withdraw from the EU, while espousing an anti-political elite discourse where parties are described as interchangeable ('LibLabCon'). Created in 1993 by Alan Sked, an academic at the London School of Economics, UKIP was at first weakened by infighting and competition from the short-lived Referendum Party created in 1997 by Sir James Goldsmith. It was originally limited to pressuring the Conservative Party into promising a referendum on membership of the EU. After 2000, as the percentage of voters ranking immigration as one of the main issues steadily grew, UKIP under the leadership of Nigel Farage widened its appeal by promising to curb immigration and oppose the established political class (Ford and Goodwin 2014: Ch. 2). The growth of UKIP started before the Great Recession of 2008–2009 but it has been amplified by it, as the weaknesses of the British neoliberal and open model were exposed, as well as the downside impact of the globalisation of the economy on low-skilled workers. Although UKIP favours neoliberalism (which separates it from other some populist parties on the continent) it (inconsistently) opposes immigration and its voters fear the consequences of globalisation on low-skilled jobs. Ford and Goodwin have shown that the party combines an appeal to traditional Conservative values with working-class concerns about jobs and social services in a context of renewed immigration (2014: 129).

As a result, UKIP has gradually emerged as a major player on the British political scene, in spite of only having only two MPs in the House of Commons at the time of writing, illustrating the various ways in which small parties can deform a political system (Copus et al. 2009). As Ford and Goodwin put it, 'they have achieved something unprecedented in modern British political history: they have taken a grassroots insurgency and grown it into a more professional political party with mass support' (2014: 9).

As we saw, UKIP's success was at first mostly in the European elections, but with the coalition established in 2010, UKIP's standing in the polls increased once again as it became the main beneficiary, at least in voting intentions, of not just disaffected Conservative but also Liberal Democrat and Labour voters. This translated into a breakthrough in the by-elections that took place in 2012–2013, where it came second three times, and in the 2013 local elections where UKIP scored 23% of the votes with 147 councillors elected. Finally, in what many commentators described as an 'earthquake', it came first in the 2014 European election, securing almost 28% of the vote (though on a very low turnout of 34%) and 24 seats, that is four more than both the Conservative Party and Labour.

UKIP is often seen primarily as a threat to the Conservative Party by splitting conservative votes, which could benefit Labour in the 2015 general election. Indeed, a poll commissioned by Lord Ashcroft found that 12% of the respondents who voted Conservative in 2010 now considered turning to UKIP in 2015.[1] Furthermore, it attracted, at least in the early years, votes in rural and coastal areas of the south and east of England which are traditional Conservative strongholds (Whitaker and Lynch 2011). Yet recently, it has managed to attract 'left-behind' voters, that is white working-class older voters worried about immigrants and changes in British society, who in the past would have voted Labour but are disillusioned about traditional parties (Ford and Goodwin 2014). Labour has lost millions of working-class votes since 1997 and it is hard to imagine a straightforward victory for the party in a general election if it cannot regain at least some of these votes. Finally, it is a threat to the Liberal Democrats, whom it appears to have replaced (with the Green Party) as the main protest party on the British political scene, to the point where, according to opinion polls, it is threatened with, if not extinction, at least a dramatic drop in the parliamentary representation.

As a result, UKIP has clearly affected the behaviour of the main parties and in particular preventing voters from switching to UKIP has become a priority for David Cameron (Wintour 2013). The Conservative backbench revolts against Cameron's European policy in 2011 and 2012 had much to do with pressure from UKIP and the feeling that public opinion was more eurosceptic than the government. This explains why Cameron made a number of concessions to hard eurosceptics in his own party and UKIP, promising a repatriation of powers, an in/out referendum, supporting a bill on the referendum, etc.

The change in rhetoric on immigration has also been striking. As early as the 2005 general election, Tory leader Michael Howard had attempted to capitalise on the supposed voters' rejection of immigration with his 'Are you thinking what we're thinking?' campaign, widely accused of promoting thinly veiled racism by its critics. In 2010 Cameron promised to cap the number of migrants allowed into the UK to less than 100,000 a year, notably by reducing the number of student visas. Theresa May, the new home secretary, duly introduced restrictions on non-EU migrants as well as controversial measures such as ad vans encouraging illegal migrants to leave the country (Lassalle 2014). In the run-up to the lifting of restrictions on the circulation of Bulgarians and Romanians on 1 January 2014, eurosceptic Conservative MPs campaigned for tougher restrictions. As a result, the government mentioned free circulation of labour – a crucial pillar of the Single Act espoused by Margaret Thatcher – as one area which the government wished to limit within the EU, with Cameron suggesting that benefits should be limited for migrants, a policy he was to implement in the UK, then suggesting imposing quotas on EU immigrants (Mason 2013).

Labour, which is targeted by UKIP in its strongholds of the North, also has adjusted its rhetoric on immigration. In a shift from Blair's policy of allowing access to EU migrants following the 2004 enlargement, Brown had already talked ambiguously of 'British jobs for British workers' in 2007. Alan Johnson, then home secretary, had acknowledged that it had been a mistake to leave UK borders open to new EU member-states. Since then the new leader, Ed Miliband, has gone further, disowning Blair's immigration policy and highlighting the stresses felt by local communities, especially on social services and the labour market, due to the influx of East Europeans. He also promised to limit the numbers of migrants from new members-states who could settle in the UK for seven years if the EU was enlarged again in the future and to increase controls on employers and recruitment agencies (Miliband 2012). Shortly after the Eastleigh by-election in which Labour came fourth and UKIP second with over 27% of the votes, he promised to reduce the number of low-skilled migrants entering the UK if Labour came to power (Grice 2013). Populist parties, along with like-minded activists of the main parties in government, have therefore forced immigration and membership of the EU to the top of the elite political agenda.

The political use of referendums

Another aspect of the rise of populism in the UK has been the increasing saliency of referendums in the political debate and the number of such votes actually organised, or promised. Thus, populism can be conveyed not only by new or fringe parties but also by sections of traditional parties or leaders of traditional parties who feel under pressure or think it in their interest, to appeal directly to 'the people'.

Referendums have no binding status in an uncodified constitution ruled by parliamentary sovereignty and in any case there is an obvious tension between the principle of representative democracy and the idea of a referendum (Balsom 1996). Yet debates about and demands for referendums are anything but new in Britain. They have been contemplated at different periods in the 20th century, as for example on the question of Irish Home Rule. A.V. Dicey supported them as a useful tool to supplement indirect democracy and prevent rash legislation when the issue at stake was particularly important and controversial (Qvortrup 2005: Ch. 2). Tony Benn, a strong defender of the British constitution, was the first politician to argue about the need for a referendum on EEC membership in the early 1970s.

The first national referendum, on remaining in the EC, was indeed organised in 1975. Since then though, there has been a flurry of referendums organised in the country, most of them in parts of the UK (Scotland and Wales in 1979 and 1997, Northern Ireland in 1998, London in 1998, the North-East in 2004, Scotland in 2014) with only one other national referendum on electoral reform in 2011. Referendums it seems have become acceptable ways to amend the British constitution (House of Lords 2010), to the point where Britain, like other Western countries, may become a 'referendum democracy' (Mendelsohn and Parkin 2001).

More importantly perhaps, *calls* for referendums and *promises* of referendums have proliferated since the early 1990s. They started with the rebellion over the ratification of the Maastricht Treaty in 1992–1993, on which Conservative eurosceptics unsuccessfully demanded a referendum. This was followed by the creation of the Referendum Party by Sir James Goldsmith in 1994 to campaign for a referendum on UK membership of the EU. The party stood in constituencies where no (Conservative) candidate supported a referendum in the 1997 general election, attracting 3% of the vote. It disappeared soon after the death of its founder that same year, but its main policy was taken up by UKIP. Before that, John Major had at first resisted calls from eurosceptic MPs to promise to organise a referendum on the European single currency if the government chose to give up the opt-out on the EMU negotiated in the Maastricht Treaty, before finally giving in to the pressure and making the promise in the misplaced hope of uniting the party.

New Labour made the same promise of a referendum on the single currency in its 1997 manifesto, which effectively ensured that the future Labour government would not adopt the euro since opinion polls showed a clear majority against it. This was followed by a promise, under pressure from the Conservative Party and the eurosceptic press, to organise a referendum on the future European constitutional treaty in 2004, which was overturned by his successor, Gordon Brown, after the treaty was usefully rejected by French and Dutch voters and replaced by the Lisbon Treaty, on the ground that it was no longer a constitutional issue. Both opposition parties at the time also promised referendums. In its 2010 manifesto, even the europhile Liberal Democrats pledged to organise an in/out referendum 'the next time a British government signs up for fundamental change in the relation between the UK and the EU' as well as on the euro if the decision was taken to adopt it (Liberal Democrats 2010). As for the Conservative Party, David Cameron promised a referendum on the constitutional treaty, then on the Lisbon Treaty, which he reneged on when the treaty came into force. Instead he promised yet another referendum on any significant new transfer of powers to Brussels, which was, as promised, included in the EU Act of 2011. Finally, in his January 2013 Bloomberg speech, Cameron committed a future re-elected Conservative government to organise an in/out referendum on or before 2017 following a renegotiation of the UK's status in the EU.

We will not discuss here whether referendums are the best way to answer complex political or constitutional issues, or whether voters actually answer the questions asked in this type of voting (Nairne 1996, Marshall 1997). What is relevant here is whether referendums reinforce or undermine the existing UK political system, in other words whether they contribute to the crisis in legitimacy described above, or rather alleviate it. Organising referendums is often defended by proponents of participative or deliberative democracy as a way to reconnect with voters by raising awareness of issues, giving citizens a direct voice in the decision-making process and making them responsible for the result, thereby re-establishing real popular consent in the democratic process (Barber 1984, Budge 1996, Smith and Tolbert 2010). Nick Clegg, the then new deputy prime minister, shared this idea when he explained the constitutional reforms that would be introduced by the coalition government in Parliament:

> We want people to be able to initiate debates here in the Commons through public petitions, we want a new public reading stage for Bills, we want people to be able to instigate local referendums on issues that matter to their neighbourhoods, and we want people to decide directly if they want to change the system by which they elect their MPs, which is why there will be a referendum on the alternative vote.
>
> (House of Commons Parl. Debates, Vol. 411, Col. 44, 7 June 2010)

In this view, constitutional changes in particular require the direct consent of the people: when the constitution is altered, a simple majority vote in parliament can be seen as inadequate or insufficient to legitimate major changes in the political system because these changes will modify the identity of the *demos* (Tierney 2009). Indeed, the Scottish referendum of 18 September 2014 proved a good example of civic re-engagement, with huge participation in public debates during the campaign and an impressive turnout of 85% on election day, 20 points above the turnout for the 2010 general election in Scotland.

Yet resorting ever more frequently to referendums or at least calling for them on a regular basis has been, in the UK in general, less about giving power to the people and more about gaining a tactical political advantage over opponents or papering over internal party divisions (Mendelsohn and Parkin: 19). This was true of the Labour Party in the 1970s and of the Conservatives today. The long-term effect of endlessly debating the need for popular votes in a system which, more than in other advanced democracies, is based on *parliamentary* sovereignty and thereby the principle that a parliament cannot bind its successors, has too often been neglected. Although in the UK the principle of parliamentary sovereignty is legally upheld by the fact that referendums are not binding, in practice this has been very much a fig leaf, especially when referendums were organised before the passage of the bill, as in the 1997 Scottish and Welsh referendums. In practice popular votes bind any Parliament and probably also its successors – it is hard to imagine, for example, Westminster voting to abolish the Scottish Parliament or the Welsh assembly. As a result, the principle of accountability of elected representatives, which is crucial to the theory of the British constitution, is necessarily weakened (Sartori 1987). Referendums also undermine the authority of law and of law-makers by suggesting that their vote can be by-passed. It is ironical that Conservative MPs and leaders, seemingly unaware that they would be undermining their own legitimacy as parliamentarians, have used calls for referendums in a way which Margaret Thatcher herself exposed in 1975: 'It is frequently the case that those who are against a change in the law put up the proposition of a referendum when they think that, by having one, they can defeat the change in the substantive law. That is the usual reason for such a suggestion' (Thatcher, House of Commons Parl. Debates, 11 March 1975).

In short, referendums have become a tactical instrument in the British inter-party confrontation and yet, by their plebiscitary nature, they provide only an ambiguous and awkward response to the perceived lack of legitimacy of representative democracy and the much reduced level of voter trust towards the political class. They may well reinforce the trend they are meant to respond to, by sending the signal that politicians are indeed incompetent, not to be trusted for important decisions and that only 'the people' can make an informed choice. The more frequent use of referendums can have a long-term effect on institutions which politicians, obsessed with short-term advantage, ignore. Finally if the result is anything like close, it leaves the question of legitimacy unanswered and open to further attack, as in the Scottish referendum result.

Devolution and the possible end of the British state

The uncertain future of Britain as a *United* Kingdom is another aspect of the current tensions in the political system. Since the UK is a union-state rather than a nation-state, any threat to its unity becomes existential (Bulpitt 1983). Originally, devolution to Scotland and Wales was presented in the New Labour project as a way of modernising the British constitution and adjusting it to a world where citizens wanted power to be closer to them whenever possible, while embracing the benefits of economic globalisation (Mandelson and Liddle 1996). It was also a democratic response to demands made by the population in Scotland – it was less clear in Wales at first, as shown by the low turnout in the 1997 referendum – which would in the end strengthen, not weaken, the Union by increasing the level of satisfaction among Scottish and Welsh voters (Labour Party 1997).

At first it seemed this scenario would develop as planned. The new Scottish Parliament and Welsh Assembly were created and soon became entrenched and legitimate in the eyes of voters (Paterson 2002: 24–25). The Scottish Parliament, in particular, passed a number of distinctive laws in the devolved areas, especially on free university tuition and care for the elderly, while avoiding any damaging conflict with London. This was made easier by the fact that Labour governed both in London and in Edinburgh (in coalition with the Liberal Democrats). Devolution was seen at the time as possibly providing new alleys for a regeneration of the British political system: a different electoral system which would lead to a less adversarial system, more transparency in the workings of the Scottish Parliament, greater involvement of the citizens, all of which could pave the way for a widespread modernisation of political practices in Britain as a whole.

Things changed in several respects after 2007 (Schnapper 2011: Ch. 1). First, the SNP won the Scottish Parliament election, partly as a result of the Labour government's growing unpopularity, and between 2007 and 2011 was able to govern as a minority party, in spite of a proportional electoral system (the additional member system) which was supposed to prevent any party from winning a majority on its own. The new first minister, Alex Salmond, used this power to introduce even more distinctive popular (if not populist) policies in Scotland, such as scrapping bridge tolls and freezing council taxes. Unlike the previous Scottish governments' agenda, the nationalists' agenda was to show the Scottish public that devolution was an unsatisfactory answer to the specific needs of Scotland and that full independence was necessary. Disputes with London were therefore stressed by the SNP, for example on nuclear armament, the protection of Scottish interests in the EU or North Sea oil. The minority government introduced a draft Referendum bill in the Scottish Parliament in November 2009, which was rejected by the three unionist parties.

The second stage in the process in Scotland started with the return of the Conservative Party to joint power in 2010, which reinforced the divergence in policy outlook between London and Edinburgh as the Scottish government opposed the coalition's drastic cuts to public spending. The SNP was able to argue successfully that the London government was not legitimate in Scotland, where the Conservative Party still had only one MP, and that Scotland's distinctive social-democratic identity and policy choices were not respected. Whatever the truth of this assertion, Alex Salmond made the most of its symbolic value, speaking of 'our Scottish social democracy' to justify his claim for independence (Curtice and Ormston 2008, Salmond 2013).

Finally, the political rift between England and Scotland was widened by the SNP's overall majority in the Scottish Parliament in May 2011. This time, the central government could no longer refuse a referendum on Scottish independence. An agreement was reached between Edinburgh and London in November 2012 paving the way for a referendum on 18 September 2014. Although the result was negative, the momentum towards further changes in the relation between the centre and periphery in the UK has not subsided. With future powers being transferred to Edinburgh, pressure will increase in Wales, possibly Northern Ireland, but above all in England for a rebalancing of power between and within the different entities. Uncertainty about the future of the British state remains in the backdrop of widening divisions between the Scottish and British polities (Harris 2014). The vexed West Lothian question, by which Scottish and Welsh voters continue to vote in Westminster on issues which are devolved in Scotland

and Wales and therefore only affect the English population, will not disappear.

The first ten years of devolution have therefore led on the one hand to progress in the democratic representation and governance of Scotland and Wales, but on the other exposed or reinforced differences between the three entities on many accounts. Devolution has accelerated the polarisation of English, Scottish and Welsh policies and identities. In the devolved matters such as health, distinctive policy communities have emerged (Keating 2009). Different political arenas have developed in Scotland and Wales, with different actors and different priorities from Westminster. Media reports have also changed, with national newspapers largely ignoring the Welsh and Scottish political debates, including during the first stages of the debate on independence in Scotland. The SNP constantly stresses the different Scottish political culture, more social-democratic and Scandinavian in its outlook than both Conservative 'hyperglobalist' neoliberalism and New Labour's open regionalism (Baker et al. 2002). Furthermore, the quasi-disappearance of the Conservative Party in Scotland means that a Conservative government in London will always struggle to be accepted in Scotland, fuelling recurring tensions. Similarly a Labour government elected thanks to Scottish and Welsh votes but in a minority in England would face a major legitimacy issue in Westminster.

The *British Social Attitudes Survey* of 2013 also shows evidence of a strong sense of Scottishness, to the detriment of Britishness, where since 1997 between 70% and 80% of Scots have defined themselves as Scottish rather than British in 'forced choice' questions (Curtice et al. 2013). In itself that should not be cause for worry since a strong regional identity can be combined with a national one. Indeed, this is what the so-called Moreno question, which offers several combinations of identity, shows. In 2012 30% of Scottish respondents defined themselves as equally Scottish and British, only 3% less than in 1992; 53% felt either only Scottish or more Scottish than British, which was less than in 1992, when it was 59% (Curtice et al. 2013).

Devolution in itself has therefore not increased the differences in identity. But the figures show a weakening of Britishness since the late 1970s which is more worrying because this is what is supposed to bind the four nations together in spite of their distinctive identities. This is true also in England, where Englishness has increased since the early 1990s: whereas over 60% of respondents defined themselves as British and 30% as English in 1992, the figures were both at around 42% in 2012 (Curtice 2013). Between 1992 and 2012, the percentage of respondents defining themselves as 'English not British' has risen from 7% to 17%, much less than the 44% describing themselves as 'equally English and British' but still significant (Curtice et al. 2013: 148).

The process of devolution, therefore, has unleashed significant forces for change in the balance between the different parts of the UK which could turn out to be mostly benign, even positive, but clearly have the potential to undermine the sense of collective belonging in the country as a whole. In short, Anderson's 'imagined community' may have to be seriously reimagined.

Conclusion

Although the British political system appears stable and solid on the surface and in its often arrogant self-image projected towards Europe and the wider world, it has experienced a weakening of popular support in the last 20 years which should be of concern to all parties. Lower political participation, higher contempt for politicians and parties, geographical and generational divides are some of the symptoms of this underlying crisis slowly undermining the British polity. Traditional parties have, consciously or not, participated in this evolution in encouraging debates about referendums and using them as political footballs to score short-term points, ignoring the longer-term effects of undermining the principles of representative democracy.

One of the more worrying manifestations of the crisis is the rise in populist parties, especially UKIP, which mirrors developments taking place in most other EU member-states. UKIP is particularly relevant in this study as a symptom of this malaise, because it illustrates *both* the rejection of traditional domestic ways of governing and the EU, seen as an undemocratic and bureaucratic monster stifling the British/English nation. It could also prove to be a major catalyst in any future move towards separation between the UK and EU with huge ramifications for the British state and the remaining EU.

5
Britain and the Political Crisis in the European Union

The previous chapter has attempted to show the link between a national democratic crisis in the UK and a wider disaffection towards the EU. In this chapter, we explore further this connection between national and supranational politics by looking at the widespread public questioning of the legitimacy of the European project throughout the EU and its consequences on the position of the UK.

The EC/EU has experienced political crises in the past before, from the failure of the French Parliament to ratify the treaty on the European Defence Community in 1954 to the 'empty chair' crisis provoked by General de Gaulle in 1966 to, more recently, the tensions over the Iraq war in 2003. The main difference between these past episodes and the present situation is that in the former cases these crises were mostly diplomatic and dealt with at the elite level, whereas the present one involves the European public at large, a proportion of which now rejects the European project as a whole against the backdrop of a renewed saliency of national identity issues.

This is a type of organic crisis that mainstream political elites find much more difficult to respond to because it questions the top-down approach to integration that had been used in the first decades, to the detriment of representative democracy (Majone 2009). The acquiescence among member-state populations that existed in the 1950s and 1960s and was identified by Lindberg and Scheingold as 'permissive consensus' (1970) has given way to what Hooghe and Marks call a 'constraining dissensus', a result of the politicisation of European issues which affects the whole of the EU and impacts on national party competition and government policy (Hooghe and Marks 2009). The deferential approach to politicians which had made the permissive consensus possible in the first place has largely evaporated with the EU increasingly perceived as undemocratic and illegitimate in sections of the public, well beyond the traditional eurosceptic countries like Britain. They also show how important the identity dimension, including national culture and national sovereignty, is to understand recent developments in popular attitudes to Europe, a premise that we share.

In the first section of this chapter, we provide a brief, non-exhaustive summary of the academic discussion about the so-called 'democratic deficit' in Europe. Then we examine the disenchantment with European politics which has affected most member-states in the 1990s and early 2000s. Section three will show how the economic and financial crisis has exacerbated the pre-existing political crisis, mainstreaming the British position on European integration while threatening deadlock at the Community level. The fourth section will look at (mostly failed) attempts since the start of the 21st century to address the 'democratic deficit' and reconnect citizens through the strengthening of the EP and/or national parliaments, greater citizen participation and the 'politicisation' of Community institutions. The last section will explain their failure by the European elites' inability to confront the real source of the problem, which is less in the EU itself than in a more general sense of anxiety among European citizens about the consequences of globalisation on their material conditions and identities.

An ongoing academic debate

The notion of 'democratic deficit' was first used by David Marquand in the late 1970s and has become ubiquitous in the European debate. In the academic literature, several arguments are often put forward to describe it. One is the expansion of executive power at the supranational level by the European Council and Commission, but also the European Central Bank and the Court of Justice, operating without proper control by national parliaments and the lack of a parallel development of a political legitimating discourse (Siedentop 2001). The second is the lack of political accountability at the EU level, since the EP, the only directly elected body at the supranational level, has limited powers in this respect (Majone 2009: 152–153). Another suggestion concerns the lack of truly pan-European elections which trans-national parties would contest on European issues (Follesdal and Hix 2006) and the absence of meaningful opposition within the European institutions (Mair 2013). The lack of a clear ideological divide over policy in the EU leads to a muddled consensus which some, especially in the UK, find too regulatory and bureaucratic while others, especially among continental left-wing parties, consider too neoliberal and insufficiently protective of welfare. Finally, the complexity of decision-making at the EU level and the multiplicity of actors involved are seen as increasing the distance from voters, which neither national politicians nor national medias are making much effort to bridge.

Yet several scholars have questioned the premise of the 'democratic deficit'. For Andrew Moravscik,

> if we adopt reasonable criteria for judging democratic governance, then the widespread criticism of the EU as democratically illegitimate is unsupported by the existing empirical evidence. At the very least, this critique must be heavily qualified. Constitutional checks and balances, indirect democratic control via national governments, and the increasing powers of the European Parliament are sufficient to ensure that EU policy-making is, in nearly all cases, clean, transparent, effective and politically responsive to the demands of European citizens.
> (Moravscik 2002: 605)

He suggests that comparing the EU to traditional models of parliamentary democracy is misleading as it

> obscures the social context of contemporary European policy-making – the real-world practices of existing governments and the multi-level political system in which they act. This leads many analysts to overlook the extent to which delegation and insulation are widespread trends in modern democracies, which must be acknowledged on their own terms. The fact that governments delegate to bodies such as constitutional courts, central banks, regulatory agencies, criminal prosecutors, and insulated executive negotiators is a fact of life, one with a great deal of normative and pragmatic justification.
> (Moravscik 2002: 605–606)

In this view the EU is no less 'democratic' than the EU's component national governments in a complex technological world. Indeed, there are no reasons why the problems identified in the earlier chapter at the national level – disillusionment with government and parties, lower turnout, a return to identity politics – should not affect and even be exacerbated at the European level, which appears even more removed and opaque to most citizens than their national institutions. Going further, Vivien Schmidt makes the important claim that the democratic deficit is at the national, not European, level, as national institutions have failed to adjust their discourse to the realities of Europeanisation:

> the oft-cited democratic deficit is indeed a problem, but not so much at the level of the European Union per se as at the national level. This is because national leaders and publics have yet to come to terms with the institutional impact of the EU on the traditional workings of the national politics... That national leaders have chosen not to engage their publics in deliberations about the effects of Europeanization on national democracy attests to the fact that the short-term political costs are high and the benefits low. Ironically, this failure allows national publics to hold their leaders accountable for policies for which they are not fully responsible, over which they may not have much control, and to which they may not even be totally committed. It also contributes to citizens' disenchantment and provides populists with grist for their mill.
>
> (Schmidt 2006: ix, 3)

Majone also argues that standards applying to national institutions should not be used to describe an EU which is *sui generis* and limited in its competences, so that it is unrealistic to apply national standards to an institutional architecture defined by 'the impossibility of mapping functions onto specific institutions' (Majone 2005: 31). Indeed, both executive and legislative powers are exercised, for the purpose of avoiding divisions and conflict, by several institutions (Bourlanges 2014). Since European integration has followed a mostly economic path and since the member-states are not ready to cede it more sovereignty, the democratic deficit will remain a necessary evil (Majone 1998: 2005).

In spite of certain analytical failings, the idea of a lack of legitimacy of the EU has nevertheless become ubiquitous in the public debate, even more so since the onset of the financial and economic crisis. In the words of Jack Hayward and Rüdiger Wurzel, the European project now threatens 'to turn from European Union mode and into European disunion in the face of demands for greater sovereignty and solidarity' (Hayward and Wurzel 2012: 2). This was particularly illustrated in the results of the EP elections on 25 June 2014, which saw right-wing populist parties gaining ground in many member-states, most particularly in France, Denmark and the UK where they came first, and a range of soft and hard eurosceptic parties on the right and left of the political spectrum winning over a quarter of the seats in the Parliament.

Disenchantment with Europe

The current debate about the democratic legitimacy of the EU really started in the wake of the Maastricht Treaty, as a result of several developments. First, with the end of the Cold War, the European project took a decisively integrative turn with the single currency project, European citizenship, an intergovernmental political union and the prospect of enlargement to Central and Eastern European countries. The European project was inexorably moving, it seemed, towards 'an ever closer union', a phrase used since the early days of European integration (in the Rome Treaty) but which to some, especially in the UK, now seemed to threaten precious national identities. Second, a severe crisis affected the European economies in the early 1990s, undermining the claims of the EC/EU to be providing economic and social benefits to the European peoples in all circumstances, with the EU seemingly powerless to stop the relative decline of the continent. Finally, the failure to prevent or stop the wars in the former Yugoslavia after 1991 underlined the gap between Europe's lofty ambitions to be a world power and the reality of its divisions and weaknesses on the regional, let alone international, scene.

The first anti-European populist parties appeared and made electoral gains in some countries around that period – the Lega Nord in Italy, which joined a coalition government with Berlusconi's Freedom Party, the Freedom Party (FPÖ) under Jörg Haider in Austria, the Front National (FN) in France, whose first breakthrough was in the 1986 parliamentary election, and Vlaams Blok in the Netherlands (1988). Although different in origin and nature, they shared a nationalist, anti-immigration and anti-EU rhetoric (except for the Lega Nord at first) which started to attract votes in their respective countries. They marked the renewed salience of identity issues after the end of the Cold War, especially of the exclusive kind, which has been shown to correlate with a higher degree of euroscepticism (Hooghe and Marks 2004). Euroscepticism, which had mostly affected far-left parties in some countries before the 1990s (especially Communist parties), was extended to more countries and to the right of the political spectrum, and among Green and regionalist parties, especially in Italy and Spain (Verney 2011).

The emerging gap between the elite and the masses in Europe was also brought to the fore by a succession of negative or almost negative votes on the Maastricht Treaty in Denmark and France in 1992. This was also a sign of the emergence of 'direct democracy' at the EU level and the politicisation of this issue. As Taggart put it, referendums have become more popular as the European integration project has become less popular... the demise of the permissive consensus, at least as something that could be assumed, seems to have marked the emergence of the move to plebiscitary politics to legitimate that which would previously have been legitimated through consensus.

(2006: 12)

In contrast with previous positive referendums on accession in 1973 and the Single European Act in 1986, Denmark voted 'no' by a small majority of less than 51% in June 1992. The symbolic effect of this result was felt throughout the EC and emboldened British eurosceptics even though – having secured opt-outs from the EMU, defence and Home and Justice Affairs – Danish voters ratified the treaty on 18 May 1993 with a 57% majority. Meanwhile in September 1992, France, a founding member of the EC, only ratified the treaty by a *'petit oui'* of 51%.

The failed referendum and the lower turnout in the EP elections – going down from over 61% in 1979 to 56.7% in 1994 and only 49.5% in 1999 – contrasted with the large majorities which had ratified the Maastricht Treaty in the different national parliaments. They confirmed, as Vernon Bogdanor put it, 'that the EU was beginning to give rise to that deepest and most intractable of all political cleavages, a cleavage between the people and the political class' (Bogdanor 1996: 104).

The EU's failure to bridge the distance with its citizens was becoming a major issue in the Union. Turnout for EP elections continued to decline in the EU as a whole to only 45.5% in 2004. The drop was particularly striking in Germany, France, Italy, Spain and Portugal, countries with traditionally strong pro-European electorates.

Even before the financial crisis, opinion polls showed widespread dissatisfaction with democracy in the EU. Only 34% of respondents in the Eurobarometer poll published in 2007 thought that their voices counted in the EU – and only 22% in the UK (Eurobarometer 2007: 100). The percentage of people trusting the EU had declined from 50% in 2004 to 45% in 2007 against 40% who did not trust it on average. The UK was at the bottom of the list with only 26% of respondents trusting the EU (Eurobarometer 2007: 110). Nevertheless, support for membership of the EU remained fairly strong on average (53%), and not significantly different from ten years earlier. It was highest in Ireland, the Netherlands, Belgium, Spain and Poland; it was lowest and in sharp decline in the UK and Hungary (Eurobarometer 2007: 118). Similarly, while trusting it less, respondents were on the whole positive about the benefits of membership of the EU (54%), with Britain trailing far behind again (39%).

However ambiguous these poll responses were, the feeling of a political crisis in Europe was compounded by the failed referendums set to ratify the Nice and constitutional treaties in Ireland, France and the Netherlands. On 7 June 2001, Ireland, the only country holding a referendum to ratify the Nice Treaty, rejected it by 54% of the votes on a very low turnout of less than 35%. Enlargement (which would reduce Ireland's receipts from the EU), the fear of big countries exercising too much power and plans for a common European defence (against a tradition of Irish neutrality) played an important part in the first negative result (Garry 2005). A second referendum was more successful in the following year, after the government had secured assurances from its partners about the Irish voters' main worries.

The constitutional treaty, signed in 2004 following a lengthy negotiating process and a much larger degree of transparency than for previous treaties (see below), was rejected in May 2005 by a majority of 55% in the French referendum of ratification and on 1 June by Dutch voters by a majority of almost 62%, in spite of all major parties supporting the 'yes' vote – although it was easily ratified by referendums in Spain and Luxemburg. European integration was widely debated during both campaigns – although sometimes topics were discussed which had nothing to do with the treaty itself, such as the threat of social dumping by the 'Polish plumber' or Turkish membership of the EU. In the Netherlands the sovereignty issue and the feeling that the country was contributing excessively to the EU budget played an important role in the 'no' vote (Nijeboer 2005). In France, as in the Netherlands, the ballot gave the opportunity to voters to express themselves on other European issues such as the euro, on which they had not been consulted. Turnout was relatively high, showing more interest for the European debate than had been anticipated: 63.3% in the Netherlands, more than double the turnout for the European election of 1999, and almost 70% in France, against 42% in the European election of 2004. The immediate effect of the referendums was to stall the ratification process and start intense soul-searching across the EU. Tony Blair captured the general mood in a speech to the EP on 23 June:

> Just reflect. The Laeken declaration which launched the constitution was designed 'to bring Europe closer to the people'. Did it? The Lisbon agenda was launched in the year 2000 with the ambition of making Europe 'the most competitive place to do business in the world by 2010'. We are half way through that period. Has it succeeded? I have sat through council conclusions after council conclusions describing how we are 'reconnecting Europe to the people'. Are we? It is time to

give ourselves a reality check. To receive the wake-up call. The people are blowing the trumpets round the city walls. Are we listening? Have we the political will to go out and meet them so that they regard our leadership as part of the solution not the problem?

(Blair 2005)

By the time the financial crisis burst in 2007–2008, the problem was therefore well identified, but it had not affected all member-states equally. Public opinion in some countries, like Germany (Lees 2008) Spain and Ireland, despite the 2001 referendum (Gilland 2008), did not show the same signs of disenchantment with Europe that were becoming prevalent in Britain, France and the Netherlands.

Consequences of the financial and economic crisis

The financial and economic crisis soon turned into a political crisis as well, suggesting the failure of the European project as a whole to shield the population from global turbulence, and even seen as making it worse. There were several ways in which voters' discontent was fuelled.

First, the euro was seen as having been flawed from the start, with its founders unable to create adequate economic and political governance of the EZ to complement the currency union and failing to bridge the imbalances in competitiveness between the different member-states. There was also the failure to enforce the growth and stability pact, which was supposed to ensure that budget deficits would not exceed 3% of the GDP and debts-to-GDP ratios would not exceed 60% of GDP, in several countries including Germany, Greece and France. The failure to redress public accounts in times of growth was widely condemned, leading to austerian measures to reduce debt in the midst if a recession.

But beyond criticism of the governance of the euro, it was the effect of the austerity measures adopted throughout the EU as a response to the sovereign debt crisis and the rise in interest rates paid by governments which increased opposition to the EU and divisions within and between member-states.

The fate of southern European countries after 2008, which saw unemployment soar to over 25% in Greece and Spain as public spending was brutally cut, was particularly cruel. As massive popular protests erupted in Greece in mid-2011, the population turned against the German government, accused of imposing these harsh measures. Conversely, opinion in Germany and other creditor countries like Finland resented the bail-outs to 'profligate' southern countries which had not kept their accounts in order, when they themselves had made great sacrifices to improve competitiveness with the Agenda 2010 reforms.[1] Economic solidarity between EU countries, one of the crucial principles on which the European project had been based, was therefore in jeopardy while in southern Europe the trade off between 'solidarity' and 'discipline', at the basis of their participation in the EMU, was shattered (Bull 2012). The growing power of Germany within the EU, due both to its economic success and to the weakening of its traditional partner in leadership, France, also increased resentment in a number of countries most affected by the sovereign debt crisis (Guérot and Leonard 2011). This feeling was reinforced by the fact that Germany was one of the main beneficiaries of the single currency and yet was slow to come to the rescue of Greece in May 2010, failing to prevent the spread of the crisis to other southern countries and Ireland (Young and Semmler 2011).

So the economic difficulties were compounded by the feeling that austerity measures had been imposed from outside the countries by unelected officials who had by-passed the normal democratic procedures. Democratically elected governments in Southern Europe were seemingly powerless in the face of reforms imposed by the 'troika', all technocrats unaccountable to any electorate. The fact that countries like Britain and Germany (at first) had also cut spending (albeit to a much smaller degree) without such pressure was not considered.

The effect of the crisis on the popularity of the EU was soon felt, especially in countries which had traditionally benefitted from membership of the EU, like Spain, Greece and Ireland. The case of Greece was the most spectacular, with approval ratings of EU leadership collapsing from 60% in 2009 to 19% in 2013. In Spain it dropped from 59% in 2008 to 27% in 2013 and in Ireland from 70% to 47%. The level of approval was also below a third in some countries which had not been bailed out, such as the UK, Sweden and the Czech Republic. There was also a drop, though starting from a higher level, in France. Other countries, like Germany, Belgium, Denmark and Austria, which suffered little in the way of deep austerity cuts, remained much more favourable to EU leadership (Gallup 2014). Thus, it was claimed that euroscepticism had spread 'across the continent like a virus' (Torreblanca and Leonard 2013). Looking in more detail at the effect of the economic crisis on levels of trust towards the different EU institutions as measured by Eurobarometer, Roth et al. found a marked decline in trust for the Commission, –17% on average between 1999 and 2012. It was even more spectacular for the EP, with –30% on average and, as one would

122 *Britain and the Crisis of the European Union*

expect, even greater in Spain, Portugal, Ireland and Greece (Roth et al. 2013: 398, see also European Commission 2014).

More generally, the image of the EU clearly deteriorated between 2006 and 2013, as the following figure from Eurobarometer shows, with positive and negative views almost identical at around 30% (Figures 5.1 and 5.2):

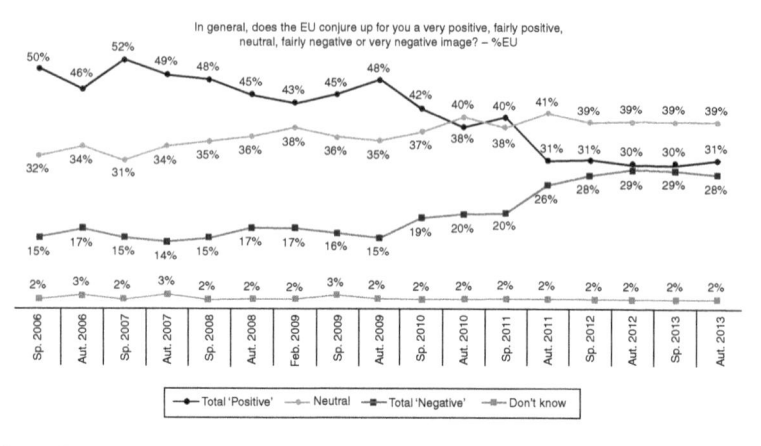

Figure 5.1 Survey results on the perception of the EU
Source: European Commission (2013: 6), © European Union, 1995–2014.

Equally worrying, a growing majority of two-thirds of the European population felt that their voice was not heard in Europe:

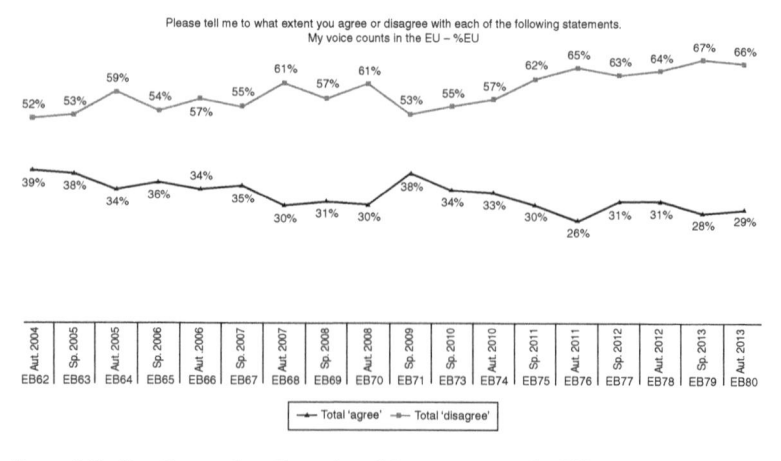

Figure 5.2 Pew Research poll results of the survey on the EU
Source: European Commission (2013: 7), © European Union, 1995–2014.

65% of respondents to a PewResearch poll in 2014 stated that the EU did not understand their needs and 63% found it too intrusive. The highest rate of such negative perception, over 85%, was in Greece (PewResearch 2014).

In this context, it is hardly surprising that existing populist parties throughout the EU thrived in the crisis nor that new anti-European parties emerged in Greece, Germany, Italy and Spain. Eurosceptic parties focused their criticism on the euro, with some parties like the FN in France and the Five-Star Movement (M5S) in Italy demanding a referendum on the euro. Whereas Jean-Marie Le Pen, then leader of the FN, got only 10.4% of the votes in the first round of the 2007 presidential election, his daughter Marine Le Pen won over 18% of the votes five years later, though coming third after François Hollande and Nicolas Sarkozy. In some, though not all, southern European countries the contestation of the EU expressed itself by the creation of new protest parties rejecting the pro-European consensus of mainstream parties, although their attitudes to the EU in general differed. Syriza in Greece and Beppe Grillo's M5S, launched in 2009, are cases in point. M5S was a politically ambivalent internet-based grassroots movement, with elements of a left-wing agenda, for example on the environment, as well as right-wing agendas, especially on taxation and immigration (Corbetta and Vignati 2013). It obtained spectacular results in the 2013 Italian general election, arriving a close second behind the centre-left PD with 25% of the votes and shaking the majoritarian system that had emerged with difficulty in the 1990s (Chiaramonte and Baggini 2013). In Greece, Syriza was instead a more traditional radical left party rejecting the austerity measures imposed by the 'troika', but not membership of the EU. It tripled its share of the votes between 2009 and 2012, when it secured 27% of the votes, coming second after the centre-right New Democracy. In Greece too, a neo-Nazi party which had existed under different guises since 1980, Golden Dawn, received 7% of the popular vote in the general election in 2012 and became represented in Parliament for the first time, with 18 seats.

No new populist party emerged in Portugal, Ireland and Spain, though in the latter case opposition to the EU austerity programmes took the form of a social movement, *Los Indignados*, which eventually turned into a new party, *Podemos*, for the 2014 European election. But Germany, which had escaped the worst of the crisis, saw a new anti-euro (though not anti-EU) party, *Alternative für Deutschland* (AfD), appear on the political scene, reaching just under 5% of the vote in the 2013 general election.

Results in the May 2014 European elections confirmed the trends that opinion polls had identified in the previous months. Eurosceptic parties in general increased their representation throughout the EU and populist parties came first in France with 25% (FN), in Britain with 26.8% (UKIP) and in Denmark with 26.6% (People's Party). Although different in nature and degree of euroscepticism, parties critical of the EU increased their tally in Germany (AfD), Austria (FPÖ), Belgium (Vlaams Blok (VB)), Hungary (Jobbik got 14% of the vote, on top of the already eurosceptic and nationalist party in power, Fidesz), Italy (M5S) and Sweden (Sweden Democrats (SD)), confirming the increasingly 'embedded' nature of contemporary euroscepticism (Usherwood and Startin 2013). Even though they remained a minority in the EP and shared little except their opposition to the EU (as the subsequent failure of the FN to create a parliamentary group demonstrated), their relative success and high profile testified to the depth of the legitimacy crisis faced by the European project whose supranational ideal seemed increasingly at odds with the reality of a popular retrenchment to nationalism and real or imagined sovereignty.

Immediate reactions to these results illustrated the disarray and divisions among European leaders. Numerous voices mentioned the need to 'reform' the EU to make it more palatable to European voters but there was no consensus as to what these 'reforms' should be. For the British government this meant reducing the powers of the EU, returning power to the states and reducing intra-EU immigration. For the French and Italian governments it meant reducing the burden of austerity and adopting measures to boost growth, whereas the German Chancellor saw no reason to change tack and argued that the best response to popular discontent would be to improve the EU economy, denying that the crisis might go beyond the effect of the economic crisis.

By 2014 therefore, the EU political crisis manifested itself in the rise of eurosceptic populist parties, popular distrust towards the EU and a lack of shared vision about the future path of European integration. Tensions between governments, which had always existed, seemed more difficult to accommodate as Germany, who had emerged as the main power in Europe, was unwilling to exercise its leadership and provide such a vision. With regard to the British government under David Cameron, it considered that its traditional intergovernmentalist vision of Europe had been vindicated by the crisis, while distancing itself increasingly from the Union and its partners, unable and unwilling to exercise any influence. The political crisis in the EU was therefore left unaddressed, except by a number of attempts to improve the accountability of the EU institutions to its citizens.

Attempts to respond to the 'democratic deficit'

It would be unfair to argue that European elites were deaf to the popular discontent that expressed itself about Europe from the 1990s onwards. A number of institutional changes in the EU decision-making process were attempted. In 2001 the European Commission published a White Paper on governance to address the issue of the disconnection between Europe and its citizens. It identified openness, participation, accountability, effectiveness and coherence as the key principles of EU governance (European Commission 2001). It proposed 'opening up the policy-making process to get more people and organisations involved in shaping and delivering EU policy', especially regional and local governments as well as civil society. It also pledged to improve communication with the general public and enforce Community law more effectively – all worthy aims, but the document was woefully short on specific ways to achieve them (Cygan 2002).

That same year, the European Council met in Laeken and adopted a declaration which set a number of principles for the future Convention on the future of Europe, the first step to an IGC on a European constitution. The declaration first acknowledged that:

> the European institutions must be brought closer to its citizens. Citizens undoubtedly support the Union's broad aims, but they do not always see a connection between those goals and the Union's everyday action. They want the European institutions to be less unwieldy and rigid and, above all, more efficient and open. Many also feel that the Union should involve itself more with their particular concerns, instead of intervening, in every detail, in matters by their nature better left to Member States' and regions' elected representatives. This is even perceived by some as a threat to their identity. More importantly, however, they feel that deals are all too often cut out of their sight and they want better democratic scrutiny.
> (European Council 2001: annex 1)

The Convention would look at ways to improve 'the democratic legitimacy and transparency' of the EU institutions. The simplification of the treaties into a single constitution was one way in which this could be done. The opening of the Convention to a forum, a website where civil society organisations could post contributions, was another way of attempting to reduce the gap with citizens by encouraging a form of participative democracy which had hitherto not been in use at the EU level. The Convention was composed of representatives of the national governments, but also of the national parliaments, EP and European Commission, as opposed to traditional IGCs in which only national governments take part. The proceedings of the Convention would also be broadcast, as opposed to the oft-criticised backroom deals by national governments. In June 2002 hearings of NGOs were also organised by the Convention in a number of plenary sessions.

Yet although a great number of organisations (around 500) participated in the project, most of them were already Brussels-based and not representative of all countries or all interests. There is also little evidence that the civil society input had much effect on the workings of the Convention or indeed on its outcome, the constitutional treaty. Ironically there were no replies or feedback from the members of the Convention to their suggestions (Lombardo 2007). The draft treaty introduced the principle of participative democracy, with the possibility for at least one million citizens to sign a petition to propose legislation at the EU level (but not a referendum), but on the whole, the Convention worked on the same principles of inter-state bargaining as in the previous IGCs (Menon 2003, Magnette and Nikolaidis 2004).

The Lisbon Treaty later encouraged more participation in the EU policy-making process through article 11.4, which states that:

> Not less than one million citizens who are nationals of a significant number of Member States may take the initiative of inviting the European Commission, within the framework of its powers, to submit any appropriate proposal on matters where citizens consider that a legal act of the Union is required for the purpose of implementing the Treaties.

Under the treaty, the European Citizens' Initiative was established, which enables citizens to propose legislation to the European Commission, provided it is supported by at least seven member-states. But proposals need to be based on existing treaties and they remain not binding, since the Commission has the sole right of initiative. This limits the extent of the contestation of the EU that they may convey and their potential impact (Raffenne 2015).

Attempts to increase citizen participation have therefore remained limited.

Another path which was followed to reduce the democratic gap between the citizens and the EU was to increase the powers of the EP, the only directly elected European body, therefore in theory at least depository of greater democratic legitimacy than, for example, the Commission. Indeed, in the traditional view of representative democracy, the democratic deficit, due to the excessive power of the executive in the EU, would be reduced if the powers of the EP were reinforced (Majone 2005: 31). The powers of the Parliament have indeed increased steadily with, first, the Single Act, which introduced the cooperation procedure, then the Maastricht Treaty which installed 'co-decision', therefore a veto power. Co-decision, already the rule for 46 legal bases, was then extended in the Nice Treaty to 40 new policies, including in the areas of freedom, security and justice, external trade, environmental policy and the CAP. Under the Lisbon Treaty, the Parliament now has budgetary authority on equal terms with the Commission. It must approve the appointment of the president of the Commission, who under the Lisbon Treaty must be chosen 'in accordance with the results of the European elections'. This amounts to a substantial increase in the role played by the Parliament in relation to other European institutions, although still falls short of the usual functions of a parliament such as choosing the government and initiating legislation.

Following criticism that there was no left/right nor majority/opposition divides in the EP, which would allow for a familiar political competition similar to what happens at the national level, an attempt was made to politicise the EP in 2014. In the run-up to the election, the main pan-European political groups in the Parliament chose leaders who would then run for the presidency of the Commission if the party came first – Jean-Claude Juncker for the EPP, Martin Schultz for the Socialists, Guy Verhofstadt for the Liberal group, etc. This was to increase the role of Parliament to the detriment of the European Council. It is therefore not surprising that, after the May 2014 election which saw the EPP win, several heads of governments sitting in the European Council, including David Cameron, the Dutch and Swedish prime ministers, resisted at first the move to immediately appoint Jean-Claude Juncker, though in the end Cameron was the only one to actually vote against him. This illustrates the ambiguity of governments bemoaning the 'democratic deficit' on the one hand while declining to endorse what could seem a legitimate step to reduce it and to politicise the Parliament on the other. In any case, if European elections were supposedly turning into a left/right competition as a result, a cleavage which corresponds to what voters experience at the national level, that is hardly relevant at the EU level, where the europhile/eurosceptic cleavage is much more relevant. The electorate seemed in any case oblivious to these changes, on which neither national politicians nor the media have really dwelt. Indeed, most MEPs are hardly ever mentioned in national media, nor is the work of the EP much covered except for a few exceptions, such as phone roaming, or the regulation of dangerous chemicals, while elections to the EP remain, more than ever, 'national second-order' elections.

Another path that has been explored to reduce the 'democratic deficit', particularly supported by both Conservative and Labour British politicians, is to reinforce the role of *national* parliaments in the EU decision-making process, overturning an evolution which dated back to the 1979 direct election of the EP and the loss of competences of national parliaments to the EP and European Council. Tony Blair had suggested creating a second chamber made up of national parliamentarians to oversee the implementation of subsidiarity in his Warsaw speech in 2000. In spite of the efforts of the British representatives in the Convention, Peter Hain and Gisela Stuart, no such institution was created, but the Lisbon Treaty introduced a new limited procedure to increase the role of national parliaments in the EU decision-making process (Menon 2003b). National parliaments can object to a draft legislation within eight weeks if they think it does not comply with the principle of subsidiarity. This would trigger a 'yellow card' if a third of national parliaments were involved. The relevant institution (Commission, EP, European Court, ECB) must then review its proposal and withdraw, amend or retain its draft (article 5.3). The fact that these warnings are non-binding obviously limits the influence of national parliaments. Article 33 also confirms that national parliaments should always be part of a treaty revision procedure, as was the case with the Convention. A protocol also extends the number of documents which must be provided to national parliaments. All of this remains therefore limited, maintaining national parliaments on the fringe of EU policy-making (Zalewska and Gstrein 2013). David Cameron, in his Bloomberg speech, continued to argue in favour of more powers for national parliament as the best way to reduce the 'democratic deficit', on the grounds that:

> It is national parliaments, which are, and will remain, the true source of real democratic legitimacy and accountability in the EU. It is to the Bundestag that Angela Merkel has to answer. It is through the Greek Parliament that Antonis Samaras has to pass his government's

austerity measures. It is to the British Parliament that I must account on the EU budget negotiations, or on the safeguarding of our place in the single market. Those are the Parliaments which instil proper respect – even fear – into national leaders. We need to recognise that in the way the EU does business.

(Cameron 2013)

This was supported by the Dutch and Danish governments. A report by the House of Lords European Affairs Committee also suggested ways to improve the role of national parliaments in the scrutiny, formulation and implementation of EU policies, insisting that no treaty changes were necessary and that more could be done by parliamentarians themselves under the present procedure. Yet these ambitions are limited in practice by the difficulty of scrutinising and holding governments to account on such complex and often technical issues as EU matters (House of Lords 2014). There is also a risk of paralysis in giving too much power over EU legislation to 28 different parliaments with different agendas and priorities. Finally, we have seen that national parliaments are not always considered in much more favourable terms by citizens than the EP. In 2007, before the economic crisis, only 35% of EU respondents on average trusted their national parliament (Eurobarometer 68, 2013). This means that giving them a bigger role in the EU might not make a significant difference in terms of voters' interest in and acceptance of the EU, which leads us to our last section about the wider significance of the crisis.

Domestic crises and the fear of globalisation

Several points need to be made here. First the European political crisis is also the result of a number of *national* political crises, such as the one described in the chapter about Britain, which both share a number of features and present specific national traits. Instances abound of the interplay between national and European factors in manifestations of dissent across Europe. In the case of the Maastricht referendums, for example, research showed that short-term national political considerations were the main factors explaining the results, with pro-EU parties in opposition failing to mobilise their voters in favour of the treaty and these voters expressing dissatisfaction with national governing parties through their negative vote. The treaty had been 'hijacked' for partisan and national ends, 'thereby shutting out public discussion of European issues' (Franklin, Marsh and McLaren 1994: 470).

Similarly, Mark Franklin identified structural factors which needed to be taken into account to qualify the downward trend in turnout for European elections. First, the lower percentage of countries using compulsory voting in the EU following enlargement in the 1980s led to an almost mechanical drop in participation. He also noted that the drop in turnout after the first election to the EP occurred in *all* countries, as if the excitement of the new institution had subsided. Finally, the point in the national election cycle when the election to the EP takes place is a factor, with turnout being lower when the European election takes place shortly after a national election (Franklin 2007: 15). Non-EU-related factors could therefore explain the trend.

Domestic factors were also important in the 2001 Irish referendum, particularly the non-campaigning by the 'yes' camp and the lack of communication about the actual content of the treaty (Sinnot 2001). In 2005 in France, dissatisfaction with the incumbent centre-right government mid-way through the electoral cycle played a part in the negative result, with left-wing voters turning up against the constitution in spite of the Socialist party's official support for it (Ivaldi 2006, Qvortrup 2006, Taggart 2006, Startin and Krouwel 2013). It was interpreted as another sign of the crisis of legitimacy of the political class, already apparent in the first round of the 2002 presidential election, where Jean-Marie Le Pen came second, ahead of the socialist candidate, Lionel Jospin. But reasons for voting 'no' were different in France and the Netherlands, making it difficult to draw conclusions about a similar rejection of the EU: in France it was mostly a protest against a 'neoliberal' Europe whereas neoliberally inclined Dutch voters wanted to pay less for Europe, therefore seemingly demanding a less 'social' Europe (Taggart 2006: 19). As Taggart put it, 'it is increasingly difficult (if it was ever possible) to talk in universal terms about a single contest over European integration. The way Europe is contested varies fundamentally according to the context in which it takes place' (2006: 19). It is therefore particularly difficult to provide an adequate summation of this multi-faceted discontent.

The second important point is that dissatisfaction with politics, both at the national and European levels, is linked to much deeper changes to the socio-economic structures throughout the continent, of which globalisation is one aspect. This is not a new phenomenon – Seymour Martin Lipset analysed the factors which could lead working classes to support authoritarian movements in the 1950s and he identified economic insecurity and low political participation as key factors (Lipset 1981: 109). He demonstrated that extremism could also appeal to those middle-class voters who feared and revolted against modernity, seen as a threat to their upward social mobility (p. 135 and foll.). This analysis, originally applied to the 1930s, is to a large extent relevant when analysing the transformations of the global economy since the 1970s. Betz, in his book about right-wing populism in Europe, described the restructuring of the economy which has taken place, especially in the Western industries, with increasing individualism and competition leading to dramatic changes in the social structures and the value systems of the different countries (Betz 1994: 27). These new 'post-industrial' societies experience a bifurcation of the labour market between those who have attractive jobs, job security and promotion prospects on the one hand and those who are either unemployed or under-employed, have low pay and little prospect of improvement on the other. They are the 'winners' and 'losers' of globalisation, according to how successful they are in the new economic competition taking place in an increasingly culturally diverse environment. Indeed, Kriesi et al. add a cultural dimension to this dichotomy which can also explain the rise of nationalist anti-European parties:

> Individuals who possess a strong identification with their national community and who are attached to its exclusionary norms will perceive a weakening of the national political institutions [resulting from globalization] as a loss. Conversely, citizens with universalist norms will perceive this weakening as a gain, if it implies a strengthening of supranational political institutions.
> (Kriesi et al. 2005)

They describe a changing cleavage structure, along integration/demarcation lines, cross-cutting the traditional class cleavage, which mainstream parties struggle to adjust to, especially when it comes to addressing the 'losers'. In other words, the 'bargain' identified by Alan Milward, according to which European citizens after 1945 accepted economic modernisation in exchange for welfare protection, is now broken (Milward 1992).

Populist movements in Europe are in a position to fill this vacuum by supplying policies advocating the end of immigration and protectionism – though not UKIP in Britain, even if a distinction needs to be drawn between its leader's hyper-globalist discourse and the views of many of its voters on this topic (Ford and Goodwin 2014). Fear of globalisation expressed itself indirectly in the 2005 referendum campaign in France, with worries about the end of the European social model and social dumping from new East European members (Startin and Krouwel 2013). Polls showed that in France and the Netherlands in 2005 and in Ireland in 2008, an overwhelming majority of manual workers and unemployed people voted against the Constitutional Treaty (Startin and Krouwel 2013). They are more likely to be attracted to the defence of the nation and the closure of borders which these parties advocate. The FN describes the French political establishment as *élites mondialisées*. The Austrian National FPÖ has also moved to a protectionist line as well as the Lega Nord in Italy, which combines it with an anti-central government stance.

As Swank and Best put it:

> Radical right-wing parties may well have gained electorally from nationalist foreign economic programmes, anti-immigrant policies and strident anti-establishment themes as international economic integration proceeded and as mainstream parties broadly participated in the 1980s and 1990s liberalization of restrictions on international economic activity.
>
> (Swank and Betz 2003: 223)

European institutions bear the brunt of this discontent as none of them seems able to shield these vulnerable populations from economic insecurity. Responses to these fears, research by Betz and Swank suggests, lie also at the national level, where national political institutions and welfare state structures have an impact on populist votes (2002). Targeting social groups negatively affected by globalisation would be desirable but difficult to combine with current harsh austerity policies.

Conclusion

The crisis in the EU is not just about the economy, nor is it really about an institutional 'democratic deficit' at the European level. It reveals a wider questioning of the *finalité* of the whole project, with public opinion no longer acquiescing to further integration and expressing increasing mistrust towards EU institutions and its leaders. The two landmarks in this process were the Maastricht Treaty in 1992 and the constitutional treaty in 2005, which showed an increased politicisation of the debate and the weakening influence of national parties in shaping it. The increased use of referendums to ratify treaties or enlargement has contributed to both these developments.

As a result, euroscepticism is now 'embedded', to use Simon Usherwood's term, not just within national party systems but also across European societies. This has enabled eurosceptic and populist parties to make spectacular gains in European elections, although falling short of being able to influence the Parliament agenda (Taggart and Szczerbiak 2013).

The main effect of this growing opposition has been to stall any movement towards further integration or substantial reforms, as national leaders fear opening new negotiations on treaty change. It has also led several countries, especially Britain, to advocate a limitation on some EU powers, such as the free movement of people – in other words calling for a redirection if not partial unravelling of the whole integration project. Indeed, uncertainty about the future of the EU has seldom been as great.

Finally, this chapter has also shown that European and national political crises are closely intertwined, not just in the UK but in many other member-states as well. It is therefore probably futile to think that national politics can in some way overcome the EU crisis, as British eurosceptics believe, and perhaps more fruitful to address the underlying grievances about economic security and globalisation, though they are much more difficult to tackle.

6
Britain and the Economic Crisis of the European Union

In this chapter we are interested in how economic and social perceptions of the EU fed into growing levels of euroscepticism and outright europhobia in the UK, identified in the previous chapters, which led to increasingly aggressive and ultimately unsuccessful, government intransigence in Brussels after 2010.

Since 2008 a number of factors have come into play, including the sovereign debt crisis and the growth in largely Eastern European economic migration to the UK. This gave added credence to the eurosceptic message that EU membership has been actively harmful to Britain's economic interests and therefore injected new life into both hard-line Tory eurosceptics and UKIP's long-running campaigns for complete withdrawal. In 2013 this pushed David Cameron into offering an 'in/out referendum on Europe', subject to prior negotiations to repatriate powers over the Charter of Fundamental Rights, criminal justice, and social and employment legislation. In addition, the recovery of the UK economy while most of Europe was still languishing in near recession strengthened the neoliberal economic case for Britain going it alone in the global economy as a 'Hong Kong of the Atlantic', usefully linked (from a eurosceptic perspective) to growing anti-German sentiment across the EU.

In the first section, we describe the perception of the EU crisis from the point of view of British political elites and the eurosceptic media. This is explained, in the second section, by traditions of British exceptionalism as far as issues of nation and sovereignty are concerned, which are particularly potent in the Conservative discourse about Europe. We then recall the distinction in British attitudes towards Europe between hyperglobalism, open regionalism and intergovernmentalism before showing, in section four, how dominant the hyperglobalist approach has become in the Conservative Party and UKIP. This leads us to understand the often counter-productive policy pursued by the Cameron government in Brussels, leading to an unprecedented isolation of the UK in the EU.

The view from London

The EU's sovereign debt crisis and subsequent austerity woes, lowering growth rates, tipping millions into unemployment and poverty across the EU, and sparkling popular protests across Europe, emboldened Britain's growing army of neoliberal and sovereignty-obsessed eurosceptics and silenced many pro-European voices. The eurosceptics linked Europe's economic problems and proposed currency union treaty changes with the traditional core issues of loss of sovereignty and moves towards federalism. The 'F' word has long been the *bête noire* of British eurosceptics, a symbol of all that is bad about the EU. During the Maastricht Treaty negotiations in 1991, politicians and officials of other states were astonished by the dogged and ultimately successful British fight to remove the 'F' word from the treaty, replacing it with the founding Rome Treaty's phrase of an 'ever closer union among the peoples of Europe'. As Charter observes, this is because 'to the British government, federalism stood for the surrender of national sovereignty and rule from Brussels. To the continental mind, it was simply a description of the way in which functions of government were apportioned to the relevant level – local, regional, national or supranational' (Charter 2012: 34).

Of equal significance to strengthening eurosceptic voices has been the re-emergence of the 'New German question' in the EU (Guérot and Leonard 2012). This is because accelerated moves towards an increasingly federal Europe, provoked by the failure of the existing EZ system and the need to reform it, bear a decidedly German stamp. As currently envisaged the new more federalised EU core will be centred on the inner elite of creditor states, led by Germany with a second tier of chastened and reformed debtor states, bound together by strict monetary and fiscal rules along German ordoliberal lines. This is not an entirely novel development, since the earlier fiscal compact represented a looser version of what is proposed, but it includes new forms of centralised oversight based on the *Bundesbank* model. As Guérot and Leonard suggest, this sense of growing existential German economic power since the sovereign debt crisis also comes from within Germany.

"Underlying Germany's reluctance to be the deep pocket of Europe is a growing sense in economic circles that Germany is outgrowing the Single Market. It was one thing to invest disproportionately in an EU that was central to Germany's economic future, but quite another proposition to invest in the fiscal stimulus of southern European states when Germany's economic growth increasingly depends on its trade with rising powers like China. This sense was encapsulated in the claim that 'Germany needs the BRICS more than the PIIGS', which did the rounds at the Bundesbank in 2010. This claim is not supported by the economic evidence: Germany still trades more with the EU than any countries outside it, and its trade with the south of Europe has grown massively since the euro was introduced – but it represents a growing body of opinion which extends across the German media (2011: 5)".

We referred earlier to Angela Merkel's 2012 speech calling for 'more and not less Europe', based upon a much closer and comprehensive 'political union' in order to make workable economic and monetary union (Merkel 2012: 6) implying, as Fazi suggests, 'a game-changing transfer of sovereignty from the nation to the supranational level' (Fazi 2014: 150). In Britain such developments have legitimised the familiar eurosceptic discourse of the UK being absorbed into a German-dominated federal economic super-polity with the loss of sovereignty and economic independence this implies.

Britain is far from alone, of course, in fearing a German-dominated EU, many committed mainland European federalists share such sentiments, with an uneasy sense that a German *Europa* may finally be realised through the overwhelming force of German 'soft' economic power. The problem, as Guérot and Leonard suggest, is that 'Germany is too big to fail – it is the biggest country in Europe, but still not big enough to be Europe's hegemon' (2011: 10). However, in the wake of further weakening of many EZ states, this conclusion appears less certain and this uncertainty offers an opportunity to British eurosceptics (and those in other European countries) to use the possibility of Germany becoming the unrivalled hegemon within the EU as a weapon against continued membership. This is not a new phenomenon – in 1990 Nicholas Ridley colourfully referred to monetary union as 'all a German racket designed to take over the whole of Europe. It has to be thwarted. This rushed take-over by the Germans on the worst possible basis, with the French behaving like poodles to the Germans, is absolutely intolerable' (Ridley 1990).

Rhetorical expressions of 'iron will' and 'fixed intent' emerging from German politicians and officials, albeit mixed with reassuring noises about 'accommodating the British', have alienated several UK constituencies, and not simply the died-in-the-wool eurosceptics who view this as a final and fatal loss of sovereignty and British democratic control to our traditional rival for European hegemony. The prospect of binding the relatively uncompetitive UK economy into a European super-economy centred on the German production-centred export-led economy, where fiscal and monetary policy would be kept within rigid limits, has also alarmed some pro-Europeans (Owen 2012).

This has also been forcefully expressed by various left sceptics who reject the imposition of neoliberalisation, including the version emerging from the rebooted and rule-bound EMU's Fiscal Compact and competition-infused Single Market (Radice 2013), while in response to such developments root-and-branch British sceptics have redoubled their efforts for Britain to leave the EU, with the extra weapon of a German-dominated and reconstructed federal EU to employ as a potent weapon in their struggle.

British exceptionalism in the European Union

We have stated that British engagement with Europe has been generally half-hearted, self-interested and defensive in nature, in the face of an increasingly successful European economy, on which the UK was highly dependent to sell its goods and services. Even the City of London has become reliant on trading in European markets, attracting considerable investment from its European partners, especially in the Eurobond markets (Kynaston 2012: 461–477).

Joining the EU caused much soul-searching, particularly amongst Conservatives, but also among some Labour politicians, partly because of strong historical, political, and ideological attachment to the USA (often referred to as Atlanticism) but also due to continuing historical and emotional ties to the Commonwealth. But with disparate and relatively weak links to the Commonwealth, the real centrifugal pull was and remains towards the USA. In fact: 'No other political elite or party elite [in Europe] has the same kind of material links, or the same kind of ideological attachment to the United States as do the British Conservatives, and New Labour would arguably come second in such a comparison' (Baker et al. 2002: 423).

We argued in our methodological introduction for acknowledging the deep and enduring power of historical and ideational forces. The development and the peculiar nature of British economic thought offer a classic case of historical and discursive ideational path dependency, especially in relation to US economic thought. A powerful multi-layered Anglo-American umbilical cord, mixed with a vision of Britain as a nation with a historic economic liberalising mission, has created a highly distinctive political economy trope amongst the British political elite, especially, but not exclusively, within the Conservative Party. In varying degrees this has coloured the political economy positions of all the main UK political parties and added to their separation from their continental Christian and Social Democratic European equivalents.

Nation and Atlanticism: The exceptional community

The appeal of the UK as a nation outside the traditions of mainland Europe reflects in good part the legacies of Britain's past history which have shaped the exceptionalism (real and imagined) of the British political elite (Krieger 1999: Ch. 8). This is largely a legacy of Britain's hegemony in the global economy of the 19th century exercised through military strength and an 'open seas' policy, emphasising free trade and free movement of capital and labour, made possible by Britain's military and productive ascendancy over all rivals. Crucially the folk memory of this hegemony has continued to colour the beliefs of the leaders of the three major parties and of wider civil society too.

In addition, the domestic free market is remembered as being created with the minimal government involvement – a *laissez faire* state – beginning with the removal of most of the mercantilist and guild restrictions on economic activity that had blocked competition and entrepreneurial innovation. As a result this policy regime has come to be viewed as the natural form of capitalism, in a simplistic and caricatured version of the writings of Adam Smith, seen as reflecting the best possible organisation of industry, finance and commerce to maximise the wealth of any nation. Andrew Gamble suggests that this was always in its core an essentially *English* projection, but that it proved so intellectually powerful and economically successful that it became a self-image that the British and many others succumbed to:

> Although England was never in reality a true geographical island, its special path of development made it a world island in its own perception of itself, and in the perception of others. It was an empire of territory and an empire of trade, a system of power extending over Britain and Ireland and large parts of the world, as well as an empire of ideas, the representation of an ideal and the creator of a model, the pioneer of institutions, principles and practices which were widely imitated throughout the world. In these ways *England shaped the world and was in turn decisively shaped by it*, while remaining in important respects insulated from it, a world island, and therefore

an insular world of idiosyncratic customs, practices and beliefs. This paradox has been responsible for many of the peculiarities of English and British development.

(2003: 2, emphasis ours)

Britain's bedrock open-seas policies came under increasing challenge from the 1880s onwards from domestic social imperialism, and US, German and later Japanese completion in global market and on the high seas. In response social imperialists aimed at transforming Britain's empire into a protected trading, financial and industrial bloc within the world economy, along the lines of Bismarkian Germany (Gamble 1994a). But attachment to the liberal open-seas policy remained strong along with the staunch defence of the City of London as the commercial core of British liberal capitalism, surviving through depression and the loss of the gold standard, economic exhaustion through war and the loss of empire, to enjoy an unexpected revival after 1945 under US tutelage, so entrenching open-seas Atlanticism as a key element of Britain's liberal free-market political economy 'imagined community' (Anderson 1983).

After 1946 these beliefs became intertwined with shared Anglo-American values of anti-Communism, which saw Britain fighting the Cold War as the principal junior partner of the US, acting (Wilson's refusal to send troops to Vietnam aside) as its most loyal and supportive ally, in spite of the trauma of the Suez debacle at the hands of the Americans.

This nexus of economic and foreign-policy factors, plus the common language, explains the Atlanticist exceptionalism (both in economic and political terms) of the British political elite, especially in relation to the process of European political economy and the rise of the EU as a nascent rival to US economic hegemony (Baker et al. 2002: 423). Gamble again:

British national identity and political economy have been shaped by Anglo-America for over three hundred years... This has been of particular importance in relation to Europe. In the twentieth century in particular Anglo-America came to represent an alternative to involvement in Europe for the British state, a means of preserving its long standing ideal of an open, free-trade, liberal world order, and for many in the British political class it does so still. For them the narratives of Anglo-America retain their potency... Many of the characteristics of the Anglo-American model have stemmed from this approach, in particular its voluntarism and short-termism, as well as the liberal character of its welfare system and corporate governance, and the relative importance of its financial institutions, particularly its stock markets.

(Gamble 2003: 88 and 105)

In terms of political economy, UK elite-sponsored Atlanticism is also rooted in the writings of a number of influential Anglo-liberal economists, some fleeing Nazism, most notably Friedrich von Hayek, who travelled between the great centres of liberal economics learning in the US and UK, developing and spreading the open-seas and unfettered free-market messages across the Anglosphere, in so doing reinforcing the sense of an epistemic community of shared beliefs centred on maximising the freedom of markets and fostering open competition (Blyth 2002, Dumenil and Levy 2005, Mirowsk and Plehwe 2009).

The demise of empire was also significant in the initial turn towards Europe since it occurred at a time when US interests were preoccupied in Indo-China and elsewhere. In 1962 during the post-war transition period, Dean Acheson the US secretary of state acutely observed that: 'Great Britain has lost an Empire and has not yet found a role' (West Point 5 December 1962). During this period the USA also adopted a new strategic conception of its Atlantic interests (inspired by the Cold War) which included partnership with a united Western Europe, under West German economic leadership, relegating Britain to a subordinate position (Gamble 2003: 98).

This changing situation was widely recognised amongst the British political elite, as was the fact that the Commonwealth would not be able to provide the same levels of bilateral trade under the terms of US-led open-seas policies. With the EEC's economy growing much faster than the UK's which was mired in a stop-go rhythm of industrial decline, the importance of the EU and Britain's relationship with it was fully recognised, leading to entry in 1973 under Edward Heath, after De Gaulle's resignation had removed the final stumbling block. During the next 20 years Britain set about appearing to vindicate De Gaulle's feeling that the British represented an Anglo-American Trojan Horse at the heart of Europe, carving out a reputation as an awkward partner (George 1992).

Nationhood and sovereignty

A feature of Conservative political discourse on Europe distinguishing it from its continental conservative counterparts, which to some extent cuts across party boundaries, is the narrative of Britain's special path to nationhood and its relation to the British state. Most of the forms of political identity which they have traditionally promoted include the idea of this British nationhood. These have been closely linked to an appeal to the sovereign British nation-state and, in particular, inviolable parliamentary sovereignty, seen as increasingly threatened by political, legal and administrative encroachments emanating from Brussels and Strasbourg.

Conservative attitudes to Europe have always been marked by the significance they allocate to the British nation-state. Colley's study of British identity traces this back to an 18th century fear of Catholic France towards the supposed freedom-loving traditions and institutions of British national life. The symbolisms of Britannia and the 'free born Englishman' – re-enacted in the Last Night of the Proms, the Royal Opening of Parliament and the Trooping the Colour – all emerged in this period and, while largely English and London metropolitan in focus, were carefully widened in appeal to allow for the construction of a united British national identity around empire, the Crown and Parliament, as symbols and the guarantors of sovereignty (another word for freedom) and independence – usually from Europe (Newman 1987, Colley 1992, Haseler 1996, Lynch 1999).

Conservative accounts of the British nation extoled the values of shared institutions and history, common values and a unified national culture. In the process they constructed and succumbed to an idealised 'imagined community' stretching in an unbroken line from Magna Carta to Dunkirk (Anderson 1984). In fact, as Peter Scott has pointed out: 'Britain is an invented nation...not much older than the United States' (Scott 1990: 168). It is not, of course, exceptional to succumb to national myths. France, Germany and the USA have their own national tropes which are necessary to bind nations together through their civic culture, but the British-imagined community is closely intertwined with an open-seas commercial trading and essentially free-market liberal political economy.

Also at the core of British Conservative statecraft lies a powerful defence of executive autonomy, expressed as parliamentary sovereignty, and 'strong government' (Gamble 1971, Bulpitt 1986, Lynch 1999). Sovereignty therefore becomes a matter of huge practical and symbolic importance in the Conservative politics of nationhood, since both democracy and legitimacy are located in the British nation-state created organically as the repository of all legitimate democratic politics. At best this implies a strongly intergovernmentalist and decentralised stance towards the EU, the default position of successive British governments.

However, once the process of integration is perceived to have dangerously encroached upon British national sovereignty, the only choice for many Conservatives (and others like Tony Benn seeking to preserve parliamentary freedoms to legislate for their chosen policies) is a complete restoration of British parliamentary sovereignty through withdrawal from the EU, since the core powers of British sovereignty are viewed as inviolable and indivisible.

Recent Commission proposals to fully federalise core parts of the EU in the wake of the EZ sovereign debt debacle are viewed by many British Conservatives as a threat not only to British sovereignty and national identity, but also to the global liberal economic order which Britain first created and has since sustained via its historic alliance with the USA. By threatening to replace the nation-state as the core sovereign in monetary and fiscal policy (taxation policy has long been the red line for British eurosceptics) the EU is viewed as a clear and present danger to British national freedoms and, incidentally, to the governing project of British Conservatism. Therefore, the coming Europe as presently envisaged is no longer the half-acceptable alternative to empire, a larger political space to be judiciously managed under British leadership, where British national interests could best be defended and extended, that it once appeared to be.

An alternative for Britain in the global economy?

As Andrew Gamble has pointed out,

> What is at stake in the European controversy in British politics is a major choice about Britain's role in the global political economy, which involves questions of interest, ideology, and identity. Such choices occur rather rarely but when they do they often trigger political realignments which can constitute major turning points in the life of parties and governments.
>
> (1998: 12)

Narratives of English exceptionalism have abounded in British political discourse for over 200 years. In investigating the core ideological difference between British and continental European views on political economy (setting aside for now the strong Atlanticist currents), we have adopted a perspective derived from research by Baker et al. which has mapped in detail the trajectory of British economic exceptionalism, taking in the views on Europe of all the main parties and setting this in British historical perspective by looking at past examples of major disputes over strategic political economy issues amongst the British political elite (Baker et al. 2002: 1993a). The most significant historical examples occurred in 1846 (over Corn Law repeal) and 1903–1906 (over Tariff Reform), both involving a crucial strategic choice over Britain's role in the evolving international political economy, in which Britain itself played a central role as the leading imperial and commercial power.

The former represented a dispute between the aristocratic landowners who wanted continued protection for their corn prices and the rising class of industrialists who wanted to import cheap corn for their workers. The latter case represented a struggle between the social imperialists who wanted to create the Empire as a close protective bloc against rival German and US imperialisms, and laissez faire open-seas liberals who wanted to maintain low tariffs and trade in world markets through open competition.

In each case the clash occurred between rival interests and elite visions of the correct future to maintain Britain's wealth and power. Both disputes caused splits in the Liberal and Tory parties and led to electoral defeat and ideological and political marginalisation for the losing sides. In each case it was the open-seas liberalisers, arguing that free-market liberalism and laissez faire was in harmony with the natural instincts and ancient traditions of the British nation, who won the day (Baker et al. 1993a).

Ironically these strategic decisions to prioritise a liberalised world order over the British Empire saw the beginnings of the gradual decline of Britain as a great power enjoying a global reach. As Linda Colley remarked: 'crucially, both commercial supremacy and imperial hegemony have gone. No more can Britons reassure themselves of their distinct and privileged identity by contrasting themselves with impoverished Europeans (real or imaginary), or by exercising authority over manifestly alien peoples. God has ceased to be British, and Providence no longer smiles' (Colley 1992: 374).

However, there is a crucial difference between these disputes and the contemporary clash of visions over Britain's place in the EU, since these earlier clashes over Britain's future in the global political economy 'did not involve questions of sovereignty directly, but rather the balance of interests within the British state. Europe has managed to involve both' (Gamble 1988: 12).

The early years of Britain's membership of the EEC/EU did not appear to raise deep questions of Britain's divergent form of liberal political economy, nor threats to its sovereignty. These years were marked by the demonstrable economic advantages of being inside the Community's economic trading bloc and tariff walls, accompanied by a strong sense in the UK that the EU was necessary to bind Germany into a democratic bloc and reinforce it as a bastion against Soviet Communism in the East. This made europhile arguments solid and difficult to question, especially for British conservatives.

However, since the early 1990s the debate over Europe has occurred under less favourable circumstances for British pro-Europeans. The collapse of Soviet communism in Europe and the reunification of Germany ended the Cold War, and the stagnation of the EU's economy relative to other regions of the world economy started, latterly the BRICS nations – Brazil, Russia, India and China – and also the fast-growing UK economy by the late 1990s. And when the destabilising after-effects of the global financial and EZ sovereign debt crises were added to the mix, the traditional claims of Britain's pro-European lobby that the EU represented a shining regionalist example for the future development of global capitalism and democracy appeared relatively weak. This opened the door to plausible-sounding alternative open-seas economic strategies for the UK outside the EU, based upon deregulation, low taxation, flexible labour markets, open trade and investment and bilateral trade agreements with the most dynamic economies in the global marketplace (Spicer 1992, Holmes 1996, Bannerman 2011, Kwarteng 2012).

It is necessary to understand the nature of the belief systems which underpin such an alternative vision of British political economy and to bear in mind that since the collapse of the Bretton Woods international financial system in the 1970s, the context for the discussion of national economic policy-making and European regional integration has been dominated by the growing issues of globalisation and regionalisation (Gamble and Payne 1996, Krieger 1999). Taking this into consideration, Baker et al. suggest that the bulk of British views on Europe cluster around two ideological and policy nodes, one *hyperglobalist*, and largely the preserve of British Conservatives, and the other *open regionalist*, favoured by New Labour and many Liberal Democrats. These are contrasted with a third *intergovernmentalist* position adopted by many mainland European elites and some in the UK.[1]

Hyperglobalism

During the 1980s Thatcherite politicians highlighted what they saw as the superiority of the Anglo-American neoliberal model of capitalism over its European rivals, centred on flexible labour markets, deregulation of financial markets, privatisation, low taxes, shareholder value and the minimal state. This was thrust upon the UK's European partners as by far the most democratic and efficient method of creating a prosperous economy in a world dominated by globalisation which ruled out all other alternatives, since neither national governments nor regional blocs could control global economic forces (Gamble 2003: 107).

This position drawn from the first wave of Conservative hyperglobalist rhetoric today represents the most powerful eurosceptical political economy strand in a right-wing eurosceptic-dominated coalition, seen as the only rational response to the changing political economy of the globalised world economic system (Perraton et al. 1997, Held et al. 1999). Hyperglobalist values are also clearly visible in UKIP, as one would expect from a fundamentalist anti-EU breakaway faction from the Conservative Party, with close links to powerful hyperglobalists in the City of London.

In the extensive theoretical literature on globalisation the hyperglobalist position can be summed up as a belief that national and even regional economies are becoming deterritorialised, global and transnational, through the increasingly free mobility of capital across national boundaries, promoted by transnational corporations, especially in the financial, knowledge-based and communications industries, and also by increasing manufacturing interdependency and outsourcing between different national economies (Held et al. 1999, Hay and Marsh 2000, Hay and Rosamond 2002, Scholte 2005, Martell 2012 and 2007).

Scholarly theorists of hyperglobalism argue that the changes the process has introduced are extremely far reaching, altering irrevocably the political economy environment of state policy-making by 'hollowing out' the fiscal and monetary powers of nation-states through the massive increase in the volume and speed of computerised financial and shadow investment banking system and container-based trade flows, so creating a truly mobile global economy whose course and future direction are beyond the control of any national government or regional bloc, no matter how powerful. In addition: 'National economic, political and cultural forces are transformed and have to share their sovereignty with other entities (of global governance and international law, as well as with mobile capital, multi-national corporations and global social movements) but they are not removed' (Martell 2007: 179–180). The more extreme forms of hyperglobalist discourse is often apolitical and/or fatalistic, not to say utopian with regard to the benefits of completely unregulated global markets (Ohmae1995, Wolf 2004, Friedman 2005).[2]

Of course, not all of the above is palatable to British Conservative hyperglobalists who also wish to preserve national sovereignty. So how do British sovereignty obsessed ultra-nationalists manage to live with markets beyond the control of nation-states? One key to understanding this is the fact that hyperglobalisation rules out interventionist policies for manipulating the economy. In short, Keynesian economic management to promote employment is deemed no longer practical or effective. The hyperglobalist message is therefore music to the ears of Conservative eurosceptics since it rules out the un-British social engineering project of social democracy. It also dooms the European federalist project to irrelevance and eventual failure, because the federal super-state levies high levels of taxation, spending and market regulation, rendering its component states (including Britain as a member) uncompetitive in global markets.

The real get-out-of-jail card now emerges, since there does, however, remain a viable role for a strong nation-state from this perspective, freed from managing the economy to concentrate on controlling inflation and maintaining a healthy fiscal balance and also ensuring that markets are left alone to be truly free, so maintaining the confidence of the financial markets, without which a run on the currency will occur. So the role of government resides largely in keeping markets as free as possible (Gill 1998). This perspective offers its adherents a perfect neoliberal solution to globalisation in which 'frictionless' markets operationalise perfect competition, eliminating all need for positive state interventions and instead resolute and democratic nationally based governments maintain the night-watchman state (Portillo 1998).

British Conservatives remain the only major European party to contain a large faction actively promoting the hyperglobalist position, although there are signs in some of the new Eastern member states, especially Estonia, of a similar form of national market fundamentalism (Bohle and Greskovitz 2007).

This eurosceptic/hyperglobalist position considers national political and economic independence as the only way to create and police a liberalised market economy, able to take full advantage of the entrepreneurial opportunities of globalisation, while (crucially) remaining democratically accountable in the process to the national electorate rather than an EU remote from its citizens and deeply undemocratic, since the sovereign British state is directly monitored and controlled (in theory) through parliamentary accountability.

Under this model the only rational policy for Britain to pursue therefore is to re-establish parliamentary sovereignty, either wholly or substantially, in order to become a deregulated, privatised, light-tax, and light-welfare economy taking full advantage of links with the most dynamic global markets (Holmes 1996). Taken to its logical conclusion this implies withdrawal of Britain from the EU, or, at the very least, setting the clock back to before the Maastricht Treaty.[3] Conservative MEP David Campbell Bannerman offers a textbook example of the hyperglobalist Conservative economic case for the benefits of withdrawal:

> We would be free from increasing EU attempts to interfere in management of the British economy such as proposals for the EU to vet British budgets before they are shown to the British people and plans to 'harmonise' taxes across the EU, such as with the EU-imposed Value Added Tax (VAT) and the proposed Financial Transactions Tax (FTT)... Freedom to improve the British economy and generate more jobs by stripping out reams of unnecessary red tape... and related excessive Health & Safety and Employment legislation which bear most heavily on small businesses, the lifeblood of jobs and the economy, the British economy will be stimulated and many more jobs will be created. Major plants producing steel, aluminium, chemicals and electrical power will be reprieved by the ending of excessive and unrealistic emissions targets... Free of EU membership, the UK will be able to seek far more advantageous globalised visions, for example, to pursue the concept of a Commonwealth Free Trade Area... There are no benefits of being in the EU that could not be achieved through a Free Trade Agreement and friendly international relations, and without the ever increasing membership cost... Over time the economy would benefit from withdrawal through lower taxes and/or more public spending, reduced national debt, lower consumer prices, reduced business regulation, and enhanced job and trade opportunities, better trade deals... On leaving the EU, Britain would secure a similar, if not better, free trade agreement with the EU as its biggest customer and a major world economy. Our trading position will benefit from reduced regulation and taxes, and more appropriate free trade agreements with other countries.
> (Bannerman 2011: §14–36)

Including several questionable, not to say utopian, claims, this expresses perfectly the British populist hyperglobalist case for leaving the EU. His mention of harmonising taxes across the EU and the proposed Financial Transactions Tax are a direct reference to the changes coming about due to the sovereign debt crisis (although Britain would actually be exempted from the former unless it joined the EZ). One missing element in much of the hyperglobalist anti-European literature is a critique of the austerity policies of the EU's troika backed by Germany, since it is difficult for Conservative eurosceptics to openly attack a policy that the UK coalition stands firmly behind in the domestic British context.

Open regionalism

The open regionalism perspective towards the EU is associated in the UK with many in Labour, Old, New and post-New, most Liberal Democrats and many in the dwindling pro-European wing of the Conservative Party. Tony Blair is perhaps the most high-profile open regionalist, but David Cameron has also demonstrated many of the characteristics in his rhetoric.

Open regionalists accept the thesis that international capitalism has become globalised, but reject the more extreme versions of the hyperglobalisation thesis (Perraton et al. 1997). From this perspective nation-states remain central political actors on the global stage; however open regionalists accept that there has been a progressive hollowing out of the policy-making capacity of nation-states which is irreversible, especially in the area of global financial markets, which they accept have radically modified the context of national economic policy-making. In short, certain policy stances and policy choices are no longer viable at the level of the nation. This does not mean however that all policy choices are ultimately dictated by exogenous global market forces, as the hyperglobalists suggest, nor that they cannot be restored at the regional level by a powerful regionalist bloc such as the EU (Baker et al. 2002).

Thus the open regionalist perspective is centred on the positive relationship of the UK to the process of European integration and the opportunities this brings for resisting the more extreme neoliberal aspects of the process of globalisation. Indeed, the development of regional trading blocs is not seen as running counter to the process of globalisation; rather it compliments and strengthens this process by adding areas of political and economic space within the global system. In addition, open regionalists reject interpretations which view regional blocs as heralding a return to a world of rival protectionist military-industrial and currency blocs, since open regionalism is by definition 'open' to world trade and the accepted rules of such trade.

The EU is seen as pioneering the development of novel forms of control and regulation of the global economy, creating new spaces for the discussion of common concerns and the elaboration of new forms of governance (Gamble and Payne 1996). Since this process is most advanced in Europe (according to Rugge the first 'post-modern state') it is seen as representing a crucial test-bed for the success or failure of open regionalism and must, therefore, engender widespread support from European elites and populations, since the alternative is to face the neoliberal race to the competitive bottom envisaged and welcomed by the anti-EU hyperglobalists (Baker et al. 2002).

Thus, from the open regionalist perspective the goals of national economic management are, wherever feasible, best pursued at the collective level of the EU. In many ways the turning point in this direction for the UK Labour Party and trade union movement came with Commission President Jacques Delors' speech to the TUC conference in 1988 in which he outlined his vision of a social Europe, whilst admitting the forces of globalisation needed to be accommodated:

> Your organization has played a pioneering role in the history of the trade union movement. It has served as a model for other trade unions in neighbouring European countries in their fight for the rights of workers and for the defence of their dignity. This historic achievement helped to forge in Europe a new model for society, a model based on a skilful balance between society and the individual. This model varies from country to country, but throughout Europe we encounter similar mechanisms of social solidarity, of protection of the weakest and of collective bargaining... In recent years it had been threatened by adverse economic developments, some of which have an external origin. Europe has grown increasingly vulnerable. We must now rely on our own forces. The globalization of markets and new technologies affect our perceptions and our way of life. All those concerned with the organization of our society must adapt. This of course includes the Trade Unions of Europe... The countries of Europe are responding to the challenge in more or less the same way. They have rejected drastic reductions in wages and levels of social protection. They have sought to adapt to the new world situation through an increase in productivity. They have succeeded in part, but at the price of massive unemployment... Unemployment is our major challenge.
>
> (Delors 1988)

The delegates gave him a standing ovation and chanted 'Frère Jacques' and Mrs Thatcher condemned the speech, thus cementing it into the labour movement's folk law. As Ben Rosamond suggests: 'the contribution of Delors was vital to the recognition that effective exploitation by unions of the new European agenda could have an important part to play in undermining the dominance of Thatcherism in the UK' (Rosamond 1998: 134).

Thus open regionalism, in theory at least, promises multi-level governance where co-operation at the EU level to achieve and support macroeconomic stability and competitiveness also secures high domestic spending on education, health and welfare, making global-market driven disciplines less painful and unacceptable. To quote Lipietz:

> Harmonized ecological regulations; united capital taxation and labour norms; Europe-wide social welfare insurance; more extensive inter-regional net transfers on the transnational European scale; maintenance of 'air chamber' between regions or nations which want to keep a particular aspect of a satisfactory 'social compromise' – this simply means the building of a European 'grand compromise', to be negotiated between citizens residing in Europe.
>
> (1992: 140)

This is a model of *progressive* interventionism achieved at the regional level, where new opportunities abound for making cross-national alliances and constructing protective institutions against the encroachments of globalisation. As Strange puts it:

> European regionalism in a 'second movement' period leaves open the possibility of a non-hegemonic world order characterised by competing welfarisms in which the EU's relatively distinct social model may, against neoliberalism, develop in the direction of negotiated or 'inclusive' openness as suggested by Lipietz. Such a model would seek the development of transnational social inclusion as part of a new, European-sponsored, multilateralism. It would, for example, move towards the reform of the world economic institutions through the assertion of the EU's increasing transnational actor capabilities. This would (for example) provide the basis for strategic alliances with emerging bloc actors in the developing world through which a new global social democracy could, conceivably, be forged. In the absence of such a strategy, a global shift towards new protectionisms is, as Cox (1981) warned, also conceivable. Either way, further moves towards the consolidation of global neoliberalism are not an inevitable outcome of EU regionalism.
>
> (2009: 27–28)

This form of 'deep regionalism' is not predicated on the disappearance of the nation-state, rather it is an acceptance that the nation-state is being transformed by the forces of globalisation and competition, and that regionalism is a positive response, offering a new political space for progressive politics to develop and grow. The new regionalism embodies a belief that a regional framework of governance is an indispensable weapon in the attempt to protect and regulate national economies under the fierce challenges posed by globalisation.

To open regionalists, globalisation does not necessarily imply a linear progression towards a world economy dominated by frictionless markets. In fact, increased regionalisation of economic activity and associated democratic governance is viewed as an integral part of the intensification of global economic activity. This perspective also rejects the hyperglobalist suggestion that in a globalised world left to market forces, trade and investment flows will naturally converge and growth and employment levels rise creating a 'global market civilisation'. Elements of this position can be seen in this speech by Tony Blair:

> Above all, those opposed to Britain's role in Europe argue about sovereignty: that the gains we have made are outweighed by the fact that in many areas national sovereignty is no longer absolute. My answer is this: I see sovereignty not merely as the ability of a single country to say no, but as the power to maximise our national strength and capacity in business, trade, foreign policy, defence and the fight against crime. Sovereignty has to be deployed for national advantage. When we isolated ourselves in the past, we squandered our sovereignty – leaving us sole masters of a shrinking sphere of influence.
>
> (Blair 2001)

Blair was espousing a form of regional economic realism, seeking a successful strategy to maintain Britain's economic and diplomatic power and influence, and also to maximise prosperity by ceding certain aspects of British sovereignty to the open regionalist EU bloc. Open regionalists are not necessarily opposed to Britain joining a federalised Europe, providing it protects the Single Market model that Blair and other British open regionalist neoliberals often favour. The Labour leadership and the bulk of the Liberal Democrats remain wedded to the open regionalist position, although the impact of the sovereign debt crisis has been to remove much of their past enthusiasm towards monetary and fiscal integration.

Intergovernmentalism

Intergovernmentalism is sceptical of both the hyperglobalist and open regionalist arguments for globalisation, viewing the world economy and its component states and regional blocs as still largely international in nature, largely managed through bilateral and multilateral negotiations between states. From this perspective the sovereign nation-state remains the key administrative and political institution within the EU.

> If 'globalization' is conceived as a process that promotes cross-border exchanges and transterritorial agencies at the expense of nation-states, then it would be deeply problematic...A truly global market system, in which international competitive pressures and market forces subsume national economies, and in which transnational agencies and networks reduce states to the equivalent of local authorities, would be vulnerable to multiple political and social threats that it had no means to counter: international terrorism, commercial piracy, crime, protest movements and national backlash strategies of local withdrawal from the global system.
> (Hirst and Thompson 2002: 249)

British intergovernmentalists are often pro-European *and* anti-federalist, accepting pragmatic arguments for European co-operation in securing new markets and a greater say in world affairs and are therefore strongly against withdrawal from the EU, but not prepared to cede sovereignty to the EU over areas such as monetary and fiscal policy or foreign policy. This position has been most forcefully expressed by David Owen, founder of the cross-party group New Europe to oppose Britain's participation in the euro.[4] In his recent book *Europe Restructured*, he argues for reorganising the EU to allow for those states that wish to be part of a more integrated federal EZ to do so, while those like the UK who wish to belong to the Single Market coexist alongside them (Owen 2013).

Cameron's stated position on Europe, as expressed in his Bloomberg speech of 23rd January 2013, is a classic statement of parts of the intergovernmentalist and open regionalist positions in five basic principles:

> The first: competitiveness. At the core of the European Union must be, as it is now, the single market. Britain is at the heart of that Single Market, and must remain so...I want us to be at the forefront of transformative trade deals with the US, Japan and India as part of the drive towards global free trade...In a global race, can we really justify the huge number of expensive

peripheral European institutions?...The second principle should be flexibility...Competitiveness demands flexibility, choice and openness – or Europe will fetch up in a no-man's land between the rising economies of Asia and market-driven North America. The EU must be able to act with the speed and flexibility of a network, not the cumbersome rigidity of a bloc...let's start from this proposition: we are a family of democratic nations, all members of the European Union, whose essential foundation is the single market rather than the single currency...We believe in a flexible union of free member states who share treaties and institutions and pursue together the ideal of co-operation...My third principle is that power must be able to flow back to Member States, not just away from them...In Britain we have already launched our balance of competences review – to give us an informed and objective analysis of where the EU helps and where it hampers...My fourth principle is democratic accountability: we need to have a bigger and more significant role for national parliaments...My fifth principle is fairness: whatever new arrangements are enacted for the Eurozone, they must work fairly for those inside it and out...Our participation in the single market, and our ability to help set its rules is the principal reason for our membership of the EU...that is why Britain has been so concerned to promote and defend the single market as the Eurozone crisis rewrites the rules on fiscal coordination and banking union.

(Cameron 2013)

The main problem for him is that this vision is no longer shared by most of his hyperglobalist and little Englander backbenchers.

Hyperglobalism: Winner takes all?

Hyperglobalist discourse has become by far the most important of the three main British perspectives towards the UK and Europe, representing the views of a major proportion of Conservative MPs and enjoying strong support at ministerial level too. It also encompasses the economic case promoted by UKIP, buoyed up by growing electoral success and growing influence over the debate on Europe, as well as much of the populist media and influential sections of business, including parts of the City.

It was clearly in evidence in the two public debates between Nigel Farage of UKIP and Nick Clegg of the Liberal Democrats in April 2014, on whether Britain would be better in or out of the EU, when Farage suggested:

> When we joined the Common Market...we were living in a world of tariffs, high manufacturing tariffs. That's all disappeared with globalisation and we now find ourselves actually incapable of making our own trade deals with the emerging economies of the world, so trade with Europe – and don't forget, they sell us more than we sell them – trade with Europe but let's open ourselves up for a bigger 21st century world.[5]

As the European sovereign debt crisis worsened those pushing for complete withdrawal from the EU based on a version of this perspective (sometimes called the Hong Kong solution) have grown considerably louder and bolder. The austerity-led troika-imposed solutions (leading to slow or negative growth, mass unemployment, abject poverty, social unrest and the rise of the extreme right) have added to the scepticism of the already jaundiced (and often ill-informed) perception of the EU in the UK.

There is little doubt that the appeal of hyperglobalist euroscepticism in the UK reflects the legacies of Britain's past history as an open-seas trading commercial community which has shaped the exceptionalism of the British governing elite, including those from Labour administrations (Krieger 1999: Ch. 8, Gamble 2003). But above all it reflects and reinforces the traditional populist electoral and governing statecraft of the Conservative Party (Buller 2000, Heppell 2014). With regard to this, Gamble has noted that the key to the party's unrivalled electoral success from the mid-19th century onwards has lain in the manner in which it has aligned the 'politics of power' with the 'politics of support':

> Presiding over the state...and winning the support of the nation are two separate activities in the modern political system...Electoral perspectives are the ideology of the leadership. Through them the leadership attempts to reconcile the conflicting demands of the politics of power and the politics of support, the state and the nation. But they do not seek to strike an equal balance. In an electoral perspective, political questions are always viewed from the standpoint of the state and the requirements of the politics of power. The task of this kind of political perspective is to reconcile such [state centred] requirements with winning support in the political market.
>
> (Gamble 1974: 8)

The genius of Conservative Party managers and leaders has been to harmonise support in Parliament and party with that of the expanding electorate, many of whom had little or no obvious stake in preserving *laissez faire* capitalism, which was achieved by merging the 'nation' (defined as a Conservative nation based on Empire, military success and free trade) with the requirements of the state (which in Britain since the 18th century has been an open-seas liberal state) convincing them that these two interests coincide. Disraeli was well aware of the delicate balancing act between the nation and state that electoral politics required as expressed here in his Crystal Palace speech of 1872: 'it must be obvious to all who consider the condition of the multitude with a desire to improve and elevate it...The great problem is to be able to achieve such results without violating those principles of economic truth upon which the prosperity of all States depends' (quoted in Seawright 2010: 3). Bulpitt also examined the record of the first Thatcher administration in terms of their 'statecraft' – basically the art of winning elections and achieving a measure of 'governing competence' in office. He suggests that the Thatcher administration aimed to achieve governing competence by achieving autonomy in matters of 'high polities' (Bulpitt 1986, 1992, Buller 2000).

This power/support state/nation balancing act has not always been easy to achieve, especially when major strategic political economy choices of national importance occur and even more so where the core sovereignty of the nation is considered under threat, as now with Europe.

Prime ministers of any party, when faced with divisive issues of fundamental significance to the future direction of the nation's political economy, lack the luxury of being able to neatly marry electoral support and the loyal support of their activists/representatives with that of the requirements of the state as they judge them, since whatever their private preferences they must attempt to govern the nation without threatening its economic health, which remains the most salient voting issue at most general elections – usually leading to the placing of pragmatism before ideological purity.

Thus, while the current politics of Conservative support, both electoral and within the party itself, is strongly aligned with a rapid exit from the EU, the politics of power and existential national interests are much less clear cut and still point, on balance towards the advantages of remaining in the EU, albeit on the periphery. As such

Cameron is a pragmatic pro-European intergovernmentalist and open regionalist:

> Britain's interest – trading a vast share of our GDP – is to be in those markets. Not just buying, selling, investing, receiving investment but also helping to write the rules. If we were outside, we would not be able to do that. It comes back to this, who are going to be the winning nations for the twenty-first century? If your vision of Britain was that we should just withdraw and become a sort of greater Switzerland, I think that would be a complete denial of our national interests.
> (Cameron 2012)

Unfortunately, however, Cameron was heading a strongly hyperglobalist and highly eurosceptic party in no mood to allow the requirements of Tory statecraft and high politics to fob them off.

In response to this the 2010 Conservative manifesto promised to negotiate the repatriation of powers in areas such as employment and social affairs. But this was dropped from the coalition agreement to appease Lib Dem europhiles and instead a promise was made to examine the balance of legal competences between the UK and EU. Even the passage of the 2011 European Union Act into law with its 'referendum lock' specifying that any future transfers of powers to Brussels would automatically trigger a referendum was undermined by ministerial powers to define exactly what was 'significant' (albeit subject to judicial review) but above all by the rule that no Parliament can bind its successor (Liddle 2014: 199–200).

The one advantage for the Conservatives over past eruptions of internal party disagreements over the European issue is that with successive new intakes the party has become more or less uniformly eurosceptic in nature, with the pro-European wing reduced by retirements and reversion to the back benches to a rump faction, and a largely silent one at that (Bale 2010 and 2012, Heppell 2014). However, this has not yet signalled a move by the leadership towards hard withdrawalist euroscepticism, a fact underlined in two edited books written by several of the new Tory intake (Kwarteng et al. 2010 and 2012). The general position advocates remaining in the EU, but seeking to reform the structure by placing much greater emphasis on the liberalising forces of the Single Market with Britain remaining on the periphery since the EZ countries wish to adopt a more federalist structure. Of course, this is a very British version of the Single Market as distinct from that of mainland Europe where it is not viewed 'as a simple economic trading system but rather as a complicated political construct involving many social checks and balances in order to function acceptably' (Charter 2012: 139).

Cameron's diplomacy in Europe and the failure of Tory statecraft

As Johal et al. point out, the greatest impact of the financial crisis for the UK, supranationally speaking, has been on UK–EU relations, ruling out the euro currency indefinitely and largely eliminating the major fault line between those who support and those who reject monetary union, while introducing a whole new debate over the future of the EU and Britain's role within, or outside it (Johal et al. 2012: 70).

Hyperglobalist Conservatives would never allow the pound to be replaced by the euro under any foreseeable circumstances and neither Labour not the Liberal Democrat's stance betrays any serious deviation from this position. In addition, the UK electorate has watched with horror the sovereign debt/austerity-led implosion of many southern European states, while being constantly reminded by eurosceptic politicians and many in the populist UK media of the potential loss of fundamental sovereignty surrounding any further integration. This has also been accompanied by a distasteful anti-German sub-text in certain populist quarters including UKIP. As a result membership of the euro and any further substantive integration of the UK into the EU appears off the agenda of all the governing parties as things stand and for the foreseeable future.

In terms of the dominant discourse of the crisis in the UK, Johal et al. highlight a key paradox, namely that the financial crisis has actually strengthened the underlying structural power of the City of London and the trope of continuing superior UK economic success, while the image of the EZ is largely of mass unemployment, mounting inequality, slow or negative growth, all overseen by ineffective crisis management and economic stagnation, so boosting the neoliberal eurosceptic ideology of the superiority of Anglo-Saxon open market capitalism over its 'bureaucratic' and 'undemocratic' European alternative (Johal et al. 2012: 79).

But there is a double paradox at work here, because this stagnation is arguably largely the result of the EU being driven by a form of doctrinaire supply side neoliberalism uncomfortably close to the British ideal. Thus, as Schmidt and Thatcher suggest:

> After a brief neo-Keynesian moment at the very inception of the crisis, far from abandoning neo-liberal ideas, European policy makers

responded with calls for their extension. They accepted or even embraced ideas of reducing public expenditure, delegating greater powers to supranational bodies, increasing liberalisation and imposing 'market discipline' through austerity.

(Schmidt and Thatcher 2013: xv–xvi)

Indeed, the IMF and World Bank worked hand in glove with the EU Commission, ECB and other EZ authorities to broker a deal to solve the sovereign debt crisis that would have done justice to the current British Treasury under the Cameron administration.

This is hardly surprising since, as Schmidt and Thatcher demonstrate, neoliberalism has proved to be an exceptionally resilient ideology which comes in many forms, some of them contradictory in nature. It is a philosophy and ideology which possesses the ability to metamorphose, reinterpreting its failures as successes, and consequently spreading out from market-obsessed liberal parties of the libertarian right to successfully colonise other parties and groups, including the more corporatist Christian and Social Democrats in the EU and the British New Labour Party under Tony Blair (2013: 26–33). What makes this ironic is that domestic British political circumstances have conspired to place Britain at risk of quitting the EU at the very time that neoliberalism has made major inroads into the EU/EZ.

In the domestic debate there was the usual British sense in the coalition's rhetoric that Europe was largely a foreign policy issue rather than an integrated part of the UK's domestic political system. This allowed George Osborne to sound detached from the EZ crisis and offer his strong support for further integration necessitated by the 'remorseless logic' of the single currency: 'I think we have to accept that greater eurozone integration is necessary to make the single currency work and that is very much in our national interest... We should be prepared to let that happen' (quoted in the *Financial Times*, 20 July 2011). Of course, this was diametrically opposed to Osborne's rejection of federal integration as a legitimate form of European integration. But it was deemed essential at that time since if the EZ fails to restore growth and provide sufficient demand for British goods and services this could have very serious implications for Britain's own austerity-mired recovery. Gavin Hewitt sums this up very well:

> One of the ironies of the crisis is that it turned British ministers into champions of further European integration. The Chancellor of the Exchequer, George Osborne, said the remorseless logic of monetary

union was to co-ordinate taxes and spending in a fiscal union. The British were in the curious position of opposing Brussels gaining further powers whilst telling other Europeans they needed a closer union if that is what it took to restore confidence in the currency. The party that had once fought to save the pound was now campaigning to save the euro. The ailing British economy needed Europe to succeed.

(Hewitt 2013: 219)

This air of lofty detachment and encouragement for the EU to get its act together was undermined by the sovereign debt crisis which triggered new heights of eurosceptic rhetoric against the federalising logic of the German-imposed solutions. A sign of this was the backbench motion of October 2011, demanding an immediate in/out referendum (which was heavily defeated) where a Conservative three-line whip was defied by over 80 Tory MPs. Cameron came under severe pressure from powerful eurosceptics in his party, and the earlier policy of encouraging further integration to solve the EZ crisis was gradually abandoned.

By the end of 2011, responding to pressure from Tory and UKIP eurosceptics and the realisation that the German solution to the EZ crisis was to accelerate deeper federal integration, Cameron was refusing to sanction the means to achieve this by vetoing the necessary EU Treaty modifications. At the December European Council, Cameron 'vetoed' the so-called 'fiscal compact', an amendment to the Lisbon Treaty which would enshrine binding rules about budget discipline and economic policy coordination in the EZ. Cameron claimed that Britain's partners had refused to secure the interests of the City (in other words to give him the power to block unwelcome regulation from Brussels), and therefore he acted to protect 'the British national interests', as he stated in the Commons on 12 December. The supposed threat from the European Commission was hard to sustain since, as *The Economist* noted, most rules adopted on the financial industry before then had been agreed by the British government (9 December 2011). It is therefore hardly surprising that Cameron, who had hoped to get support from Sweden, Hungary and the Czech Republic on this, soon found himself isolated as the 26 other member states went ahead with the fiscal compact outside the treaty procedures. In spite of gleeful cheers from his backbenches and the eurosceptic parts of the UK media, the reality of Cameron's decision was a total failure, although Germany had originally wished to accommodate British preferences.[6] In February 2012, in a much less well-publicised humiliation, Cameron did a U-turn and allowed the treaty to include the Fiscal Stability elements, since there was nothing he could do to prevent it.

Cameron also signally failed to take either formal or informal leadership of the group of ten member states outside the EZ. From late 2011 he became more and more shrill and intransigent in his dealings with the EU, taking an increasingly hard line on the rules governing economic migration from the Eastern European states and attacking interference from the European Convention on Human Rights on issues relating to terrorism and national security (Geddes 2014, Heppell 2014: 158–161). In so doing he antagonised Eastern European countries who originally shared many of the traditional British priorities, such as economic liberalism and military Atlanticism.

The British government's voluntary marginalisation was also made brutally obvious again when Cameron failed to assemble a blocking minority over Jean Claude Junker's appointment as head of the Commission during the summer of 2014. At one level, the Junker fiasco offers a textbook example of diplomatic bungling. In Cameron's portrayal, Junker, Europe's longest-serving prime minister, became an enemy of European progress and a fanatical federalist. He was indeed a European federalist, but then so was every previous head of the Commission and every one of his rival candidates for the post. As Ian Tryanor suggests: 'The former Luxembourg prime minister has been a less-than-colourful fixture of European politics for more than 20 years, the embodiment of consensus, compromise and coalition-building that is the daily grind of EU deal-making.'[7] Junker was a complex figure, supporting German-style fiscal and budgetary rigour, while standing on the left 'social' faction of Christian democracy, supporting a minimum wage across the EU, and a European contribution to national unemployment benefits, aimed at lessoning the impact of mass unemployment, particularly across southern Europe and especially amongst the young. Ironically Juncker was also the only candidate for the position making overtures to the British, including in his election manifesto of April 2014 a promise to try to solve the 'British question' by positively negotiating with the UK ahead of any in/out referendum.

In fact, for Cameron, and several other EU leaders, the more fundamental problem was the novel manner, described in the previous chapter, through which Junker became the frontrunner for heading the Commission, viewed as a power grab by the EP, radically altering how the EU is administered and where core power resides. This is because a new system had come into operation, largely unnoticed by the national leaders. Devised by the Social Democrat deputy head of the EP, it allowed the various party groupings in the EP to head their joint EP election campaigns lists with a pre-chosen candidate for the Commission headship. Junker headed the list of the European People's party grouping of the Christian Democratic parties which won the election, so he was automatically selected for the post, requiring only the rubber stamp of approval from the Council of Ministers.

This was viewed by Cameron (and some others) as a parliamentary coup, deleting the prerogative of national leaders to bargain amongst themselves and agree on the nomination. Cameron proved so aggressive in his opposition that he failed to turn this widespread feeling among heads of government into a success. He achieved this by insulting Junker and threatening to campaign to leave the EU in a doomed bid to block the appointment. He had relied on what he assumed to be cast iron promises made by German Chancellor Merkel to bloc Junker's appointment when the time came. But Merkel's sudden loss of enthusiasm for Junker's appointment brought considerable and sustained attacks on her from across the political spectrum in Germany for reneging on her electoral promise to honour the new and more democratic appointment system and she soon backtracked.

Cameron's defeat was of historic proportions. Never before had a British prime minister suffered such a high-profile rejection in Europe and his performance throughout smacked of petulance, blackmail and bullying. As such the UK's standing in Europe was further damaged even amongst potential allies such as the Germans, Danes, Dutch and Swedes. It was also widely pointed out that his earlier decision to take the Conservatives out of the centre-right European People's Party (EPP) had removed him from any influence over events in the EPP as they unfolded prior to the Junker affair. After this series of errors, detoxifying the British brand in Europe has become much harder.

Once Junker's appointment was inevitable Cameron returned to the default position of promising to campaign in the future referendum to keep the UK in the EU, providing he could negotiate 'serious concessions' while quietly withdrawing his meaningless veto. This left an impression of a vacillating and weak leader on EU matters and furthermore, one who could not be trusted by his Europhobe back benchers to deliver a 'Brexit' in the next parliament. Such conclusions redoubled the determination of many in his party to vociferously agitate, plot and campaign to leave the EU, if necessary in alliance with UKIP.

At the same time the cumulative rise in the levels of frustration with the UK amongst fellow member states rose considerably. Easily the most graphic illustration of this was provided in June 2014 by Polish Foreign

Minister Radoslaw Sikorski who, in a secretly taped and leaked conversation about Cameron's fiscal pact manoeuvres with former Polish Finance Minister Jacek Rostowski, said: 'It's either a very badly thought through move, or, not for the first time, a kind of incompetence in European affairs. Remember? He fucked up the fiscal pact. He fucked it up. Simple as that. He is not interested, he does not get it, he believes in the stupid propaganda, he stupidly tries to play the system.' To which Rostowski replies: 'His [Cameron's] problem is that this isn't his objective, just a short-term propaganda effect.' Sikorski also criticised what he saw as the British leader's attempt to appease British eurosceptics with soundbites: 'You know, his whole strategy of feeding them scraps in order to satisfy them is just as I predicted, turning against him; he should have said, fuck off, tried to convince people and isolate [the sceptics]. But he ceded the field to those that are now embarrassing him.'[8]

This revelation was all the more revealing and damaging for Cameron because Sikorski has close links with senior British Conservatives and was an Oxford University student and member of the Bullingdon Club contemporaneously with Boris Johnson. The German mass-readership newspaper *Bild* compared Cameron to Wayne Rooney in the World Cup: 'He lines up, he loses, he flies home,' while Jochen Buchsteiner of the *Frankfurter AllgemeineZeitung* observed that Cameron was the Don Quixote of the EU, pandering to a eurosceptical public at home: 'A majority of Brits see him as a hero – even when he comes back home beaten.'[9]

Cameron's actions were, of course, entirely explicable from a UK domestic politics perspective, where the gesture politics of his veto (both pointless and later rescinded) was given widespread media approval and lavishly praised by British eurosceptics of all hues. Boris Johnston suggested that: 'David Cameron has done the only thing that was really open to him to do. He has played a blinder.'[10] In the case of Mr Juncker, the *Sun* slandered him as – 'the most dangerous man in Europe', the son of a 'Nazi'.[11] But although understandable in purely domestic political terms, this attitude was extremely damaging for British interests in Europe.

Semi-detachment or 'Brexit'?

As things stand, Britain could vote to leave the EU in the near future. Alternatively it may remain in simply through inertia if sufficient face-saving concessions are given to the UK by the Germans and/or no referendum takes place, thereby continuing as a peripheral member of the EU outside the EZ and excluded from most of the major decisions concerning the future economic development of the EU. But whatever happens, it does appear that a historic juncture in Britain's relations with the EU is about to occur based principally upon a strategic choice over the future direction of the UK's political economy. And, as Andrew Gamble suggests, as in the past the main choice will be between Europe and Anglo-America:

> With Empire gone the future of Britain as an independent nation now depends on the multilateral relationships it forges with the rest of the world, and to which of those it chooses to give priority. Europe and America in this sense offer different futures. The choice is not an exclusive one, because Europe and America are not monolithic, but highly complex and differentiated political spaces... Yet although Britain will always be part of both Europe and of Anglo-America, there remains a question of priority... England will never be an Empire again. Its identity and its political economy will be determined primarily by its relationship with Europe and with America. The mould has been broken and cannot be reset.
>
> (Gamble 2003: 220)

In terms of Britain's future political economy strategy, a choice to leave the EU could mean the UK economy becoming a satellite to the US economy, arguably in a weaker position in terms of maintaining its *de facto* national sovereignty than its present semi-detached position within the EU. Indeed, a Scottish style devo-max solution for Britain inside the EU could be the best way of ensuring the future strength of the UK economy by giving the economy continued access to the Single Market, albeit with limited protection for the City of London, while retaining fiscal and monetary sovereignty.

A Brexit decision would have one certain political economy ramification; it would cause untold economic disruption and a period of great uncertainly (and global financial markets hate uncertainty) while the UK negotiates a series of bilateral trade arrangements, largely with the Anglophone countries, as well as with the EU (Charter 2012: 244). How the pound would fare during such a period can only be surmised, but a run on the pound is quite possible. Shares in UK companies could well take a sizable cut in value in the immediate aftermath too. The UK has also become very reliant upon foreign direct investment in recent years, attracting $53.9 billion in 2011 (the highest in Europe) and this could also go into decline after a Brexit. Just under half of foreign investors in 2010 admitted that their decision to invest in the British economy was due to its links to the European market and the fact it is an English-speaking country (Charter 2012: 256). Nor could the City of London be guaranteed its present pre-eminence as the *de facto* private banking hub of Europe. One senior banker observed:

> It is possible that London, being outside the EU, could still survive as an offshore financial centre in the way that Singapore is a major centre or Hong Kong is outside mainstream China. It is not clear if being outside would be the death knell for London, but it would certainly not be as beneficial as being on the inside.
> (Charter 2012: 260)

Once outside the EU, City access would have to be renegotiated by the British government along the lines of the WTO's 'Most Favoured Nation' status. And while a trade war with the EU looks unlikely as both would stand to lose, this does not mean that the EU would prove a pushover in such negotiations, given that the UK would have abandoned it so recently. David Charter has suggested that even after a Brexit the UK would find it impossible to withdraw from its very close economic ties to the EU. Engaging in *post hoc* history, as if Britain had already left the EU, he writes:

> Since there was no possibility of uprooting the British Isles and floating off closer to the United States, Canada or Mexico, the UK had no option but to try and stay as closely intertwined as possible with its continental partners on numerous levels. The familiar pattern of frequent arguments, muddles and joint initiatives that have always marked Britain's relationship with the continent continued unabated. It was not *adieu*. It was *au revoir*, Europe.
> (Charter 2012: 306)

Conclusion

In this study we have analysed the effects of the global crisis on the EU and the UK, and the inevitable interactions between all three geopolitical spheres, in particular the political spillover of the EU crisis into UK politics and vice versa. In short, what is often referred to as 'Britain in Europe' and 'Europe in Britain' has, we argue, developed on dangerous new dimensions because of the economic crisis (Geddes 2014: 12–16).

As we have seen, both the EU and UK have been experiencing overlapping crises of political economy, governance and democratic legitimacy, while the wider global crisis has centred on political economy issues and the move from a bi-polar (East–West) global environment to a multi-polar world, where new power relationships have weakened US economic and military hegemony without replacing it with a decisive new system (Gamble 2014: 76–129). Gramsci famously wrote in his *Prison Notebooks* that: 'The crisis consists precisely in the fact that the old is dying and the new cannot be born; in this interregnum a great variety of morbid symptoms appear' (Gramsci 1971: 276).

We have demonstrated that the UK has been powerfully impacted upon by the crisis of the EU: partly as a leading dissenting memberstate, often chafing against its rules and procedures, partly because the EU is the UK's single largest trading partner, making the UK heavily reliant upon a strong European recovery in order to maintain its own growth rate, and partly because British political culture contains powerful eurosceptic elements which have taken advantage of the economic and social disintegration and political discontent triggered by the crisis across the EU. In particular, as we have demonstrated, fundamentalist eurosceptic elements have strengthened their grip on the Conservative Party, spawning UKIP in the process and attracting the support of a growing section of the UK electorate to the hard eurosceptic cause, especially in England. Finally, we have indicated that the UK's response to the EU in crisis has impacted on the wider EU crisis, giving succour to mainland euroscepticism and antagonising European political elites, with high-profile British eurosceptics attacking moves towards a closer federal union, dismissing the social Europe dimension in favour of the Single Market and attempting to align with and encourage burgeoning eurosceptic movements across the EU. Much of this impact has been negative, alienating nations traditionally friendly and sympathetic towards the British, increasingly viewed as arrogant, out of touch and un-European in their lack of solidarity, and in the process further isolating the UK in European affairs.

Continuity and change in the dynamics in the European Union

In the recent crisis, after an initial period exhibiting a degree of contrition for encouraging market failure, and aggressively employing state powers and resources to rescue the entire global financial system, those social and political forces supporting a return to the status quo in the UK and the EU (largely varieties of conservative hyperglobalisation, neoliberalism and ordoliberalism) recovered themselves sufficiently rapidly to escape the most damaging accusations of complicity and failure, by successfully deflecting blame on others (mistakes by past governments and central bankers, profligate borrowers in the debtor states, inflated state expenditure on welfare and grand projects, etc.) enabling them to forge the dominant narrative of the crisis and command continued electoral mandates for their chosen austerian solutions.

In the process the post-crisis governing elites of the UK and EU have partially restored their image of governing competence, seizing a golden opportunity to further advance their supply-side economic policies and implement more radical market expansion and state reduction policies than were possible before the crisis struck. The outcome has seen solutions based upon highly questionable 'austerity-led growth' models linked (in theory) to rapid sovereign debt repayment, along with enforced market-based economic restructuring, representing an archetypical case of a successful post-crisis struggle for political power.

At first glance it may appear perverse to argue for continuity with pre-crisis politics, since most European governments that were in office at the time the crisis broke were subsequently ejected from office and, as we saw, Europe has also witnessed the rise of a plethora of anti-EU and anti-regime parties, some of whom – like Golden Dawn in Greece –

reject democracy as well. However, a remarkable degree of continuity with the pre-existing economic orthodoxies has been maintained by the fact that so far all of the discredited governments with the exception of the election of a Syriza-dominated left wing anti-austerity government in Greece in January 2015 have been replaced by equally or, in some cases, even more orthodox governments, often located further to the right of the political spectrum than their predecessors; or are technocratic in nature. Meanwhile, in Germany and some other creditor states the ruling parties have not been judged by their electorates as culpable, since their economies have not suffered the worst effects of the crisis in shouldering the main burdens of austerity and restructuring.

However, the successful maintenance and even strengthening of neoliberal and ordoliberal orthodoxies does not, as we have shown, mean that the underlying problems that caused the crisis of the EU and UK have disappeared. Indeed, the chosen solution of austerity in order to pay down debt and restore sustained economic growth and wealth creation, along with an attempt to stabilise the euro system by common rules and further integration has, so far at least, simply postponed and in some cases exacerbated these underlying problems.

We have also argued that long before the present crisis the balance of inter-member-state power was altered radically by the EU's post-Maastricht broadening, widening and deepening processes, which introduced qualified majority voting in the Council and elsewhere and greatly increased the number of member-states, diluting the voting power of the 'big three' (Germany, France and the UK) in so doing encouraging new and shifting alliances across a number of member-state groupings, often driven by complex intergovernmental deals struck at the level of heads of government and/or ministerial conferences. Equally, many of the new Eastern European member-states brought with them a strong desire to bolster the freedom of movement of workers across the EU, since they had underemployed populations eager to find work in the wealthier parts of the EU, and especially in the UK where the native English language holds the possibility of further onward movement to the USA and elsewhere in the future.

In relation to the changing dynamics of the EU spurred on and consolidated by the crisis, Dyson and Sepos have identified six post-Maastricht informal member-state groupings: Nordic; Baltic; Visegrad; Club Med (France, Spain and Italy); Carolingian; and Anglo-American (Dyson and Sepos 2010). The Carolingian grouping, which includes Germany, remains the most powerful, but as we have seen it is more difficult than in the past in most areas to force through changes and assemble blocking minorities under conditions of limited veto power. In this respect the crisis has been very useful to Germany since it has lifted the solution into the high politics of intergovernmental, ECB, troika and Commission-led policy-making, thus isolating it from democratic pressures and allowing German diplomacy to carry the day.

As a result Germany has been able to achieve far more of its strategic national goals than would otherwise have been possible, while the influence of France and the UK has been diminished. This was also made possible because new strata of divisions and asymmetries of post-crisis power have emerged between the 'creditor' and 'debtor' states of the EZ since 2010, making the creditor states led by Germany sufficiently powerful to overrule any opposition from the debtors, if necessary by threats of withholding necessary bail-out funding, or expulsion from the EZ. Life for David Cameron has been made considerably more difficult as a result, leading as he does a large but peripheral EU state outside the EZ. As we witnessed, this inherent weakness became brutally obvious during his humiliating failure to assemble a blocking minority over the appointment of Jean Claude Junker as the new head of the Commission in the summer of 2014.

Another spin-off of this longer-term process has been a damaging divergence between the economies and perceived national interests of the two pre-crisis guiding spirits of the EU, Germany and France. France lacks the German ordoliberal high savings, low wage, vertically and horizontally integrated technocratic and export-driven economy and therefore is exposed to austerity measures while operating within a German-valued currency system. This has placed France in objective alignment with the 'Club Med' Southern European debtor states. However, even under a socialist president France remains bound into a Franco-German alliance, lacking the political will to break free, leaving the French economy in near recession, while in Italy youth unemployment remained at an unsustainable 43% in 2014, and is in its third recession in six years and still facing the prospect of an economic collapse in the future (Traynor 2014).

France's long-term erosion of strategic power as a counterweight to Germany is deeply ironic in respect to the UK's position within the EU, since the UK's supply side and austerity-focused Conservative-dominated coalition government might be considered to be well placed to forge an alliance with the Germans to dictate the future development and direction of the EU. After all the EU currently being reconstructed under German leadership is not the liberal-market-destroying social-market-economy monster depicted by British eurosceptics rather, as we saw, it represents many of the ideas put forward by British market liberals, centred upon a liberalised and free internal market system. However, the huge gulf which exists between the German federalist and British intergovernmentalist positions over forging and managing Europe makes any such alliance to lead Europe quite impossible to achieve in the foreseeable future. It is an interesting paradox that while it agreed with the ordoliberal austerity policies pursued on the continent, the UK's coalition government has become further estranged from its natural North European 'Carolingian' partners.

The crisis of governance and legitimacy

We have suggested throughout that the present crises of the EU and UK represent much more than simply an economic phenomenon. As we saw, the EU's governance and legitimacy crisis, across all member-states, especially in the UK, predates the banking crisis of 2008 and the sovereign debt crisis of 2010. We have also shown that there are similarities between the essentially political crises of legitimacy and democracy in the UK and EU as a whole, with regard to the well-publicised widening gap between traditional governing parties and their once loyal electorates, with space opening up for extremist parties formerly kept to the fringes of politics. The scandal-prone nature of governing politicians and the widespread sense of the remoteness of EU officials mean that they are no longer trusted to look after the interests of their citizens, appearing increasingly elitist, self-serving, corrupt, technocratic and remote in their governing posture. In response, many centrist political parties have been driven to offer more extreme policies in order to match those of their radical populist rivals, and placate their own more extreme members, raising once again the spectre of officially sanctioned populist cultural racism and exclusive nationalism in Europe.

We have revealed many damaging asymmetries of institutional and political power across the EU/EZ, created by the path-dependent elite-driven nature of past integration and the collision of the resulting institutions and practices with the global banking and sovereign debt crises. One, perhaps *the*, chief political consequence of the ongoing crisis has been the heightening of pre-existing levels of popular 'dissensus' spreading across the member-states of the EU, mirroring much older traditions of dissensus evident in the UK. We have argued that this trend has quickened and deepened since the sovereign debt crisis overwhelmed the EU's capacity to respond in a decisive or suitably intra-communal manner which highlighted the harsh technocratic side of EU governance for many EU citizens.

Dissensus over the EU's governance of UK matters long predates 1991 and lies in an essentially English and conservative political culture, infused with beliefs supporting the maintenance of national sovereignty through intergovernmentalism and an absolute necessity to protect the inherently superior Anglo-American political economy based on market neoliberalisation, as well as the Atlantic alliance denoted under the 'special relationship' (Gamble 2003: 83–107, Gamble 2014).

The British situation

Paradoxically neoliberal governments in the UK (and the USA) have from the beginning of the crisis ignored the supposedly 'scientific' dictates of the self-correcting 'efficient markets hypothesis' and exercised flexibility in using state assets and powers while, it must be noted, talking tough about austerity and paying down debt. This can be seen from the unprecedented amount of taxpayers' money aimed at stabilising the banks through QE, in continued high levels of government borrowing, and the maintenance of ultra-low interest rates. Also, in the UK the deepest austerity cuts were astutely delayed by the coalition until after the 2015 election, while encouraging a housing bubble to stimulate demand in the economy through debt-fuelled privatised Keynesianism, with high-speed rail investment promised and extra military Keynesianism thrown in in the form of two new aircraft carriers (Crouch 2012, Hay 2012, Blyth 2013). In addition, the pound which is outside the EZ has been allowed to devalue by up to 30% to boost exports[1] and London has been made more fiscally attractive to the super-rich to invest in property as a hedge against lower returns on capital elsewhere. As a result, the UK economy was growing relatively strongly by 2014, in contrast to the economies of the EZ countries, many of which were mired in stagnation due to the application of inflexible austerity in a monetary system where the very architecture of the single currency reinforces deflationary pressures. Consequently the recovery in the UK has been patchy to say the least, restricted largely to major cities and their hinterlands, with most workers seeing their living standards falling along with worsening conditions of work. Many of the UK jobs that have been created have been part-time or zero hours and low waged, meaning that average living standards were still falling in the UK in 2014 along with the tax take.

The continuing political and economic crisis in the UK was made especially clear through the Scottish referendum where, although the 'No' vote won relatively comfortably by 55–45%, popular anger at the shortcomings of the London-centric wealth creating and absorbing British state were reinforced. Irvine Welsh puts it vividly:

> Scots are showing they won't go on committing their taxes or oil monies to building a London super-state on the global highway for the transnational rich, particularly when it's becoming unaffordable to their Cockney comrades, driving them out of their own city to the M25 satellites... The yes movement hit such heights because the UK state was seen as failed; antiquated, hierarchical, centralist, discriminatory, out of touch and acting against the people.
> (Welsh 2014)

The political crisis is also reflected in the state of the Tory party. With regard to this we have repeatedly indicated that the Conservative Party and its obsession with the EU lies at the heart of the crisis in relations between the UK and the EU. UKIP is itself a symptom of this obsession, representing a breakaway faction of the Tory neoliberal and little Englander right, dissatisfied with the party elite's progress on leaving the EU. With regard to the issue of Europe, traditional Conservative 'statecraft' has not proven up to the task allotted to it by Jim Bulpitt, of insulating governing conservative elites from popular democratic pressures (including those within the Conservative Party and its electorate) in order to be free to make strategic decisions at the level of 'high politics' on behalf of the 'national interest' (Bulpitt 1983, 1991). Instead, after four years in office, Cameron has managed to unite most of his party and many former and present Tory voters in the suspicion that his statecraft represented a thinly veiled plot to keep the UK in Europe by duping the British people into voting in a referendum to stay in the EU which, even if untrue, means that it represents a dismally failed form of statecraft. At root this failure serves as an illustration of the impossibility of maintaining a workable strategic form of statecraft in the face of the dangerous obsession with Europe which has continuously wracked the Conservative Party from within since the mid-1980s, ending the careers of a number of party leaders, senior ministers and most notably Prime Minister Thatcher (Ludlam and Smith 1996, Baker and Seawright 1998). In many ways the Conservative Party has become increasingly trapped inside a post-Thatcher legacy on Europe, unable to move beyond it to take account of changing circumstances and national needs.

During 2013–2014 in response to such fears, a hard core of socially Conservative MPs, in alliance with their hyperglobalist neo-Thatcherite colleagues, went further advocating an electoral pact with UKIP in order to keep Labour from obtaining power through the divisions on the right over the EU and to guarantee a future 'Brexit', which they no longer trusted Cameron to deliver. In any case, the Conservative Party remains held in stasis by the issue of Europe, unable to move on unless and until the UK is outside the EU, whatever this means for the 'national interest', in so doing arguably placing party and ideological obsessions above those of the nation (Ludlam and Smith 1996, Baker and Seawright 1998, Gamble 2014).

We have suggested that UKIP has been the chief political beneficiary in the UK of these developments, drawing support from those who are most conscious that 'we' are not 'all in it together'. In particular UKIP have drawn support from groups which feel most threatened by largely East European economic low-wage migration and from a domestic political crisis caused by the concentration of austerity and the forces of globalisation onto poorer, low-skill, renting and indebted groups, including the farming communities of the East of England from Kent to Lincolnshire, and struggling northern industrial towns like Doncaster in South Yorkshire (Blyth 2013, O'Hara 2013, Ford and Goodwin 2014).

The rise of continental forms of euroscepticism has also been spun by UKIP as legitimising its own sovereignty-obsessed, free market, cultural racist stance, in spite of the fact that many of the continental eurosceptic parties do not advocate complete withdrawal from the EU, or in some cases even from the euro, and that many are also hostile to free market, low-tax globalisation.[2] Indeed, many continental eurosceptic movements and parties are against further economic liberalisation, either favouring nationalistic and/or state-centred solutions, or a return to 'social Europe', rather than being the natural allies of Tory or UKIP-style euroscepticism. This explains the difficulties UKIP and the Conservative Party have experienced in forging links with like-minded eurosceptic parties in the European Parliament, leading in both cases to some extreme political bedfellows. Nevertheless British eurosceptics continue to peddle the claim that continental eurosceptic parties and movements support their hyperglobalist neoliberalism and cultural racism.

We have also analysed another form of political spillover from the growth of European-wide euroscepticism, namely its effect upon many mainstream governing parties desperately seeking to protect and expand their shrinking core electoral support which has become disillusioned and dealigned through austerity and falling living standards. As we saw, this explains why Cameron became more and more intransigent in his dealings with the EU offering a straightforward 'in/out' referendum if the party was re-elected to govern alone in 2015, and seeking cast-iron guarantees for protection of the City of London from new legislative interference from Brussels, while taking an increasingly hard line on the rules governing economic migration from the Eastern European states and attacking the ECHR for curbing potential laws on terrorism (Heppell 2014: 158–161).

As we saw, while Cameron originally intended to campaign in his promised in/out referendum for staying in a renegotiated 'reformed EU', he switched position during the Junker appointment fiasco, threatening to campaign to leave in his doomed bid to block the appointment. Aside from his vacillations and perceived weakness on the EU, many in his party will vociferously agitate, plot and campaign to leave, alongside or in alliance with UKIP, which will undoubtedly remain a potent populist force in UK politics over the coming years (Ford and Goodwin 2014: 268–289). If Cameron fails to win an outright victory in the 2015 election, he would face a leadership challenge organised by the powerful eurosceptic faction in his party in order to install a leader such as Boris Johnson, willing if necessary to lead the party into a pact with UKIP to secure a majority government in order to take the UK out of the EU.

But the EU is not simply a Conservative Party problem. Relentless pressure from UKIP and the Tory eurosceptic right, plus a populist right-wing media-led drive against 'benefits tourism' (essentially a modern myth) and foreigners taking 'British jobs', has caused all the main parties in the UK to offer to resist and if possible roll back EU-wide open borders legislation. Equally, if Miliband's Labour falls into line and offers a post-election referendum (which it has resisted) and then gains victory (either outright or in coalition with the Lib Dems) this could also favour a 'Brexit'. Referendums (as witnessed in the Scottish case) often see unpopular governments punished by a section of the voters, and they also encourage faith in a new future over those advocating a return to a tired and discredited status quo. Thus, with Labour broadly accepting future deep austerity cuts promised by the coalition after the next election, a 'better together' style referendum campaign led by a deeply unpopular Labour administration could easily lead to a landslide vote to leave the EU, especially with a largely hostile press and united eurosceptic Tory party attacking and ridiculing the government on all fronts.

Since the late 1990s the constant drumbeat of a largely eurosceptical national print media and endless anti-EU messages delivered in interviews by leading politicians on the broadcast media have almost drowned out most positive views on Britain's membership of the EU. The EZ crisis has reinforced this trend, further muting if not completely silencing many pro-European voices. Against the background of unrest in the streets of Southern Europe, with statistics of falling growth and record levels of unemployment in the EZ and while the UK's growth figures are touted as the highest in the EU, it is extremely difficult to convincingly argue the case for staying in.

Against this, it should be noted that most UK voters remain primarily concerned with the economy and the NHS, with Europe further down the list of salient domestic political issues. William Hague discovered this in his attempt to lead the Conservative Party to victory in 2001 on an anti-EU 'Save the Pound' ticket, which failed. However, the Scottish Referendum campaign gave a forewarning of how a referendum radically changes the political salience dynamic, especially in any referendum concerning national self-determination, making life very difficult for those seeking to argue for, or openly support, the status quo. Of course, in Scotland's case the silent majority of 'no' won the day by a clear 10% and a majority of UK voters do not see the EU in UKIP's zero sum terms, rating other issues more highly in their decision to vote (Ford and Goodwin 2014: 274–283).

However any UK-wide self-determination referendum over membership of the EU would most likely see the crucial high turnout of older voters on the exit side, and whereas in Scotland only one newspaper came out on the yes side, there would be a clear majority of mass-market UK newspapers vociferously advocating exit. In addition, the role of Salmond would be well filled by Nigel Farage and leading populists in the Conservative Party including Boris Johnson (who may by then be leading the party, if not the government). Equally, whether the dire warnings and thinly veiled threats that would certainly be issued by the EU, from some leading international banking and business leaders, and from the US and supranational organisations such as the IMF would provide a sufficient 'fear factor' to swing the vote towards staying in, as in Scotland, is a moot point. And unlike Scottish membership of the larger UK, where a proportion of Scots feel genuine dual identity with Scotland and the UK, only a small number of British people feel any real warmth towards the EU, let alone consider their primary identity to be bound up with it.

David Marquand has written eloquently of the dangers posed by the exclusive and insular nationalism associated with British euroscepticism and the relatively subdued opposition voices of pro-Europe centrist politicians:

> The myth of insular self-sufficiency has little appeal to the centre and the left, but neither of them has challenged it emotionally or ideologically. In the debate over Britain's future relationship with the continent of which she is part, Europhobes speak to the heart and Europhiles only to the head. 'Brexit', British secession from the European Union, is no longer a distant dream for some and an equally distant nightmare for others; it is a real possibility. If it happens, the odds on the survival of the union state will be poor: Scotland and Wales would probably wish to stay in the European Union even if England and Northern Ireland seceded.
>
> (Marquand 2014: 64)

Britain on the sidelines

As a result of these domestic pressures, the British government's role since the sovereign debt crisis broke out in 2010 has been, as we have seen, largely restricted to engaging in megaphone diplomacy, initially in urging the EZ members to speed up economic integration reforms to solve the economic crisis, since it impacted negatively on the speed of the British recovery. By 2012, however, responding to pressure from Tory and UKIP eurosceptics and the realisation that the German solution to the EZ crisis was to accelerate federal integration, Cameron was refusing to sanction the means by vetoing the necessary EU Treaty modifications, in spite of the fact that the UK would have been allowed to opt out from these provisions.

We have also highlighted the growing dangers for the UK in managing negotiations at the EU level from a position outside the consensus and on the periphery, in relation to the 2014 EU Commission Presidential appointment fiasco. As one German commentator put it:

> 'German politics is full of ex-politicians who placed their trust in the lady [Chancellor Merkel]. Cameron should have been warned about this. With Germany inside the eurozone, and Britain seemingly forever out, there are limits of the extent to which Germany and Britain can forge a strategic relationship inside the EU.'
>
> (Munchau 2014)

As we saw, this serious miscalculation followed two years of badly misjudged diplomatic posturing from Cameron, threatening that unless serious concessions were made towards his party's hyperglobalist and intergovernmentalist preferences, he might be unable to win an in/out referendum, even if he personally campaigned for Britain to remain in the EU. We also noted that since such concessions are unlikely to be available at any time in the near future, 'Brexit' appears a possibility if the Conservatives win the 2015 general election or Labour gives in to eurosceptic pressure for a referendum, given the overwhelming political and media forces that would line up to support a populist campaign for 'Brexit' in a referendum held under such circumstances, and the fact that the Tory party could split over the issue shortly after the 2015 election, replacing Cameron with a hard-line populist eurosceptic in the process.

Where next? The known unknowns

Prediction and futurology is *the* most difficult of scholarly tasks, particularly for those operating in social and human studies, since it means extrapolating from present and past events into the future. Unlike the 'hard' sciences, which deal with relationships between dead unconscious matter, subject to measurable physical forces and observable repeated reactions, social and human studies struggle to achieve any scientific predictive precision, due to the unpredictability, capriciousness and self-reflective capacities of interacting humans and their artificially constructed institutions. Thus, as Tomas Sedlacek has pointed out in relation to the economics profession which often considers itself akin to the hard sciences: 'Despite the fact that we want to explain the future, we often cannot even explain the past' (Sedlacek 2013: 307).

In order to attempt any form of predictive social science it is essential to employ a degree of *ceteris paribus*, meaning that a certain predicted outcome relies upon all else being more or less equal, or remaining much the same. In addition, it is necessary to recognise that currently projected policies may change in the future in response to unanticipated circumstances, or changing ideas, for instance the election of leaders not bound by past policies and/or of radical populist intent. Failure to take sufficient account of potential policy changes made under pressure of evolving events explains David Cameron's problems when dealing with Chancellor Merkel during the Junker appointment fiasco.

The one thing that is already clear about Britain's future is that it will continue to evolve as part of Europe, to which it is bound by ties of geography, history, culture and trade; but the real question is, will it also be as part of the EU? As things stand Britain will play only a peripheral role in the future development of the EU, unless the EU (specifically Germany) makes major concessions to the British anti-federalist position, an outcome that appears inconceivable at the present time, given German perceptions of the need to protect the euro currency at all costs, and some less wealthy EU/EZ states' manifest advantages in being able to export surplus labour to the wealthier EU states.

In terms of the post-crisis EU/EZ, as things stand the future appears to offer a number of possible scenarios, the core of which has been well expressed by John McCormick:

> The problems of the euro have spawned something of a cottage industry in scenario building, with numerous suggestions about where we might go from here. Many argue that Europe is now at the prosaic fork in the road, but the analogy is too simple and it would be more accurate to suggest that it has entered a roundabout from which – taking into consideration the wide range of political and public opinions about integration – there are at least five possible exits.
>
> (McCormick 2014: 147)

He lists the five main options as 1: the complete breakup of the EU and EZ; 2: a rollback to the Single Market alone; 3: a continuation of the post-crisis status quo – 'muddling through' with incremental multi-speed integration; 4: a fully federal EU/EZ; and 5: a permanently confederal EU (a union of states) preserving state sovereignty and enshrining nation-state governance of the EU.

The problem for the UK is that options 3 and (especially) 4 of these possible exits to the roundabout are completely unacceptable to British eurosceptics and therefore effectively off the agenda in the medium term, while in complete contrast 4 remains the preferred options of the majority of EU states, receiving a boost from the crisis through changes to the EZ system requiring further pooling of sovereignty and centralised politico-economic harmonisation. Most British eurosceptics are seeking option 1 after a British exit, while the present Conservative leadership is seeking options 2 and 5, which in any case overlap. As things stand, no member of the EU is seeking to preserve the status quo ex ante.

Cameron, in his January 2013 Bloomberg Speech, rashly (given his pragmatic 'soft' euroscepticism) committed a future majority Conservative administration (if elected in 2015) to a largely unworkable renegotiation and subsequent in-out referendum by the end of 2017. It is a sign of the radicalisation of sections of the Tory elite and disaffected former electorate that this did little to bring home past Tory voters to Cameron's Conservatives – many of whom remained loyal to UKIP in the 2014 European elections – let alone placate his hard-line backbenchers and 'no surrender' local party activists (Ford and Goodwin 2014: 283–288).

However this seemingly simple referendum scenario begs a number of burning questions: will the Tories or Labour win the next election outright, or will another coalition result and if so will it be Lab-Lib, Lab-Lib-SNP, Con-Lib or (much less likely) Con-UKIP? Also, will Labour and/or the Lib Dems match Cameron's promise before the next election,[3] in which case almost any combination of foreseeable government (Lab-SNP aside) will be committed to renegotiation and subsequent referendum? As we argued above, this would be a dangerous situation for Britain's continued membership of the EU, since the Scottish referendum underlined the power of such processes to radicalise and alienate an electorate from its political, broadcast media and business elites.

With regard to the role of the EU in the run-up to such a referendum, the crucial question will be whether Merkel can deliver for Cameron, or any other UK leader, sufficient concessions to allow them to win an in/out referendum? This depends on another unknown, whether the Eurozone crisis deepens again triggering a call for treaty changes. The French are already concerned that any such treaty changes would trigger a French referendum leading to rejection, and the Germans are acutely aware of this potentially blocking situation. Added to which there is the coalition's 2011 European Union Act, which specifies a 'referendum lock' if 'substantial powers' are deemed be transferred to the EU level.

The Germans and other member-states are also deeply concerned about the potential economic impact and disruption caused by the conscious uncoupling of a leading economic power at a time when austerity has already sucked the growth out of the EZ economies. However, as we have repeatedly argued, if Germany is faced with a zero-sum game on this issue there is no doubt they will opt for German core interests ahead of keeping Britain in the UK, and this was the tone adopted by Angela Merkel in November 2014 over Cameron's reported demands that immigration rights be curbed, and published in a leaked statement in *Der Spiegel*:

> Were Cameron to continue insisting on an upper limit for immigration from EU member states, Berlin sources said 'that would be that'.

Sources say that Merkel left no doubt about where she stands on the issue during a private meeting with the British prime minister on the sidelines of the recent EU summit... Should Cameron move to establish numerical limits on immigration from EU member states, 'there will be no going back', say sources in Berlin. First, they say, Cameron's proposal would be torpedoed in Brussels by Germany and several other EU countries and then he would return home and lose the referendum on Britain's exit from the EU.[4]

With regard to any future referendum, as we suggested above, those seeking 'Brexit' will paint themselves as attacking both the EU and the Westminster/London establishment and depict the referendum as offering the additional chance to give a bloody nose to the establishment and whatever government is in office, unless, of course, that government is actually recommending exit, in which case it would likely be game, set and match. Referendums are always a double-edge sword, empowering voters over the established party elites and therefore uber-democratic (as Harold Wilson said 'only one vote is enough in a referendum') while at the same time open to simplistic propaganda, media manipulation and utopian populist demagoguery, especially in referendums concerning matters of national identity. The mass politicisation that comes with any referendum on national self-determination always brings with it populism and utopianism. This process places the forces of continuity and traditional authority (the elite media, business and finance, and the traditional governing parties) on the defensive. Many vote in such referendums as a means of expressing their sense of powerlessness, feeling that their voice can be heard and make a real difference for once, hence the traditionally high turnouts. They also tend to unite the radical right and left in an anti-establishment, anti-'old guards' pact to overthrow hated and corrupt elites (Cardinal 2005, deVreese 2007).

Ford and Goodwin have, however, argued that there are formidable obstacles in the way of UKIP benefitting from almost any outcome of a future referendum. A Labour victory or Lab/Lib coalition, cancelling a referendum, would lead to the blaming of UKIP for splitting the right-wing vote and potentially a haemorrhaging of support. While a Tory victory followed by a vote to leave would destroy much of the party's reasons for existence, most probably reabsorbing it amongst the Tory party's right-wing factions. Finally, a vote to stay in would also weaken the party and undermine its overemphasis on the issue of the EU which is central to its activist's world view (Ford and Goodwin 2014: 286–288). The growing strength of British euroscepticism inside the Tory Party and through UKIP makes it very hard to predict what will happen after the 2015 election.

One of the most prescient analyses of the future prospects for the UK, in or out of Europe, has come from Wolfgang Münchau, who points out (as have we) that the road to the UK's potential exit from the EU started long ago:

> The real in-out decision is not the 2017 referendum, if it comes. The real decision was taken in 1991, when John Major negotiated the opt-out from monetary union at Maastricht, famously declaring 'Game, set and match.' The next acts in the drama were the pound's ejection from the European Exchange Rate Mechanism in 1992, and the decision by Tony Blair's government in 1998 to exercise the opt-out. These were the decisions that set Britain on a different path, ultimately leading to the fiasco of Cameron's isolation in the European Council [over the appointment of Junker as head of the Commission].
>
> (Münchau 2014)

This decision placed the UK permanently on the periphery of the EU, since currency union (even more than the vitally important Single Market which Britain does belong to) represents the political economy core of the European project and its main driving force since the late 1980s. Münchau believes that this was the only possible *economic* course of action for the UK at the time, benefitting the UK and the rest of the EU both in the short and medium term, since during both the credit crunch and sovereign debt crises of recent years the crisis might well have been made worse by Britain's membership of the euro, both for the EZ and for the UK. But Münchau correctly argues that this decision locked the UK out of the EU's centre of *political* gravity and long-term economic trajectory, weakening the UK's voice in Europe and encouraging right-wing euroscepticism to grow and prosper in the UK.

But his key point is that even a UK remaining 'in' the EU will not really be 'in' it since: 'The choice for Britain in 2017 is not really between in and out. If it votes to stay in, Britain will still not join the eurozone. Britain will seek even more areas of policy opt-out.' Rather the choice is between remaining on the periphery as a member-state and seeking to become even more peripheral through further opt outs, or leaving and being pulled back to the periphery as an independent nation-state through continued economic ties. Of the two options he considers the first to be unsustainable that is: 'for Britain simply to stay in the EU, not join the eurozone and hope that it will all turn out well'. His solution:

The best outcome for everybody would be a formal two-tier EU, with the eurozone at the centre, and a group of countries around it that require and prefer less integration. It would allow the eurozone to become more autonomous, more democratically accountable and more integrated. Market integration would be stronger inside the eurozone than within the EU as a whole. It is not just British demands for renegotiation which might bring this about. The EU would want to avoid a British exit.

(Ibid.)

However, we have argued throughout that such a deal, even if it was concluded, and we doubt that it could be, may well prove woefully insufficient to satisfy the hard-line eurosceptics in the Tory Party and in UKIP, who could hold the balance of power after the 2015 election, or shortly thereafter. If 'Brexit' does occur the problem would, as Münchau suggests, hinge on whether the UK could negotiate a suitably advantageous 'sweetheart' deal on exit and avoid the EEA 'solution' and economic collateral damage of having no influence over future Single Market legislation in the process.

One can certainly foresee some of the potential costs and benefits of 'Brexit'. Whatever the nature of a 'Brexit deal' the inevitable financial transaction costs and delays which would be incurred through separation could well prove a considerable drag on the UK and EU economies, while time-consuming bilateral deals were negotiated with other trading nations and blocs, including, of course, the EU itself. In addition, just how accommodating a unilaterally divorced EU would be with an ex-member-state that had just left after considerable anti-EU invective and propaganda had been hurled at it from the 'Brexit' camp is open to question. Some argue that Europe would itself be damaged unless it offered favoured status along Norwegian and Swiss lines, and many powerful EU companies with a stake in car and other high-value goods sales to the UK (especially in Germany) would undoubtedly lobby for a quick and equitable deal to be struck (Charter 2012: 246–84, Liddle 2014: 213–233).

In any case there would almost certainly be a short to medium term dip in the UK economy, probably following an initial optimistic bounce as Britain congratulated itself on obtaining its rightful 'freedom to trade' and to decide on its own laws. Markets, as we have seen, run on 'confidence' and as the Scottish referendum indicated, even the tangible fear of separation provoked a run on the pound in the last weeks of the campaign, while a Scottish exit could have caused a global investor confidence meltdown. Equally, or even more so, just the potential for a UK exit from the EU could trigger a loss of confidence in the EZ which would impact back onto the UK and perhaps also the wider global economy (Marsh 2013, Fazi 2014, Gamble 2014).

In this essentially counterfactual predictive world, one of the key unanswered questions lies over the future prosperity of the City of London and related sections of the service sector outside the EU/EZ. The UK is largely a service sector economy, with food, fuel, housing and transport accounting for the major slice of domestic GDP, with a good chunk of overseas earnings coming from 'invisible' earnings through the financial services and banking sectors and high-value services such as advertising, software services and games, music and film media. It is not clear how much short-term disruption could be caused, let alone what long-term damage.

If the EU/ECB eventually takes over the huge Eurobonds market and, in effect, discriminates against global banks based in London, or if market forces dictate in advance of any such moves that many global banks believe that they will be better off trading from Frankfurt and/or Paris, then this could badly damage the economy of London in particular and the UK economy in general. With arguments for and against on both sides, the City currently remains split on this with a small majority still arguing for the UK to remain in a reformed Single Market-focused element of the EU (Bootle 2014, Charter 2014).

Whatever the dangers that lie ahead for the UK and the EZ, David Charter is surely right to suggest that Britain outside the EU would only have said *Au Revoir* to its continental ex-partners and that everything would have changed to stay much the same:

> Since there [is] no possibility of uprooting the British Isles and floating off closer to the United States... the UK [would have] no option but to try to stay as closely intertwined as possible with its continental partners on numerous levels. The familiar pattern of frequent arguments, muddles and joint initiatives that has always marked Britain's relationship with the continent [would continue] unabated.
> (2012: 306)

Meanwhile the crisis of the EU rumbles on (evidenced by the ECB's move to implement Quantitative Easing to counter the growing threat of secular stagnation and deflation in the EZ economy and the election of the radical left anti-austerity Syriza government in Greece in January 2015) and, in our view, still contains the potential to trigger another global crisis. As Andrew Geddes has said:

The EU faces the challenge of responding to the economic crisis that brought it to its knees after 2008, and managing the effects of austerity and the search for economic growth... Not only does the EU face [an] 'internal' challenge to its economic governance... [p]ower relations in the global economy are changing. Will Europe's slow-growing economies, ageing populations and creaking welfare systems be able to respond to these challenges... There are also changed political dynamics in the EU that means the past might not be a reliable guide to the future.

(Geddes 2013: 259)

A worst-case scenario would see a future collapse of the EZ caused, for instance, by the UK's exit, and/or the collapse of the Italian or Greek economies, which could trigger a collapse in the Single Market and the EU itself, with the now independent states imposing currency, capital, trade and immigration barriers, leading to the Balkanisation of international trading, a breakdown of cooperative arrangements and the rise of competitive 'beggar thy neighbour' trade wars. Britain would certainly not escape and would be badly damaged by such developments, as would the global economy which is itself still recovering from the shocks of 2007/8.

The consequences of a 'Brexit' would not simply be economic but also political and strategic. Whether an 'independent' Britain would be able to develop new bilateral relations with emerging countries and get closer to its traditional transatlantic and Commonwealth partners, as Nigel Farage and other europhobes argue, is obviously debatable at the very least. The US administration has let it be known clearly and on several occasions that it does not wish the UK to leave the EU. Philip Gordon, the assistant secretary of state for European affairs, stated in January 2013 that Britain's voice in the EU was 'essential and critical' to the USA.[5] With US interests seen as defended by Britain in Brussels, the special relationship would probably be undermined in US eyes by a 'Brexit'.

More generally, Europe's position on the world scene would be even more reduced if the EU's main financial centre and military power was to leave the EU. Whatever the flaws of the common foreign and defence policies of the EU, it is hard to imagine its impact other than significantly reduced if Britain leaves it, notwithstanding the pursuit of bilateral military cooperations which could follow.

In contrast, Britain remaining in the EU in the immediate future would certainly help to stabilise the crisis of the EU, although whether this would stabilise British politics is most unlikely since, as we have repeatedly demonstrated, the Conservative Party and its UKIP offshoot have become increasingly focused on the EU, centring their core identities upon being eurosceptic and blaming most of the ills of modern Britain upon membership. As a result they, and their many powerful eurosceptic allies in the national media, appear likely to continue to fanatically campaign for Britain's exit, at least in the short to medium term. In light of this it is a difficult task to be optimistic about the future of Britain in Europe, or Europe in Britain at the time of writing.

We end with a May 2013 quotation from Boris Johnson, well known for his opportunistic eurosceptic rhetoric and linked ambitions to lead the Conservative Party, in which he warns that the UK's problems cannot be solved by simply leaving the EU:

> If we left the EU, we would end this sterile debate, and we would have to recognise that most of our problems are not caused by 'Bwussels', but by chronic British short-termism, inadequate management, sloth, low skills, a culture of easy gratification and underinvestment in both human and physical capital and infrastructure... Why are we still, person for person, so much less productive than the Germans? That is now a question more than a century old, and the answer is nothing to do with the EU. In or out of the EU, we must have a clear vision of how we are going to be competitive in a global economy.[6]

Notes

Introduction

1. http://www.theguardian.com/commentisfree/2014/oct/19/britain-political-class-tories-economic-fairytale.
2. https://www.gov.uk/government/uploads/system/uploads/attachment_data/file/364980/Summary_State_of_the_Nation_2014.pdf.
3. http://www.theguardian.com/news/datablog/2014/oct/22/ukips-polarising-effect-support-for-staying-in-the-eu-hits-23-year-high.
4. http://yougov.co.uk/news/2014/10/30/voters-shift-sharply-against-eu-membership/.
5. We view ideology as an endogenous factor woven into the social, cultural and intellectual fabric of all societies and institutions operating as 'a set of widely held beliefs.... whose acceptance is socially caused and provides sufficient conditions for collective action' (Callinicos quoted in Fine and Milonakis 2009: 157). We pay particular attention to ideological factors when dealing with neoliberalism, ordoliberalism and 'expansionary fiscal austerity'. We do not underestimate the difficulties in teasing out the various strands of ideas and ideology which operate in complex human interactions with political, economic and social processes (Hodgeson 2001: 14–22).
6. A concept of 'power' is linked to our political economy perspective. Acknowledging, as we do, that economic activity also produces major power imbalances, especially within the sphere of supposedly 'neutral' markets, clearly marks our political economy methodology from orthodox economics. Steven Lukes's work has been influential in this respect (Lukes 1974). We also consider Foucault's definition to be an important supplementary tool. For Foucault 'power is everywhere and comes from everywhere so in this sense is neither an agency nor a structure' (Foucault 1998: 63). Consequently a form of 'metapower' or 'regime of truth' pervades all levels of society, in ever changing flux and renegotiation. Foucault employs the concept of 'power/knowledge' to indicate that power is transmitted and generated via accepted knowledge, scientific discourse and supposed 'truths'. Foucault considers power to have both a negative/repressive side and a productive/positive side.

1 The Political Economy of the Eurozone Crisis

1. Neoliberalism, a concept we frequently employ, is highly contested since many neoliberals reject it as amorphous, value laden and insufficiently rigorous, as do some on the left who believe the concept obscures the underlying nature of class politics. Hayek, the central intellectual figure of analytical neoliberalism, strenuously denied the concept had any validity and some left-leaning critics have weakened the concept by stretching it to include every aspect of modern society from globalisation and the Washington

Consensus to the wars in Afghanistan and Iraq (Mirowski 2014: 39). The best summation of the powerful currents of thought which have constructed and promoted the neoliberal edifice through think tanks, leading university economics departments and conservative political movements is offered by Mirowski: 'from Ludwig Erhard's social "market economy" to Herbert Giersch's cosmopolitan individualism, from Milton Friedman's "monetarism" to the "rational-expectations hypothesis", from Hayek's "spontaneous order" to James Buchanan's "constitutional order", from Gary Becker's "human capital" to Steven Levitt's "Freakonomics", from Heartland's climate denialism to AEI's geoengineering project. And, most appositely, from Hayek's "socialist calculation controversy" to Chicago's efficient-markets hypothesis' (2014: 51). Although obsessed with individual market freedoms, neoliberalism is not libertarianism because it accepts the need for a strong state to police markets and provide military protection, and it also differs from classical liberalism in seeing no place for social welfare beyond what markets and charity can provide. Milton Friedman, at least in his early works, frequently employed the term and usefully contrasted it with 19th century liberalism: 'instead of the 19th century understanding that laissez-faire is the means to [limit the role of the state]...neoliberalism proposes that competition will lead the way' (Quoted in Mirowski: 39). Foucault was an early student of neoliberalism witnessed in his treatise *The Birth of Biopolitics: Lectures at the Collège de France, 1978–1979* (translated by Graham Burchell, New York: Palgrave Macmillan 2008). Foucault saw that:

> neoliberalism strives to ensure that individuals are compelled to assume market-based values in all of their judgments and practices in order to amass sufficient quantities of 'human capital' and thereby become 'entrepreneurs of themselves'... [and] social inequality is rendered invisible as social phenomena to the extent that each individual's social condition is judged as nothing other than the effect of his or her own choices and investments

Foucault also noted that American neoliberals were distinguishable from German ordoliberals in expanding market drives and norms to all social spheres (Hamann 2009: 41). Sally correctly refers to ordoliberalism as state-directed and rule-bound 'German neoliberalism' (1996).

2. It should be noted in passing that financial regulation in the EU, like defence, offers a case study of the continuing power of self-interested intergovernmentalism. Evidence from the past 30 years confirms that the largest EU/EZ stakeholders – the UK, Germany and France – all lean towards market-led and policed regulation rather than centralised rule-governed systems when protecting their perceived national interests through their national financial sectors. This is never justified exclusively in terms of national interest, with the big three all stressing that their domestic financial systems are of considerable advantage to the entire EU, especially in offering resistance and countervailing power towards Wall Street and the dollar (sometimes referred to as the Dollar Wall Street Regime DWSR).

2 British Preferences in the European Union: Unsung Success

1. Tony Blair, H. of C. Parl. Debates, 21 June 2004, Vol. 422, Col. 1079.
2. Quoted in *The Guardian*, 9 September 2004.
3. *The Guardian*, 29 January 2005.
4. H. of C. Deb., 21 January 2008, Vol. 470, Col. 1240.
5. And subsequently with the Commission's October 2014 demand for an extra £1.7 billion of budget funding from the UK due to GINI recalculations of member-state's GDP ratings.

3 Euroscepticism in Britain: Cause or Symptom of the European Crisis?

1. Although the British state is made up of separate components with different histories and within national politics with differing national histories and aspirations – especially in the case of Scotland when Scottish nationalism has played heavily on an independent Scotland in the EU – this does not mean that it is necessary to disaggregate its component parts to understand 'British' euroscepticism, since even Scottish attitudes towards the EU have been broadly in line with those in England. Thus, as Mahendran and McIver suggest: 'It is often believed that within the UK, Scotland is one of the most pro-European areas. The evidence within this review suggests that on the whole this is not the case, with people in Scotland reporting broadly similar Eurosceptic views as people in Britain as a whole' (2007: 7). However, they also highlight the important work of Ichijo who sets out three mains views: (i) Europe is a guarantor of enhanced [Scottish] autonomy or independence; (ii) Europe becomes a substitute for empire, that is, Scots are energetic and talented and need opportunities that go beyond their small country (where before they had the empire to realise this, there is now a need for something else); and (iii) Europe will create a more just Scotland – European values are actually closer to Scots than the UK (2007: 11, from Ichijo 2003).
2. The question as to whether views on UK sovereignty are any less 'ideological' than other significant issues relating to Euroscepticism would need to be resolved to fully agree with this approach.
3. See Thurlow, R. C. (1998), *Fascism in Britain: From Oswald Mosley's Blackshirts to the National Front* (London: I.B. Tauris).
4. It should be noted, however, that Brown rejected Rumsfeld's description in a speech delivered in March 2009 to the US Congress; in which he said 'There is no old Europe, no new Europe. There is only your friend Europe.'
5. See 'Former minister Gisela Stuart Says Lisbon Treaty would create "democratic deficit"', *Telegraph*, 19 September 2009; H. of C. Parliamentary Debates, 5 March 2008, Vol. 472, Col. 1909 and foll.
6. H. of C. Parliamentary Debates, 20 June 2011, Vol. 530, Col. 26.
7. Ed Balls and Peter Mandelson, 'We agree about Europe', *The Observer*, 13 May 2012.
8. See H. of C. Parliamentary Debates, 11 March 2008, Vol. 473, Col. 163 and foll.

9. 'Nick Clegg lashes out at PM and vows to rebuild ties with Europe', *The Guardian*, 11 December 2011.
10. See 'David Cameron under fire from MPs over Europe', *Telegraph*, 31 May 2012; Daniel Hannan, 'David Cameron has allowed the EU to say FU to its people', *Guardian*, 31 January 2012.
11. 'Ed Davey: Coalition will be more pro-European than New Labour', *Telegraph*, 4 April 2012.
12. 'The lure of the open sea', *The Economist*, 14 April 2012.
13. Interview with a Conservative MP, June 2012.
14. See Robert Ford, Matthew J. Goodwin and David Cutts, 'Strategic Eurosceptics and polite xenophobes: Support for the United Kingdom Independence Party (UKIP) in the 2009 European Parliament elections', *European Journal of Political Research*, 51, 2012, pp. 204–234.
15. H. of C. Parliamentary Debates, 24 October 2011, Vol. 534.
16. http://conservativehome.blogs.com/thetorydiary/2012/06/100-tory-mps-call-for-cameron-to-prepare-legislation-for-eu-referendum.html.
17. 'David Cameron, 'We need to be clear about the best way of getting what is best for Britain', *Sunday Telegraph*, 30 June 2012.
18. 'Liam Fox: Life outside European Union holds no terror', *Guardian*, 2 July 2012.
19. See also 'EU referendum: Poll shows 49% would vote for UK withdrawal', *Guardian*, 24 October 2011.
20. Graph available at https://yougov.co.uk/news/2014/10/30/voters-shift-sharply-against-eu-membership/.

4 The Crisis of Democracy in the United Kingdom

1. http://lordashcroftpolls.com/2012/12/the-ukip-threat-is-not-about-europe/

5 Britain and the Political Crisis in the European Union

1. 'German media fuels public resentment over Greek bailout', *The Guardian*, 21 June 2011.

6 Britain and the Economic Crisis of the European Union

1. We would not suggest, however, that these three ideal-type categories cover all the attitudes towards the EU in the UK. As suggested above Tony Benn represents a left-wing position which doesn't easily fit into any of these categories. Like many Conservatives Benn viewed the EU as a threat to the sovereignty of Parliament and therefore national independence. A convinced Parliamentarian in the Cromwellian tradition, he argued that a free and sovereign Parliament was the only democratic guarantee of winning a majority for pursuing a socialist programme. To Benn the EU was undemocratic, unaccountable and deeply anti-socialist. Benn fought all his life for his vision of an alternative socialist political economy resting on public ownership, a universal welfare state, progressive fiscal policies, full employment

and laws to protect trade union rights, all of which he considered to be under attack from the EU. However, aside from the early 1980s when the Labour Party's Alternative Economic Strategy was in vogue and the party's manifestos included withdrawal from the 'rich man's club' of Europe, Benn's parliamentary leftist anti-Europeanism has not been widely influential in the Labour movement.
2. For an excellent critique of this hyperglobalist discourse see Gray 2009: 55–77.
3. Of course it is impossible to know how many Conservative MPs support the hyperglobalist position out of a wish to further their careers in a party with many powerful figures strongly supporting this line and many Tory activists and voters setting this as a litmus test for party loyalty. Clearly the selection process for Conservative MPs and MEPs over the past 20 plus years has seen a sifting out of pro-European candidates and more and more candidates picked for their hard eurosceptical manifestos promoting withdrawal, or at best remaining on the periphery of the EU after repatriating key powers.
4. Intergovernmentalism is also employed within the EU to denote a theory of the process of integration itself, which considers states and the national government as the primary factors behind the European integration process, in which the principal aim of governments is to protect their national geopolitical interests, in particular in areas such as national security, defence and core sovereignty (Hoffman 1966, West 2004). Indeed, all British governments have adopted an intergovernmentalist approach to negotiations with and within the EU, innocent of any higher federal purpose.
5. Clegg vs Farage debate – transcript of the first 15 minutes, Wednesday, 2 April 2014. http://www.politicshome.com/uk/article/95721/clegg_vs_farage_debate_transcript_of_first_15_minutes.html.
6. http://www.economist.com/blogs/bagehot/2011/12/britain-and-eu-0.
7. http://www.theguardian.com/world/2014/jun/20/juncker-merkel-cameron-britain-eu-european-commission.
8. http://www.theguardian.com/politics/2014/jun/23/polish-mps-ridicule-cameron-stupid-propaganda-eurosceptics.
9. http://www.theguardian.com/world/2014/jun/28/cameron-eu-juncker-defeat-britain-exit.
10. http://www.express.co.uk/news/uk/288928/Boris-Johnson-PM-has-played-a-blinder-on-EU-treaty.
11. http://www.theguardian.com/world/2014/jun/20/juncker-merkel-cameron-britain-eu-european-commission.

Conclusion

1. The pound stood at US $2.11 in November 2007, but since the global financial crisis the pound has been allowed to depreciate at a historically unprecedented rate reaching $1.38 on 23 January 2009 and slowly rising again to $1.62 in September 2014. http://finance.yahoo.com/q/bc?s=GBPUSD=X&t=3m&l=on&z=m&q=l&c=
2. For instance the Greek protest party Syriza doesn't advocate leaving the euro, calling rather for a radical overhaul of how it operates. As a party

spokesman stated: 'We're demanding a more democratic, a more social and a more just Europe'. http://www.nytimes.com/2012/05/12/world/europe/in-greece-leftist-party-syriza-upends-politics.html.
3. In an embarrassing leaflet issued by Nick Clegg in 2008, he promised a referendum on membership of the EU, albeit specifically tied to the Lisbon Treaty: 'It's been over thirty years since the British people last had a vote on Britain's membership of the European Union. That's why the Liberal Democrats want a real referendum on Europe. Only a real referendum on Britain's membership of the EU will let the people decide our country's future. But Labour don't want the people to have their say. The Conservatives only support a limited referendum on the Lisbon Treaty. Why won't they give the people a say in a real referendum?' http://www.newstatesman.com/politics/2013/05/eu-referendum-leaflet-will-haunt-clegg-today.
4. http://www.spiegel.de/international/europe/merkel-fears-cameron-crossing-red-line-on-immigration-a-1000743.html#ref=nl-international.
5. See also http://www.huffingtonpost.co.uk/yaron-schwartz/brexit-will-weaken-us-uk-relationship_b_2813046.html.
6. http://www.telegraph.co.uk/news/politics/10052646/Quitting-the-EU-wont-solve-our-problems-says-Boris-Johnson.html

Bibliography

Abdelal, Rawi E (2007), *Capital Rules: The Construction of Global Finance* (Cambridge, MA: Harvard University Press).

Alesina, Alberto F. and Ardagna, Silvia (2009), 'Large changes in Fiscal Policy: taxes versus spending', NBER Working Paper No. 15438, Cambridge, available at http://www.nber.org/papers/w15438.

Alexander, Douglas (2011), Speech to Baltic and Nordic Ambassadors, 14 November, available at http://www.guardian.co.uk/politics/interactive/2011/nov/14/douglas-alexander-speech-policy-eu.

Alexandre-Collier, Agnès (2002), *La Grande-Bretagne Eurosceptique?* (Lille: Editions du Temps).

Allen, David and Smith, Michael (1990), 'Western Europe's Presence in the Contemporary International Arena', *Review of International Studies*, Vol. 16, No. 1, pp. 19–37.

Almond, Gabriel and Verba, Sidney (1963), *The Civic Culture: Political Attitudes and Democracy in Five Nations* (Princeton: Princeton University Press).

Alvaredo, Facundo, Atkinson, Anthony B., Piketty, Thomas and Saez, Emmanuel (2013), 'The Top 1 Percent in International and Historical Perspective', *Journal of Economic Perspectives*, Vol. 27, No. 3, pp. 3–20.

Anderson, Benedict (1991), *Imagined Communities: Reflections on the Origin and Spread of Nationalism* (London: Verso).

Anderson, Peter and Weymouth, Tony (1999), *Insulting the Public? The British Press and the European Union* (London: Longman).

Aspinwall, Mark (2000), 'Structuring Europe: Power-sharing Institutions and British Preferences on European Integration', *Political Studies*, Vol. 48, No. 3, pp. 415–442.

Aspinwall, Mark (2004), *Rethinking Britain and Europe: Plurality Elections, Party Management and British Policy on European Integration* (Manchester: Manchester University Press).

Avril, Emmanuelle (2015), 'Social Networks and Democracy: Fightbacks and Backlashes in the World Wide Agora' in Emmanuelle Avril and Johan Neem (eds), *Democracy, Participation and Contestation: Civil Society, Governance and the Future of Liberal Democarcy* (London: Routledge), pp. 223–235.

Bache, Ian, George, Stephen and Bulmer, Simon (2011), *Politics in the European Union* (Oxford: Oxford University Press).

Baker, David, Gamble, Andrew and Ludlam, Steve (1993a), '1846, 1906, 1996? Conservative Splits and European Integration', *Political Quarterly*, Vol. 64, No. 4, pp. 420–434.

Baker, David, Gamble, Andrew and Ludlam, Steve (1993b), 'Whips or Scorpions? The Maastricht Vote and the Conservative Party', *Parliamentary Affairs*, Vol. 46, No. 2, pp. 151–166.

Baker, David, Gamble, Andrew and Ludlam, Steve (1994), 'The Parliamentary Siege of Maastricht 1993: Conservative Divisions and British Ratification', *Parliamentary Affairs*, Vol. 47, No. 1, pp. 37–59.

Baker, David, Gamble, Andrew, Ludlam, Steve and Seawright, David (1996), 'Labour and Europe: A Survey of MPs and MEPs', *Political Quarterly*, Vol. 67, No. 4, pp. 353–371.

Baker, David and Seawright, David (eds) (1998), *Britain for and Against Europe* (Oxford: Clarendon Press).

Baker, David, Gamble, Andrew and Seawright, David (2002), 'Sovereign Nations and Global Markets: Modern British Conservatism and Hyperglobalism', *British Journal of Politics and International Relations*, Vol. 4, No. 3, pp. 399–428.

Baker, David, Gamble, Andrew, Randall, Nick and Seawright, David (2008), 'Euroscepticism in the British Party System: "A Source of Fascination, Perplexity, and Sometimes Frustration"' in Aleks Szczerbiak and Paul Taggart (eds), *Opposing Europe? The Comparative Party Politics of Euroscepticism* (Oxford: Oxford University Press), pp. 93–116.

Baker, David and Schnapper, Pauline (2013), 'Frozen Europe: Regulatory Responses to the Eurozone Banking Crisis', Paper given to SPERI Conference, Sheffield University, June 2013. http://speri.dept.shef.ac.uk/wp-content/uploads/2013/06/Frozen-Europe-Regulatory-Responses-to-the-Eurozone-Banking-Crisis-PDF-1032KB.pdf.

Baker, Dean, Glyn, Andrew, Howell, David R. and Schmitt, John (2007), 'Are Protective Labor Market Intuitions at the Root of Unemployment? A Critical Review of the Evidence', *Capitalism and Society*, Vol. 2, No. 1, pp. 1–71.

Bale, Tim (2006), 'Between a Hard and a Soft Place? The Conservative Party, Valence Politics and the Need for a New "Eurorealism"', *Parliamentary Affairs*, Vol. 59, No. 3, pp. 385–400.

Bale, Tim (2010), *The Conservative Party from Thatcher to Cameron* (Cambridge: Polity).

Bale, Tim (2012), *The Conservative Party Since 1945: The Drivers of Party Change* (Oxford: Oxford University Press).

Balls, Edward (2007), *Britain and Europe: A City Minister's Perspective* (London: Centre for European Reform).

Balsom, Denis (1996), 'The United Kingdom: Constitutional Pragmatism and the Adoption of the Referendum' in Michael Gallagher and Pier Vincenzo Uleri (eds), *The Referendum Experience in Europe* (Basingstoke: Macmillan), pp. 209–225.

Bates, Thomas R. (2002), 'Gramsci and the Theory of Hegemony' in James Martin (ed) *Antonio Gramsci: Marxism, Philosophy and Politics* (London: Routledge).

Barber, Benjamin (1984), *Strong Democracy: Participatory Politics for a New Age* (Berkeley, CA: University of California Press).

Baun, Michael J. (1996), 'The Maastricht Treaty as High Politics: Germany, France and European Integration', *Political Science Quarterly*, Vol. 10, No. 4, pp. 605–624.

Beck, Ulrich (2012), *German Europe* (Cambridge: Polity Press).

Benn, Tony (1975), 'Speech Given in the Cabinet Meeting to Discuss Britain's Membership of the EEC, as Recorded in his Diary (18 March 1975)' in *Against the Tide. Diaries 1973–1976* (London: Hutchinson, 1989), pp. 346–347.

Berger, Peter L. and Luckmann, Thomas (2011), *The Social Construction of Reality: A Treatise in the Sociology of Knowledge* (New York: Open Road Media).

Bergsten, C. Kirkegaard, Fred and Funk, Jacob (Jan 2012), *The Coming Resolution of the European Crisis*, Policy Brief PB12–1, Paterson Institute for International Economics, Washington, DC.

Best, Edward (2002), 'The UK: From Isolation to Influence?' in Finn Laursen (ed), *The Amsterdam Treaty: National Preference Formation, Interstate Bargaining and Outcome* (Odense, Odense University Press), pp. 359–378.

Betz, Hans-Georg (1994), *Radical Right-Wing Populism in Western Europe* (New York: St Martin's Press).

Bibow, J. (2012), 'The Euro Debt Crisis and Germany's Euro Trilemma', Working Paper No. 721, New York: Levy Economics Institute of Bard College, Annandale-on-Hudson, available at http://www.levyinstitute.org/pubs/wp_721.pdf.

Blair, Tony (1996), *New Britain: My Vision of a Young Country* (London: Fourth Estate).

Blair, Tony (1998), Speech on Foreign Affairs, 15 December, available at http://keeptonyblairforpm.wordpress.com/blair-speech-transcripts-from-1997–2007/, accessed 5 June 2012.

Blair, Tony (1999), Speech on the Doctrine of the International Community, Chicago, April, available at http://www.britishpoliticalspeech.org/speech-archive.htm?speech=279, accessed 9 October 2014.

Blair, Tony (2000), Speech to the Polish Stock Exchange, 6 October, available at http://collections.europarchive.org/tna/20060715135117/http://number10.gov.uk/page3384.

Blair, Tony (2001), Speech to the European Research Institute, Birmingham University, 23 November, available at http://www.guardian.co.uk/world/2001/nov/23/euro.eu1, accessed 5 June 2012.

Blair, Tony (2002), Speech on Europe in Cardiff, 28 November, available at http://ebookbrowse.com/a-tony-blair-speech-on-europe-cardiff-28-11-2002-pdf-d32791052.

Blair, Tony (2003), 'Speech at the Foreign Office Conference', 7 January, available at http://www.number10.gov.uk/output/Page1765.asp.

Blair, Tony (2005), Speech to the European Parliament, 23 June, available at http://www.guardian.co.uk/politics/2005/jun/23/speeches.eu, accessed 6 June 2012.

Blair, Tony (2010), *A Journey* (London: Hutchinson).

Blanchard, Olivier, Dell'Ariccia, Giovanni and Mauro, Paolo (2010), 'Rethinking Macroeconomic Policy', International Monetary Fund, IMF Staff Position Note, available at http://www.imf.org/external/pubs/ft/spn/2010/spn1003.pdf.

Blyth, Mark (2002), *Great Transformations: Economic Ideas and Institutional Change in the Twentieth Century* (Cambridge: Cambridge University Press).

Blyth, Mark (2003), 'Same as It Never Was: Temporality and Typology in the Varieties of Capitalism,' *Comparative European Politics* Vol.1, pp. 215–225.

Blyth, Mark (2013), *Austerity: The History of a Dangerous Idea* (Oxford: Oxford University Press).

Blyth, Mark, Seabrooke, L. and Widmaier, W. (2007), 'Exogenous Shocks or Endogenous Constructions? The Meanings of Wars and Crises', *International Studies Quarterly*, Vol. 51, No. 4, pp. 747–759.

Bogdanor, Vernon (1996), 'The European Union, the Political Class and the People' in Hayward Jack (ed), *Elitism, Populism and European Politics* (Oxford: Clarendon), pp. 101–120.

Bogdanor, Vernon (2011), *The Coalition and the Constitution* (Oxford: Hart).

Bohle, Dorothy and Greskovitz, Bela (2007), 'Neoliberalism, Embedded Neoliberalism and Neocorporatism: Towards Transnational Capitalism in Central-Eastern Europe', *West European Politics*, Vol. 30, No. 3, pp. 443–466.

Bond, Martyn and Kim, Feus (eds) (2001), *The Treaty of Nice Explained* (London: The Federal Trust).

Bozo, Frédéric (2012), 'The European Union at Twenty: Can Europe Be saved?' in Geir Lundestad (ed), *Twenty Years of International Relations* (Oxford: Oxford University Press).

Brittan, Samuel (1971), *Government and Market Economy*, The Institute of Economic Affairs (London: Hobart).

Brown, Gordon (2005), *Global Europe, Full Employment Europe* (London: HMSO).

Brown, Wendy (2005), 'Neoliberalism and the End of Liberal Democracy' in *Edgework: Critical Essays on Knowledge and Politics* (Princeton: Princeton University Press), Ch. 3.

Bryan, Steven (2010), 'The Historical Appeal of Austerity', *Columbia University Press Blog*, 1 October, available at http://www.cupblog.org/?p=2390.

Buffet, Warren (2002), Excerpts from the Berkshire Hathaway annual report for 2002, available at http://www.fintools.com/docs/Warren%20Buffet%20on%20Derivatives.pdf.

Bull, Martin J. (2012), 'Southern Europe and the "Trade Off": Architects of European Disunion?' in Jack Hayward and Rüdiger Wurzel (eds), *European Disunion: Between Sovereignty and Solidarity* (Basingstoke: Palgrave), pp. 283–297.

Buller, Jim (2000), *National Statecraft and European Integration: The Conservative Government and the European Union 1979–97* (London: Pinter).

Bulmer, Simon (2008), 'New Labour, New European Policy? Blair, Brown and Utilitarian Supranationalism', *Parliamentary Affairs*, Vol. 61, No. 4, pp. 597–620.

Bulmer, Simon and Burch, Martin (1998), 'Organizing for Europe: The British State and the European Union', *Public Administration*, Vol. 76, No. 4, pp. 601–628.

Bulmer, Simon and Burch, Martin (2009), *The Europeanisation of Whitehall: UK Central Government and the European Union* (Manchester: Manchester University Press).

Bourlanges, Jean-Louis (2001), 'La fin de l'Europe communautaire: Critique du traité de Nice', *Commentaire*, No. 95, Autumn, pp. 589–601.

Bourlanges, Jean-Louis (2014), 'L'imposture euro-présidentielle', *Le Monde*, 20 May.

Bréchon, Pierre (2009), *La France aux urnes: 60 ans d'histoire électorale* (Paris: La Documentation Française).

Bromley, Catherine, Curtice, John and Seyd, Ben (2004), 'Is Britain Facing a Crisis of Democracy?', Working Paper 106, Centre for Research into Elections and Social Trends, Oxford.

Brown, Gordon (2005a), *Global Europe: Full-employment Europe* (London: HM Treasury).

Brown, Gordon (2005b), 'Global Britain, Global Europe: A Presidency Founded on Pro European Realism', Mansion House Speech, 22 June, available at www.gees.org/documentos/Documen-464.pdf.

Budge, Ian (1996), *The New Challenge of Direct Democracy* (Cambridge: Polity Press).

Buller, Jim (2000), *National Statecraft and European Integration, 1979–1997* (London: Frances Pinter).

Bulpitt, Jim (1983), *Territory and Power in the United Kingdom: An Interpretation* (Manchester: Manchester University Press).

Bulpitt, Jim (1986), 'The Discipline of the New Democracy: Mrs Thatcher's Domestic Statecraft', *Political Studies*, Vol. 34, Issue. 1, pp. 19–39.

Bulpitt, Jim (1992), 'Conservative Leaders and the 'Euro-ratchet': Five Doses of Scepticism', *Political Quarterly*, Vol. 63, pp. 258–275.

Burnham, Peter (2001), 'New Labour and the Politics of Depoliticisation', *British Journal of Politics and International Relations*, Vol. 3, No. 2, pp. 127–149.

Butler, David and Stokes, Donald (1971), *Political Change in Britain: The Evolution of Electoral Choice* (Basingstoke: Macmillan).

Byrne, Paul (1997), *Social Movements in Britain* (Abingdon: Routledge).

Cameron, David (2006), 'A New Approach to Foreign Affairs – Liberal Conservatism', *Speech to the British American Project*, 11 September, available at http://www.conservatives.com/News/Speeches/2006/09/Cameron_A_new_approach_to_foreign_affairs__liberal_conservatism.aspx, accessed 8 December 2011.

Cameron, David (2012), 'I'll Never Campaign to Take us Out of Europe', *Daily Telegraph*, interview, 18 July.

Cameron, David (2013), EU Speech at Bloomberg, 23rd January 2013, available at https://www.gov.uk/government/speeches/eu-speech-at-bloomberg.

Canovan, Margaret (1999), 'Trust the People! Populism and the Two Faces of Democracy', *Political Studies*, Vol. 47, No. 1, pp. 2–16.

Caporaso, James (1996), 'The EU and Forms of State: Westphalian, Regulatory or Post-modern?', *Journal of Common Market Studies*, Vol. 34, No. 1, pp. 29–52.

Cardinal, Mario (2005), *Breaking Point Quebec-Canada: The 1995 Referendum* (Bayard Canada).

Carey, Sean and Burton, Jonathan (2004), 'The Influence of the Press in Shaping Public Opinion Towards the European Union in Britain,' *Political Studies*, Vol. 52, October, pp. 623–640.

CEO-TNI (2012), 'Stop the EU's Antidemocratic Austerity Policies – for a Different Europe', *CEO Website*, 8 May, available at http://corporateeurope.org/eu-crisis/2012/05/stop-eus-antidemocratic-austerity-policies-different-europe.

Charter, David (2012), *Au Revoir Europe: What If Britain Left the EU* (London: Biteback Publishing).

Chatham House (2012), *The Chatham House-YouGov Survey 2012: British Attitudes Towards the UK's International Priorities* (London: RIIA).

Chiaramonte, Alessandro and Maggini, Nicola (2013), 'The 2013 Italian General Election: The End of Bipolarism?', *Italian Politics and Society*, No. 72–73, Spring–Fall, pp. 27–37.

Church, Clive (2001), 'Intergovernmental Conferences and Treaty Reform: The Nice Experience' in Martyn Bond and Kim Feus (eds), *The Treaty of Nice Explained* (London: The Federal Trust), pp. 75–95.

Clarke, H.D., Sanders, David Stewart, M. and Whiteley, Paul (2004), *Political Choice in Britain* (Oxford: Oxford University Press).
Clarke, Simon (1987), *Keynesianism, Monetarism and the Crisis of the State* (Aldershot: Edward Elgar).
Clegg, Nick (2004), 'Europe: A Liberal Future' in David Laws and Paul Marshall (eds), *The Orange Book: Reclaiming Liberalism* (London: Profile).
Clegg vs Farage debate (2014) – Transcript of First 15 minutes, Wednesday 2nd April, available at http://www.politicshome.com/uk/article/95721/clegg_vs_farage_debate_transcript_of_first_15_minutes.html).
Clift, Ben (2001), 'New Labour's Third Way and European Social Democracy' in Martin Smith and Steve Ludlam (eds), *New Labour in Power* (London: Macmillan, now Palgrave Macmillan), pp.55–72.
Clift, Ben (2004), 'The French Model of Capitalism: Still Exceptional?' in J. Perrino and B. Clift (eds), *Where Are National Capitalisms Now?* (Basingstoke: Palgrave), pp. 91–110.
Clift, Ben (2006), 'The New Political Economy of Dirigisme: French Macroeconomic Policy, Unrepentant Sinning and the Stability and Growth Pact', *British Journal of Politics and International Relations*, Vol. 8, No. 3, pp. 388–409.
Clift, Ben (2014), *Comparative Politica Economy: States Markets and Global Capitalism* (Basingstoke: Palgrave Macmillan).
Coggan, Philip (2013), *The Last Vote: Threats to Western Democracy* (London: Penguin Books).
Cohen, Elie (1995), 'France: National Champions in Search of a Mission' in Jack Hayward (ed), *Industrial Enterprise and European Integration: From National to International Champions in Western Europe* (Oxford: Oxford University Press), pp. 245–72.
Coleman, Stephen and Blumler, Jay G. (2009), *The Internet and Democratic Citizenship: Theory, Practice and Policy* (Cambridge: Cambridge University Press).
Colley, Linda (1992), *Britons: Forging the Nation* (New Haven, CT: Yale University Press).
Cooper, Robert (2000), *The Post-Modern State and the World Order* (London: Demos).
Conservative Party (2001), *Time for Common Sense*, General Election Manifesto, available at http://www.conservativemanifesto.com/2001/2001-conservative-manifesto.shtml.
Conservative Party (2005), *Are You Thinking What We're Thinking?*, General Election Manifesto, available at www.conservatives.com/pdf/manifesto-uk-2005.pdf.
Conservative Party (2010), *Invitation to Join the Government of Britain*, General Election Manifesto, available at media.conservatives.s3.amazonaws.com/manifesto/cpmanifesto2010.
Copus, Colin, Clark, Alistair, Reynaert, Herwig and Steyvers, Kristof (2009), 'Minor Party and Independent Politics beyond the Mainstream: Fluctuating Fortunes but a Permanent Presence', *Parliamentary Affairs*, Vol. 62, No. 1, pp. 4–18.
Corbetta, Piergiorgio and Vignati, Rinaldo (2013), 'Left or Right? The Complex Nature and Uncertain Future of the 5 Stars Movement', *Italian Politics and Society*, No. 72–73, Spring-Fall, pp. 53–62.

Corrigan, Philip and Sayer, Derek (1985), *The Great Arch* (Oxford: Blackwell).
Couet, Isabelle (2012), 'L'aide à la Grèce ne coûte rien à l'Allemagne', *Les Echos*, 21 June.
Cowley, Philip (2000), 'British Parliamentarians and European Integration: A Re-Examination of the MPP Data', *Party Politics*, October 2000, No. 6, pp. 463–472.
Cowley, Philip (2011), 'Political Parties and the British Party System' in Richard Heffernan, Philip Cowley and Clin Hay (eds), *Developments in British Politics 9* (Basingstoke: Palgrave Macmillan), pp. 91–112.
Cowley, Philip and Stuart, Mark (2012), 'A Coalition with Two Wobbly Wings: Backbench Dissent in the House of Commons', *Political Insight*, Vol. 3, No. 1, pp. 8–11.
Cox, Michael (2001), 'Whatever Happened to American Decline? International Relations and the New United States Hegemony', *New Political Economy*, Vol. 6, No. 3, pp. 311–339.
Credit Suisse (2013), *Global Wealth Report 2013*, October, available at http://images.smh.com.au/file/2013/10/09/4815797/cs_global_wealth_report_2013_WEB_low%2520pdf.pdf?rand=1381288140715.
Crouch, Colin (2006), 'Models of Capitalism' in Anthony Payne (ed), *Key Debates in New Political Economy* (Abingdon: Routledge), pp. 11–31.
Crouch, Colin (2008), 'What Will Follow the Demise of Privatised Keynesianism', *Political Quarterly*, Vol. 79, No. 4, pp. 476–487.
Crouch, Colin (2009), 'Privatized Keynesianism: An Unacknowledged Policy Regime', *British Journal of Politics and International Relations*, Vol. 11, No. 3, pp. 382–399.
Crouch, Colin (2011), *The Strange Non-death of Neo-liberalism* (London: Polity Press).
Crozier, Michel, Watanuki, Joji and Huntington, Samuel P. (1975), *The Crisis of Democracy: Report on the Governability of Democracies to the Trilateral Commission* (New York: New York University Press).
Curtice, John (1999), 'Was It The Sun Wot Won It Again? The Influence of Newspapers in the 1997 Election Campaign', Working Paper 75 (Oxford: Centre for Research into Elections and Social Trends).
Curtice, John (2005), 'Voters Stay Home – Again', *Parliamentary Affairs*, Vol. 58, No. 4, pp. 776–785.
Curtice, John (2011), 'The Death of a Miserable Little Compromise: The Alternative Vote Referendum', *Political Insight*, Vol. 2, No. 2, September, pp. 14–17.
Curtice, John, Devine, Paula and Ormston, Rachel (2013), 'Devolution: National identity and constitutional preferences' in Alison Park, Caroline Bryson, Elizabeth Clery, John Curtice and Miranda Philips (eds), *British Social Attitudes Survey 30* (London: Nat Cen Social Research), available at www.bsa-30.natcen.ac.uk, pp. 139–172.
Curtice, John and Ormston, Rachel (2008), 'On the Road to Divergence? Trends in Public Opinion in Scotland and England', *British Social Attitudes 28*, available at http://ir2.flife.de/data/natcen-social-research/igb_html/pdf/chapters/BSA28_2Devolution.pdf.
Curtice, John and Seyd, Ben (2012), 'Constitutional Reform: A Recipe for Restoring Faith in Our Democracy?' in Alison Park, Elisabeth Clery, John Curtice, Miranda Phillips and David Utting (eds), *British Social Attitudes: the 29th Report*

(London: NatCen Social Research), available at http://www.bsa-29.natcen.ac.uk/read-the-report/constitutional-reform/introduction.aspx.

Curtice, John and Steed, Michael (1997), 'The Results Analysed' in David Butler and Dennis Kavanagh (eds), *The British General Election of 1997* (Basingstoke: Macmillan), pp. 295–325.

Curtice, John and Steed, Michael (2001), 'The Results Analysed' in David Butler and Dennis Kavanagh (eds), *The British General Election of 2001* (Basingstoke: Palgrave), pp. 304–338.

Curtice, John, Stephen, Fisher and Steed, Michael (2005), 'The Results Analysed' in David Butler and Dennis Kavanagh (eds), *The British General Election of 2001* (Basingstoke: Palgrave), pp. 235–259.

Cygan, Adam (2002), 'The White Paper on European Governance – Have Glasnost and Perestroika Finally Arrived to the European Union?', *European Law Review*, Vol. 65, No. 2, pp. 229–240.

Daddow, Oliver (2011), *New Labour and the European Union: Blair and Brown's Logic of History* (Manchester: Manchester University Press).

Daddow, Oliver (2013), 'Margaret Thatcher, Tony Blair and the Eurosceptic Tradition in British Foreign Policy', *British Journal of Politics and International Relations*, Vol. 15, No. 2, pp. 210–227.

Daddow, Oliver and Pauline, Schnapper (2013), 'Liberal Intervention in the Foreign Policy Thinking of Tony Blair and David Cameron', *Cambridge Review of International Affairs*, Vol. 26, No. 2, pp. 330–349.

Daniels, Philip (1998), 'From Hostility to "Constructive Engagement": The Europeanisation of the Labour Party' in Hugh Berrington (ed), *Britain in the 1990s: The Politics of Paradox* (London: Franck Cass), pp. 72–96.

Dalton, Russell J. (2004), *Democratic Challenges, Democratic Choices: The Erosion of Political Support in Advanced Industrial Democracies* (Oxford: Oxford University Press).

Delors, Jacques (1988), 'It Is Necessary to Work Together', Speech to Trades Union Congress, Bournemouth, 8 September 1988, available at http://pro-europa.eu/index.php?option=com_content&view=article&id=281:delors-necessary-to-work-together&catid=11:the-struggle-for-the-union-of-europe&Itemid=17.

Delwitt, Pascal (2011), 'L'introuvable électeur? La participation électorale en Europe (1945–2005)' in Anissa Amjahad, Jean-Michel de Waele, Michel Hastings (eds), *Le vote obligatoire* (Paris: Economica), pp. 17–33.

Denver, David (1994), *Elections and Voting Behaviour* (Hemel Hampstead: Harvester Wheatsheaf).

Denver, David (2011), 'Elections and Voting' in Richard Heffernan, Philip Cowley and Colin Hay (eds), *Developments in British Politics 9* (Basingstoke: Palgrave Macmillan), pp. 70–90.

Debomy, Daniel (2012), 'Do the Europeans still believe in the EU?', Notre Europe, 29 July, available at http://www.notre-europe.eu/fr/axes/democratie-en-action/travaux/publication/les-europeens-croient-ils-encore-en-lue/, accessed 3 September 2012.

Dieter, Plehwe, Bernhard, Walpen and Gisela, Neunhöffer (eds) (2006), *Neoliberal Hegemony: A Global Critique* (Abingdon: Routledge).

Draghi, Mario (2012), 'Q&A: ECB President Mario Draghi' *Wall Street Journal*, 23 February, available at http://blogs.wsj.com/eurocrisis/2012/02/23/qa-ecb-president-mario-draghi/.

Drahokoupil, Jan (2009), *Globalization and the State in Central and Eastern Europe: The Politics of Foreign Direct Investment* (Abingdon: Routledge).
Dube, Arindrajit (2013), 'Guest Post: Reinhart/Rogoff and Growth in a Rime Before Debt', *Next New Deal*, 17 April.
Duchêne, François (1972), 'Europe's Role in World Peace' in R. Mayne (ed), *Europe Tomorrow: Sixteen Europeans Look Ahead* (London: Fontana for Chatham House).
Dullien, Sebastian and Guerot, Ulrike (2012), 'The Long Shadow of Ordoliberalism: Germany's Approach to the Euro Crisis', *European Council on Foreign Relations*, Paper ECFR/49.
Dumenil, Gerard and Levy, Dominique (2005), 'The neoliberal counter-revolution', in Alfredo Saad-Filho and Deborah Johnston (eds), *Neoliberalism: A Critical Reader* (London: Pluto Press).
Dyson, Kenneth (1994), *Elusive Union* (London: Longmans).
Dyson, Kenneth (2000), *The Politics of the Euro-Zone* (Oxford: Oxford University Press).
Dyson, Kenneth (2001), *European States and the Euro* (Oxford: Oxford University Press).
Dyson, Kenneth (ed) (2008). *The Euro at 10: Europeanization, Power, and Convergence* (Oxford: Oxford University Press).
Dyson, Kenneth (2012), 'Economic and Monetary Disunion', in Hayward, Jack and Wurzel, Rudiger (eds), *European Disunion, Between Sovereignty and Solidarity* (Basingstoke: Palgrave), pp. 181–199.
Dyson, Kenneth (2013), *States, Debt, and Power: Saints and Sinners in European History and Integration* (Oxford: Oxford University Press).
Dyson, Kenneth and Featherstone, Kevin (1999), *The Road to Maastricht: Negotiating Economic and Monetary Union* (Oxford: Oxford University Press).
Dyson, Kenneth and Marcussen, Martin (2010), 'Transverse Integration in European Economic Governance: Between Unitary and Differentiated Integration', *Journal of European Integration*, Vol. 32, No. 1, pp. 17–40.
Dyson, Kenneth and Sepos, Angelos (2010), *Which Europe? The Politics of Differentiated Integration* (Basingstoke: Palgrave).
Eurobarometer (2011a), *Standard Eurobarometer 76* (Brussels: CEC).
Eurobarometer (2011b), *Attitudes Towards the EU in the United Kingdom*, Flash Barometer 318 (Brussels: European Commission).
European Commission (2001), *European Governance: A White Paper*, COM (2001)428, available at http://aei.pitt.edu/1188/1/european_governance_wp _COM_2001_428.pdf, accessed 22 May 2014.
European Commission (2008), *Global Europe: EU Performance for the Global Economy*.
European Commission (2009), 'Economic and Financial Affairs, 'Myths and facts', 30 April, available at http://ec.europa.eu/economy_finance/emu0/facts8 en.htm.
European Commission (2011a), 'Economic Governance; Commission Proposes Two New Regulations to Further Strengthen Budgetary Surveillance in the Euro Area', Press Release, 23 November, available at http://ec .europa.eu/economy_finance/articles/governance/2011-11-23-proposed-reg -strengthening-surveillance-ms-severe-financial-disturbance_en.htm.

European Commission (2011b), 'European Commission Green Paper on the Feasibility of Producing Stability Bonds', Press Release, available at http://europa.eu/rapid/press-release_MEMO-11-820_en.htm.
European Commission (2013), Standard Eurobarometer 80, Autumn, available at http://ec.europa.eu/public_opinion/archives/eb/eb80/eb80_first_en.pdf, accessed 4 June 2014.
European Commission (2014), 'Europeans in 2014', Special Eurobarometer 415, available at http://ec.europa.eu/public_opinion/archives/ebs/ebs_415_data_en.pdf, accessed 4 June 2014.
European Council (2001a), 'Presidency Conclusions of the Meeting in Laeken', available at http://ec.europa.eu/smart-regulation/impact/background/docs/laeken_concl_en.pdf.
European Council (2001b), *Laeken Declaration on the Future of the European Union*, available at www.european-convention.eu.int/pdf/lknen.pdf.
European Council (2012), 'The European Council Agrees on a Roadmap for the Completion of Economic and Monetary Union', 14 December, available at http://www.european-council.europa.eu/home-page/highlights/the-european-council-agrees-on-a-roadmap-for-the-completion-of-economic-and-monetary-union?lang=en.
Eurostat (2012), 'At Risk of Poverty or Social Exclusion in the EU27 – in 2011, 24% of the Population Were at Risk of Poverty or Social Exclusion', Press Release, 3 December, available at http://epp.eurostat.ec.europa.eu/cache/ITY_PUBLIC/3-03122012-AP/EN/3-03122012-AP-EN.PDF.
Eurostat Press Release (2013),'First Quarter of 2013 Compared with Fourth Quarter of 2012, Euro Area Government Debt up to 92.2% of GDP, EU27 Debt up to 85.9%', 22 July, available at http://epp.eurostat.ec.europa.eu/cache/ITY_PUBLIC/2-22072013-AP/EN/2-22072013-AP-EN.PDF.
Evans, Geoffrey and Butt, Sarah (2007), 'Explaining Change in British Public Opinion on the European Union: Top Down or Bottom Up? *Acta Politica*, Vol. 24, No. 2, pp. 173–190.
Evans-Pritchard, Ambrose (2012), 'Blaming the Spanish Victim as Europe Spirals into a Summer of Crisis', *The Telegraph*, 22 July.
Farrell, Henry and Quiggin, John (2012), 'Consensus, Dissensus and Economic Ideas: The Rise and Fall of Keynesianism during the Economic Crisis', 9 March, unpublished paper available at http://www.henryfarrell.net/Keynes.pdf.
Fella, Stefano (2002), *New Labour and the European Union: Political Strategy, Policy Transition and the Amsterdam Treaty Negotiations* (Aldershot: Ashgate).
Fielding, Steven (2002), *The Labour Party: Continuity and Change in the Making of New Labour* (Basingstoke: Palgrave Macmillan).
Fieschi, Catherine (2004), 'Introduction', *Journal of Political Ideologies*, Vol. 9, No. 3, pp. 235–240.
Financial Secrecy Index, 2011
Fine, Ben and Milonakis, Dimitris (2010), *From Economics Imperialism to Freakonomics: The Shifting Boundaries between Economics and Other Social Sciences* (London: Routledge).
Fitzgibbon, John (2011), *Eurosceptic Protest Movements: A Comparative Analysis between Ireland, the UK, Estonia and Denmark*, DPhil Thesis: University of Sussex.

Fishman, Robert M. (2011), 'Portugal's Unnecessary Bailout', *New York Times*, 12 April.
Foley, Stephen (2011), 'What Price the New Democracy? Goldman Sachs Conquers Europe', *The Independent*, 18 November.
Follesdal, Andreas and Simon, Hix (2006), 'Why There Is a Democratic Deficit in the EU: A Response to Majone and Moravscik', *Journal of Common Market Studies*, Vol. 44, No. 3, pp. 533–562.
Ford, Robert and Goodwin, Matthew (2014), *Revolt on the Right: Explaining Support for the Radical Right in Britain* (London: Routledge).
Foreign Office (2004), *White Paper on the Treaty Establishing a Constitution for Europe, Cm 6309*, published by TSO (The Stationery Office) London, for the Foreign and Commonwealth Office.
Forster, Anthony (1998), 'Britain and the Negotiation of the Maastricht Treaty: A Critique of Liberal Intergovernmentalism', *Journal of Common Market Studies*, Vol. 36, No. 3, pp. 347–369.
Forster, Anthony (2000), 'Euroscepticism: What, When, Why and Where?', British Council Paris.
Forster, Anthony (2002a), *Euroscepticism in Contemporary British Politics: Opposition to Europe in the British Conservative and Labour Parties since 1945* (London: Routledge).
Forster, Anthony (2002b), 'Anti-Europeans, Anti-marketeers and Eurosceptics: The Evolution and Influence of Labour and Conservative Opposition to Europe'. *Political Quarterly*, Vol. 73, No. 3, pp. 299–308.
Foucault, Michel (1998), *The History of Sexuality: The Will to Knowledge* (London: Penguin).
Foxman, Simone (2011), '20 Banks That will Get Crushed if the PIIGS Go Bust', *Business Insider*, 25 November.
Fraile, Maria and Danilo Di Mauro (2010), 'The Economic Crisis and Public Opinion about Europe', EUDO, European University Institute, available at http://eudo-publicopinion.eui.eu.
Fram, Nicholas (2006), 'Decolonization, the Commonwealth, and British Trade 1945–2004', Stanford University, 17 May.
Friedman, Thomas L. (2005), *The World Is Flat: A Brief History of the Twenty-First Century* (New York: Farrar Straus Giroux).
Franklin, Mark N. (2007), 'Effects of Space and Time on Turnout in European Parliament Elections' in Wouter van der Brug and Cees van der Eijk (eds), *European Elections and Domestic Politics* (Notre Dame, IN: University of Notre Dame Press), pp. 13–31.
Franklin, Mark N., Marsh, Michael and McLaren, Lauren (1994), 'Uncorking the Bottle: Popular Opposition to European Unification in the Wake of Maastricht', *Journal of Common Market Studies*, Vol. 32, No. 4, pp. 455–472.
Gabel, Matthew J. (1998), 'Public Opinion and European Integration: An Empirical Test of Five Theories', *Journal of Politics*, Vol. 60, No. 2, pp. 333–355.
Gabor, Daniela and Ban, Cornel (2012), 'Fiscal Policy in (European) Hard Times: Financialization and Varieties of Capitalism', paper presented at the Understanding Crisis in Europe workshop, Bristol Business School.
Galbraith, John Kenneth (1982), 'Recession Economies', *New York Review of Books*, 4 February.

Gallino, Luciano (2011), *Finanzcapitalismo: La civilta del denaro in crisi* (Turin: Einaudi).
Gallup (2014), 'EU Leadership Approval at Record Low in Spain, Greece', poll 8 January, available at http://www.gallup.com/poll/166757/leadership-approval-record-low-spain-greece.aspx, accessed 3 June 2014.
Gamble, Andrew (1974), *The Conservative Nation* (London: Routledge).
Gamble, Andrew (1988), *The Free Economy and the Strong State: The Politics of Thatcherism* (London: Macmillan).
Gamble, Andrew (1994a), *Britain in Decline* (Basingstoke: Macmillan).
Gamble, Andrew (1994b), *The Free Economy and the Strong State: The Politics of Thatcherism* (Basingstoke: Palgrave).
Gamble, Andrew (1995), 'The New Political Economy', *Political Studies*, Vol. 43, No. 3, pp. 516–530.
Gamble, Andrew (1998), 'The European Issue in British Politics' in David Baker and David Seawright (eds), *Britain for and against Europe* (Oxford: Clarendon Press), pp. 11–30.
Gamble, Andrew (2003), *Between Europe and America: The Future of British Politics* (Basingstoke: Palgrave Macmillan).
Gamble, Andrew (2009), *The Spectre at the Feast: Capitalist Crisis and the Politics of Recession* (Basingstoke: Palgrave).
Gamble, Andrew (2014), *Crisis Without End: The Unravelling of Western Prosperity* (Basingstoke: Palgrave).
Gamble, Andrew and Kelly, Gavin (2000), 'The British Labour Party and Monetary Union', *West European Politics*, Vol. 23, No. 1, pp. 1–25.
Gamble, Andrew and Payne, Anthony (eds) (1996), *Regionalism and World Order* (Basingstoke: Palgrave).
Gareth, Gore and Sudip, Roy (2012), 'Spanish Bailout Saves German Pain', *International Financing Review*, 29 June.
Garry, John (2005), '"Second-order" versus "Issue-voting" Effects in EU Referendums: Evidence from the Irish Nice Treaty', *European Union Politics*, Vol. 6, No. 2, pp. 201–221.
Garton Ash, Timothy (2001), 'Is Britain European?', *International Affairs*, Vol. 77, No. 1, pp. 1–14.
Geddes, Andrew (2002), 'In Europe, Not Interested in Europe', in Andrew Geddes and Jonathan Tonge (eds), *Labour's Second Landslide: The British General Election 2001* (Manchester: Manchester University Press).
Geddes Andrew (2013), *Britain and the European Union* (Basingstoke: Palgrave Macmillan).
George, Stephen and Deborah, Haythorne (1996), 'The British Labour Party' in John Gaffney (ed), *Political Parties and the European Union* (London: Routledge), pp. 110–121.
George, Stephen (1998), *An Awkward Partner: Britain in the European Community* (Oxford: Oxford University Press).
Giddens, Anthony (1979), *Central Problems in Social Theory* (Basingstoke: MacMillan).
Giddens, Anthony (2014), *Turbulent and Mighty Continent: What Future for Europe?* (Cambridge: Polity).
Gifford, Chris (2008), *The Making of Eurosceptic Britain* (Aldershot: Ashgate).

Gifford, Chris (2010), 'The UK and the European Union: Dimensions of Sovereignty and the Problem of Eurosceptic Britishness', *Parliamentary Affairs*, Vol. 63, No. 2, pp. 321–338.

Gill, Stephen (1998), 'European Governance and New Constitutionalism: Economic and Monetary Union and Alternatives to Disciplinary Neoliberalism in Europe', *New Political Economy*, Vol. 3, No.1, pp. 5–26.

Gill, Stephen (2008), *Power and Resistance in the New World Order*, 2nd edn. (Basingstoke: Palgrave Macmillan).

Goodhardt, Charles A. E. (1998), 'The Two Concepts of Money: Implications for the Analysis of Optimal Currency Areas', *European Journal of Political Economy*, Vol. 14, No. 3, pp. 407–432.

Gowland, David and Anthony, Turner (1998), *Reluctant Europeans: Britain and European Integration 1945–1998* (London: Longman).

Gramsci, Antonio (1971), *Selections from the Prison Notebooks*, ed. and trans. Hoare, Quintin and Nowell-Smith, Geoffrey (London: Lawrence & Wishart).

Graeber, David (2012), *Debt: The First 5,000 Years* (New York: Melville House).

Grant, Charles (2009), *Is Europe Doomed to Fail as a Power?* (London: Centre for European Reform).

Grant, Wyn and Wilson, Graham K. (2012), *The Consequences of the Global Financial Crisis: The Rhetoric of Reform and Regulation* (Oxford: Oxford University Press).

De Grawue, Paul (2012), "How Not to Be a Lender of Last Resort," CEPS Commentary, Center for European Policy Studies, Brussels, 23 March, available at http://aei.pitt.edu/34246/.

Green, Jane (2007), 'When Voters and Parties Agree: Valence Issues and Party Competition', *Political Studies*, Vol. 55, pp. 629–655.

Grey, John (2009), *False Dawn: The Delusions of Global Capitalism* (London: Granta).

Grice, Andrew (2013), 'Ed Miliband Pledges Tougher Line on Immigration after Past Mistakes', *The Independent*, 6 March.

Guérot, Ulrike and Mark, Leonard (2011), 'The New German Question: How Europe Can Get the Germany It Needs', European Council on Foreign Relations Policy Brief, available at http://www.ecfr.eu/page/-/ECFR30_GERMANY_AW.pdf, accessed 29 May 2014.

Hague, William (2009), 'The Future of British Foreign policy', 21 July, available at http://www.conservatives.com/News/Speeches/2009/07/William_Hague_The_Future_of_British_Foreign_Policy.aspx.

Hall, Peter (2002), 'Britain: The Role of Government and the Distribution of Capital' in Robert D. Putnam (ed), *Democracies in Flux: The Evolution of Social Capital in Contemporary Societies* (Oxford: Oxford University Press).

Hall, Peter and David, Soskice (eds.) (2001), *Varieties of Capitalism: The Institutional Foundations of Comparative Advantage* (Oxford: Oxford University Press).

Hamann, Trent H. (2009), 'Neoliberalism, Governmentality, and Ethics', *Foucault Studies*, No 6, February, pp. 37–59.

Hancke, Bob (2009), *Debating Varieties of Capitalism: A Reader* (Oxford: Oxford University Press).

Hanley, Seán (2002), 'From Neo-Liberalism to National Interests: Ideology, Strategy and Party Development in the Euroscepticism of the Czech Right,' 30th

ECPR Joint Sessions of Workshops, Turin, 22–27 March, available at http://eprints.ucl.ac.uk/15078/1/15078.pdf.

Hanson, Jon D. and Yosifon, David G. (2003–2004), 'The Situation: An Introduction to the Situational Character, Critical Realism, Power Economics, and Deep Capture.' *University of Pennsylvania Law Review*, Vol. 152.

Harvey, David (2007), *A Brief History of Neoliberalism* (Oxford: Oxford University Press).

Haseler, Stephen (1996), *The English Tribe: Nation and Europe* (Basingstoke: Macmillan).

Hay, Colin (1999), *The Political Economy of New Labour: Labouring under False Pretences?* (Manchester: Manchester University Press).

Hay, Colin (2001), 'The Invocation of External Economic Constraints: A Genealogy of the Concept of Globalization in the Political Economy of the British Labour Party, 1973–2000', *The European Legacy*, Vol. 6, No. 2, pp. 233–249.

Hay, Colin (2006), 'Constructivist Institutionalism' in R. A. W. Rhodes, Sarah A. Binder, and Bert A. Rockman (eds), *The Oxford Handbook of Political Institutions* (Oxford: Oxford University Press), pp. 56–74.

Hay, Colin (2011), 'Britain and the Global Financial Crisis: The Return of Boom and Bust' in Philip Cowley, Richard Heffernan, and Colin Hay (eds), *Developments in British Politics 9* (Basingstoke: Palgrave Macmillan), pp. 238–256.

Hay, Colin and Marsh, David (eds) (2000),'Introduction' in *Demystifying Globalisation* (Basingstoke: Palgrave), pp. 1–17.

Hay, Colin and Rosamond, Ben (2002), 'Globalization, European Integration and the Discursive Construction of Economic Imperatives', *Journal of European Public Policy*, Vol. 9, No. 2, pp. 147–167.

Hay, Colin and Watson, Matthew (2003), 'The Discourse of Globalisation and the Logic of No Alternative: Rendering the Contingent Necessary in the Political Economy of New Labour', *Policy and Politics*, Vol. 31, No. 3, pp. 289–305.

Hayward, Jack (ed) (1996), *Elitism, Populism and European Politics* (Oxford: Clarendon).

Hayward, Jack and Rüdiger, Wurzel (eds) (2012), *European Disunion: Between Sovereignty and Solidarity* (Basingstoke: Palgrave).

Heath, Anthony, Jowell, Roger, Taylor, Bridget and Thompson, Katharina (1998), *Euroscepticism and the Referendum Party*, Working Paper No. 63 (Oxford: CREST), available at *www.crest.ox.ac.uk/papers/p63.pdf*.

Heipertz, Martin and Verdun, Amy (2010), *Ruling Europe: The Politics of the Stability and Growth Pact* (Cambridge: Cambridge University Press).

Held, David and McGrew, Anthony (eds) (2002), *Governing Globalization: Power, Authority and Global Governance* (Cambridge: Polity Press).

Held, David and McGrew, Anthony (eds) (2003), 'The Great Globalization Debate: An Introduction' in *The Global Transformations Reader* (Cambridge: Polity Press), pp 1–50.

Held, David, McGrew, Anthony, Goldblatt, David and Perraton, Jonathan (1999): *Global Transformations* (Cambridge: Polity Press).

Henry, James S. (2012), *The Price of Offshore Revisited: New Estimates for 'Missing' Global Private Wealth, Income, and Lost Taxes* (London: Tax Justice Network) July.

Heppell, Tim (2014), *The Tories: From Winston Churchill to David Cameron* (London: Bloomsbury).

Herndon, Thomas, Ash, Michael and Pollin, Robert (2013), 'Does High Public Debt Consistently Stifle Economic Growth? A Critique of Reinhart and Rogoff', University of Massachusetts Amherst, 15 April, available at http://www.peri.umass.edu/fileadmin/pdf/working_papers/working_papers_301–350/WP322.pdf.

Herzog, Hanna (1987), 'Minor Parties: The Relevancy Perspective', *Comparative Politics*, Vol. 19, No. 3, pp. 317–329.

Hettne, Bjorn (2006), 'Beyond the New Regionalism', in Anthony Payne (ed), *Key Debates in New Political Economy* (Abingdon: Routledge), pp. 128–160.

Hewitt, Gavin (2013), *The Lost Continent: Europe's Darkest Hour since World War Two* (London: Hodder and Stoughton).

Hirst, Paul and Thompson, Graham (1996), *Globalization in Question: The International Economy and the Possibilities of Governance* (Cambridge: Polity Press).

Hirst, Paul and Thompson, Graham (2002), 'The Future of Globalization Cooperation and Conflict', *Journal of the Nordic International Studies Association*, Vol. 37, No. 3, pp. 247–265.

Hix, Simon (2012), 'David Cameron's EU Treaty Veto Is a Disaster for Britain', LSE Blog, available at http://blogs.lse.ac.uk/politicsandpolicy/archives/18436.

Hobsbawm, Eric and Ranger, Terence (1983), *The Invention of Tradition* (Cambridge: Cambridge University Press).

Hodges, Michael and Woolcock, Stephen (1993), 'Atlantic Capitalism versus Rhine Capitalism', *West European Politics*, Vol. 16, No. 3, pp. 329–344.

Hodson, Dermot (2011), *Governing the Euro Area in Good Times and Bad* (Oxford: Oxford University Press).

Hoffmann, Stanley (1966), 'Obstinate or Obsolete? The Fate of the Nation State and the Case of Western Europe', *Daedalus*, Vol 95, No. 3, pp. 862–915.

Hoffmann, Stanley (1982), 'Reflections on the Nation-State in Europe Today', *Journal of Common Market Studies*, Vol. 21, No. ½, pp. 21–38.

Holliday, Ian (2000), 'Is the British State Hollowing Out?' *Political Quarterly*, Vol. 71, No. 2, pp. 167–176.

Holman, Otto (2004a), 'Asymmetrical Regulation and Multidimensional Governance in the EU', *Review of International Political Economy*, Vol. 11, No. 4, pp. 714–735.

Holman, Otto and Van der Pijl, Kees (1996), 'The Capitalist Class in the European Union', in Goerge Kourvetaris and Andreas Moschonas (eds), *The Impact of European Integration: Political, Sociological and Economic Changes* (London: Pinter), pp. 55–74.

Holmes, M. (ed) (1996), *The Eurosceptical Reader* (Basingstoke: Palgrave).

Hooghe, Liesbet and Marks, Gary (2004), 'Does Identity or Economic Rationality Drive Public Opinion on European Integration?', PSOnline, pp. 415–420, available at http://www.olemiss.edu/courses/inst381/HoogheMarks04.pdf, accessed 29 July 2014.

Hooghe, Liesbet and Marks, Gary (2007), 'Sources of Euroscepticism', *Acta Politica*, Vol. 42, pp. 119–127.

Hooghe, Liesbet and Marks, Gary (2009), 'A Postfunctionalist Theory of European Integration: From Permissive Consensus to Constraining Dissenssus', *British Journal of Political Science*, Vol. 39, No. 1, pp. 1–23.

House of Commons Treasury Select Committee (1998), *The UK and Preparations for Stage Three of Economic and Monetary Union*, HC503 1997–98. London: HMSO, available at http://www.publications.parliament.uk/pa/cm199798/cmselect/cmtreasy/905/90503.htm.

House of Lords (2010), *Referendums in the United Kingdom*, Select Committee on the Constitution, 12th Report of Session 2009–10, HL Paper 99, available at http://www.publications.parliament.uk/pa/ld200910/ldselect/ldconst/99/99.pdf.

House of Lords (2014), *The Role of National Parliaments in the European Union*, Report of the European Union Committee, HL Paper 151, 24 March, available at http://www.publications.parliament.uk/pa/ld201314/ldselect/ldeucom/151/151.pdf, accessed 22 May 2014.

Hughes, Kirsty and Smith, Edward (1998), 'New Labour, New Europe?', *International Affairs*, Vol. 74, No. 1, pp. 93–103.

Hutton, Will (2002), *The World We're In* (London: Little, Brown).

Ichijo, Atsuko (2003), 'The Uses of History: Anglo-British and Scottish Views of Europe', *Journal of Regional and Federal Studies*, Vol. 13, No. 3, pp. 23–43.

Ichijo, Atsuko (2004), *Scottish Nationalism and the idea of Europe: Concepts of Europe and the Nation* (London: Routledge).

Ikenberry, G. John (2008), 'The Rise of China and the Future of the West: Can the Liberal System Survive?', *Foreign Affairs*, Vol. 87, No. 1, 23–37.

Ilzkovitz, Fabienne, Dierx, Adriaan, Kovacs and Viktoria, Sousa, Nuno (2007), 'Steps Towards a Deeper Economic Integration: The Internal Market in the 21st Century', *European Economics Papers 271*, available at http://ec.europa.eu/economy_finance/publications/publication_summary788_en.htm.

IMF (2010), *World Economic Outlook: Recovery, Risk, and Rebalancing*, October, available at http://www.imf.org/external/pubs/cat/longres.aspx?sk=23542.

IMF (2012), *Euro Area Policies: Article IV Consultation*, July, available at http://www.imf.org/external/pubs/ft/scr/2012/cr12181.pdf.

IMF (2013a), 'Greece: Ex Post Evaluation of Exceptional Access under the 2010 Stand-by Arrangement', 2013, available at http://www.imf.org/external/pubs/ft/scr/2013/cr13156.pdf.

IMF (2013b), Country Report No. 13/156, June, available at http://www.inif.org/extemal/pubs/ft/scr/2013/crl3156.pdf.

IMF, Laeven, Luc and Valencia, Fabian (2008), 'Systemic Banking Crises: A New Database', November, available at https://www.imf.org/external/pubs/ft/wp/2008/wp08224.pdf.

IMF Laeven, Luc and Valencia, Fabian (2012), 'Systemic Banking Crises Database: An Update', available at https://www.imf.org/external/pubs/cat/longres.aspx?sk=26015.0.

Inglehart, Ronald (1977), *The Silent Revolution: Changing Values and Political Styles among Western Publics* (Princeton: Princeton University Press).

Inglehart, Ronald (1990), *Culture Shift in Advanced Industrial Society* (Princeton: Princeton University Press).

Ivaldi, Gilles (2006), 'Beyond France's 2005 Referendum on the European Constitutional Treaty: Second-order Model, Anti-establishment Attitudes and the End of the Alternative European Utopia', *West European Politics*, Vol. 29, No. 1, pp. 47–69.

Janssen, Ronald (2012), 'Another Europe Now!' *Social Europe Journal*, 14 November.
Jacoby, Wade and Meunier, Sophie (2010), 'Europe and Globalization', in A. Egan, N, Nugent and W. Paterson (eds), *Research Agendas in European Union Studies: Stalking the Elephant* (Basingstoke: Palgrave Macmillan).
Joffe, Josef (2009), 'The Default Power: The False Prophecy of America's Decline', *Foreign Affairs*, Vol. 88, No. 5, 21–35.
Johal, Sukhdev, Moran, Michael and Williams, Karel (212): 'The Future Has Been Postponed: The Great Financial Crisis and British Politics', *British Politics*, Vol 7, April, pp. 69–81.
Jones, Bill, Trevor, Kavanagh, Michael, Moran and Philip, Norton (2007), *Politics UK*, 6th edn (Harlow: Pearson).
Kagan, Robert (2008), *The Return of History and the End of Dreams* (New York: Alfred A. Knopf).
Kaiser, Wolfram (1996), *Using Europe, Abusing the Europeans: Britain and European Integration 1945–63* (New York: St Martin's Press).
Kassim, Hussein (2004), 'The United Kingdom and the Future of Europe: Winning the Battle, Losing the War', *Comparative European Politics*, Vol. 2, No. 2, pp. 261–281.
Kavanagh, Denis (1989), 'Political Culture in Britain: The Decline of the Civic Culture' in Gabriel Almond and Sidney Verba (eds), *The Civic Culture Revisited* (London: Sage).
Kavanagh, Denis and Philip, Cowley (2010), *The British General Election of 2010* (Basingstoke: Palgrave Macmillan).
Kearney, Hugh (1989), *The British Isles: A History of Four Nations* (Cambridge: Cambridge University Press).
Keating, Michael (2009), 'The Territorialisation of Interest Representation: The Response of Groups to Devolution', in John Curtice and Ben Seyd (eds), *Has Devolution Worked* (Manchester: Manchester University Press).
Keen, Steve (2011), *Debunking Economics: The Naked Emperor Dethroned* (Croydon: Zed Book).
Kellner, Peter (2012), *Worried Nationalists, Pragmatic Nationalists and Progressive Internationalists: Who Might Win a British Referendum on Europe* (London: European Council on Foreign Relations).
Kerry, John (2013), 'Joint Press Conference by John Kerry and British Foreign Secretary William Hague'. United Kingdom Foreign and Commonwealth Office, London: US Department of State. September 9.
Kindleberger, Charles P. (1984), *A Financial History of Western Europe* (Oxford: Oxford University Press).
Kindleberger, Charles P. and Aliber, Robert Z. (2011), *Manias, Panics, and Crashes: A History of Financial Crises*, 6th edn (Basingstoke: Palgrave Macmillan).
Kinsella, Stephen (2013), 'Remember: A Country Is Not a Company', *Harvard Business Review*, 25 March.
Killian, Sheila, Garvey, John and Shaw, Frances (2011), *An Audit of Irish Debt*, University of Limerick, September, available at http://www.debtireland.org/download/pdf/audit_of_irish_debt6.pdf.
Kirchfeld, Aaron, Logutenkova, Elena and Comfort, Nicholas (2012), 'Deutsche Bank No.1 in Europe as Leverage Hits Valuation', Bloomberg, 27 March,

available at http://www.bloomberg.com/news/2012-03-26/deutsche-bank-no-1-in-europe-as-leverage-hits-market-valuation.html.
Kissinger, Henry (2014), *World Order: Reflections on the Character of Nations and the Course of History* (London: Penguin Books).
Klein, Naomi (2008), *The Shock Doctrine: The Rise of Disaster Capitalism* (London: Penguin).
Kornelius, Stefan (2013), *Angela Merkel: The Chancellor and Her World*, transl. by Anthea Bell and Christopher Moncrieff (Richmond: Alma Books).
Kriesi, Hanspeter, Grand, Edgar, Dolezal, Martin, Lachat, Romain, Bornschier, Simon and Frey, Timotheo (2005), 'Globalization and the Transformation of National Political Space: Six European Countries Compared', TranState Working Papers 14, available at http://www.econstor.eu/bitstream/10419/28264/1/497813890.pdf, accessed 27 July 2014.
Krugman, Paul (1991), *Geography and Trade* (Cambridge, Mass.: MIT Press).
Krugman, Paul (2011), 'The Demand-side Temptation', *New York Times*, 25 January.
Krugman Paul (2012a), *End This Depression Now!* (New York: W.W. Norton).
Krugman, Paul (2012b), 'What Ails Europe?', *New York Times*, February 26.
Krugman, Paul (2013a), 'The Big Fail', *New York Times*, 6 January.
Krugman, Paul (2013b), 'The 1 Percent's Solution'. *New York Times*, 25 April.
Krugman, Paul and Layard, Richard (2012c): 'A Manifesto for Economic Sense' available at http://www.manifestoforeconomicsense.org/.
Kynaston, David (1994), *The City of London: Volume 1: A World of its Own, 1815–1890* (London: Chatto & Windus).
Kynaston, David (2011), *The City of London: The History* (London: Vintage Books).
Kwarteng, Kwasi, Patel, Priti, Raab, Dominic, Skidmore, Chris and Truss, Elizabeth (2012), *Britannia Unchained Global Lessons for Growth and Prosperity* (Basingstoke: Palgrave Macmillan).
Kwarteng, Kwasi, Skidmore, Chris, Raab, Dominic, Truss, Elizabeth and Patel, Priti (2011), *After the Coalition: A Conservative Agenda for Britain* (London: Biteback).
Labour Party (1997), *New Labour, Because Britain Deserves Better*, General Election Manifesto, available at http://www.labour-party.org.uk/manifestos/1997/1997-labour-manifesto.shtml, accessed 30 May 2012.
Labour Party (2010), *Labour Party Manifesto*.
Laffan, Brigid (1997), *The Finances of the European Union* (London: Macmillan).
Lapavitsas, Costas et al. (2012), *Crisis in the Eurozone* (London: Verso).
Larsen, Henrik (2006), 'The United Kingdom: New Approach and New Influence' in Finn Laursen (ed), *The Treaty of Nice: Actor Preferences, Bargaining and Institutional Choice* (Leiden: Brill), pp. 307–322.
Lassalle, Didier (2014), 'Royaume-Uni: l'immigration sur l'agenda politique', Pages Europes, La Documentation Française, 14 January.
Lau, Lawrence J. (2010), *Regulation and Supervision Post the Global Financial Crisis*, Institute of Global Economics and Finance (IGEF) of the Chinese University of Hong Kong, available at http://www.igef.cuhk.edu.hk/igef_media/working-paper/IGEF/igef%20working%20paper%20no.%202.pdf.
Laursen, Finn (ed) (2002), *The Amsterdam Treaty: National Preference Formation, Interstate Bargaining and Outcome* (Odense: Odense University Press).
Leconte, Cécile (2010), *Understanding Euroscepticism* (Basingstoke: Palgrave Macmillan).

Lee, Lucy and Penny, Young (2013), 'A Disengaged Britain? Political Interest and Participation over 30 Years' in *British Social Attitudes Survey 30*, available at http//:www.bsa-30.natcen.ac.uk.
Lelieveldt, Herman and Princen, Sebastiaan (2011), *The Politics of the European Union* (Cambridge: Cambridge University Press).
Lequesne, Christian (2001), 'Le traité de Nice et l'avenir institutionnel de l'Union européenne', *Regards sur l'actualité*, La Documentation Française, September–October, pp. 3–14.
Leuffen, Dirk, Rittberger, Berthold and Schimmelfennig, Frank (2013), *Differentiated Integration: Explaining the Variation in the European Union* (Basingstoke: Palgrave).
Levitt, Theodore (1983), 'The Globalization of Markets', *Harvard Business Review*, May–June, pp. 92–102.
Lewis, Michael (2011), 'When Irish Eyes Are Crying', *Vanity Fair*, March.
Leys, Colin (2001), *Market Driven Politics: Neo-liberal Democracy and the Public Interest* (London: Verso).
Liberal Democrats (2010), *Change That Works For You*, General Election Manifesto, available at http://network.libdems.org.uk/manifesto2010/libdem_manifesto_2010.pdf.
Liddle, Roger (2014), *The Europe Dilemma: Britain and the Drama of European Integration* (London: I. B. Tauris).
Lindberg, Leon and Scheingold, Stuart (1970), *Europe's Would-be Polity: Patterns of Change in the European Community* (Englewood Cliffs, NJ: Prentice Hall).
Lindberg, Leon and Scheingold, Stuart (eds) (1971), *Regional Integration: Theory and Research* (Harvard: Harvard University Press).
Lindblom, Charles E. (1959), 'The Science of Muddling Through,' *Public Administration Review*, Vol. 19, pp. 79–88.
Lindblom, Charles E. (1977), *Politics and Markets* (New York: Basic Books).
Lipietz, Alain (1992), *Towards a New Economic Order* (Cambridge: Polity).
Lipietz, Alain (1996), 'Social Europe: The post-Maastricht Challenge', *Review of International Political Economy*, Vol. 3, No. 3, pp. 369–379.
Lipset, Seymour Martin (1981), *Political Man: The Social Bases of Politics* (Garden City, NY: Doubleday).
Lipset, Seymour Martin and Rokkan, Stein (1967), 'Cleavage Structures, Party Systems and Voter Alignments: An Introduction,' in S. M. Lipset and S. Rokkan (eds), *Party Systems and Voter Alignments* (New York: Free Press), pp. 1–64.
Lipset, Seymour Martin and Rokkan, Stein (1967), *Party Systems and Voter Alignments: Cross-National Perspectives* (New York: Free Press).
Lloyd, Christopher (1986), *Explanation in Social History* (Oxford: Basil Blackwell).
Lojsch, Dagmar H., Rodriguez-Vives, Marta and Slavik, Michal, 'The Size and Composition of Government Debt in the Euro Area', European Central Bank, Occasional Paper Series 132, 15 October 2011, available at http://www.ecb.europa.eu/pub/pdf/scpops/ecbocp132.pdf.
Lombardo, Emanuela (2007), 'The Participation of Civil Society' in Dario Castiglione, Justus Schönlau, Chris Longman, Emanuela Lombardo, Nieves Perez Solorzano and Miriam Aziz (eds), *Constitutional Politics in the European Union: The Convention Moment and Its Aftermath* (Basingstoke: Palgrave Macmillan), pp. 153–170.

Longstreth, Frank (1979), 'The City, Industry and the State' in Colin Crouch (ed), *State and Economy in Contemporary Capitalism* (London: Croom Helm), pp. 157–90.
Louis, William Roger (1977), *Imperialism at Bay: The United States and the Decolonization of the British Empire, 1941–1945* (Oxford: Oxford University Press).
Ludlam, Steve (1996), 'The Spectre Haunting Conservatism: Europe and Backbench Rebellion', in Steve Ludlam and M. J. Smith (eds), *Contemporary British Conservatism* (Basingstoke: Macmillan), pp. 98–120.
Ludlam, Steve and Smith, Martin (1996), *Contemporary British Conservatism* (Basingstoke: Palgrave).
Lukes, Steven (1974), *Power: A Radical View*, 2nd edn. (Basingstoke: Palgrave Macmillan).
Lynch, Philip (1999), *The Politics of Nationhood: Sovereignty, Britishness and Conservative Politics* (Basingstoke: Macmillan).
Lynch, Philip (2009), 'The Conservatives and the European Union: The Lull Before the Storm?' in Simon Lee and Matt Beech (eds), *The Conservatives Under David Cameron* (Basingstoke: Palgrave Macmillan), pp. 187–207.
Macartney, Hugh (2009a) 'Variegated Neo-liberalism: Transnationally Oriented Fractions of Capital in EU Financial Market Integration'. *Review of International Studies*, Vol. 35, No. 2, pp. 451–480.
Macartney, Hugh (2009b) 'Disagreeing to Agree: Financial Crisis Management within the Logic of No Alterative', *Politics*, Vol. 29, No. 2, pp. 111–120.
Macartney, Hugh (2011), *Variegated Neoliberalism: EU Varieties of Capitalism and International Political Economy* (Abingdon: Routledge).
Macartney, Hugh (2013), *The Debt Crisis in the European Union* (Basingstoke: Palgrave).
Magnette, Paul and Nicolaidis, Kalypso (2004), 'The European Convention: Bargaining in the Shadow of Rhetoric', *West European Politics*, Vol. 27, No. 3, pp. 381–404.
Mahendran, Kesi and McIver, Iain (2007), 'Attitudes Towards the European Union & the Challenges in Communicating "Europe" – Building a Bridge Between Europe and its Citizens', Evidence Review Paper Two, International Research, Analytical Services, Scottish Executive Scottish Parliament Information Service, Scottish Executive Social Research. http://www.scotland.gov.uk/Resource/Doc/163772/0044574.pdf.
Maier, Charles, S. (1987), *In Search of Stability: Explorations of Historical Political Economy* (Cambridge: Cambridge University Press).
Mair, Peter (2013), *Ruling the Void: the Hollowing of Western Democracy* (London: Verso).
Majone, Giandomenico (1998), 'Europe's "Democratic Deficit": The Question of Standards', *European Law Journal*, Vol. 4, No. 1, pp. 5–28.
Majone, Giandomenico (2005), *Dilemmas of European Integration* (Oxford: Oxford University Press).
Majone, Giandomenico (2009), *Europe as the Would-be World Power: The EU at Fifty* (Cambridge: Cambridge University Press).
Major, John (1994), Speech at the William and Mary Lecture, Leiden, 7 September, available at http://www.johnmajor.co.uk/page1124.html.
Major, John (2000), *The Autobiography*, 2nd edn. paperback (London: HarperCollins).

Major, John (2012), 'Major Claims Green Shoots of Economic Recovery Are Appearing', *Sunday Times*, 16 September.
Mandelson, Peter (2010), *The Third Man: Life at the Heart of New Labour* (London: Harper Press).
Mandelson, Peter (2012), 'Europe, Is It the End of the Project?', The Hands Lecture, 4 May, available at http://www.policy-network.net/news/3942/Britain-and-the-survival-of-the-European-project.
Mandelson, Peter and Roger, Liddle (1996), *The Blair Revolution: Can New Labour Deliver?* (London: Faber and Faber).
Mann, Michael (2013), *The Sources of Social Power: Volume 4: Globalizations, 1945–2011* (Cambridge: CUP).
Marks, Gary, Hooghe, Liesbet and Blank, Kermit (1996), 'European Integration since the 1980s: State-centric versus Multi-level Governance', *Journal of Common Market Studies*, Vol. 34, No. 3, pp. 341–378.
Marquand, David (2014), *Mammon's Kingdom: An Essay on Britain, Now* (London: Penguin Books).
Marsh, David (2010), *The Euro* (New Haven: Yale University Press).
Marsh, David (2013a), 'Euro Zone Needs a Truth, Reconciliation Commission', *Market Watch*, 2 July 2013.
Marsh, David (2013b), *Europe's Deadlock: How the Euro Crisis Could Be Solved and Why It Won't* (New Haven & London: Yale University Press).
Marsh, David, Richards, David and Smith, Martin J. (2001), *Changing Patterns of Governance in the UK: Reinventing Whitehall?* (Basingstoke: Palgrave Macmillan).
Marshall, Geoffrey (1997), 'The Referendum: What, When and How?, *Parliamentary Affairs*, Vol. 50, No. 2, pp. 307–313.
Martell, Luke (2007), 'The Third Wave in Globalisation Theory', *International Studies Review*, Vol. 9, No. 2, pp 173–196. Also available in draft form at: http://www.sussex.ac.uk/Users/ssfa2/thirdwaveweb.htm.
Martell, Luke (2010), *The Sociology of Globalization* (Cambridge: Polity Press).
Mason, Rowena (2013), 'UK Claims Growing Support Over Migration in Clash with Brussels', *The Guardian*, 27 November.
McDonagh, Bobby (1998), *Original Sin in a Brave New World: An Account of the Negotiation of the Treaty of Amsterdam* (Dublin: Institute of European Affairs).
McCormick, John (2014), *Why Europe Matters: The Case for European Union* (Basingtoke: Palgrave).
Meadway, James (2011), 'Greece Should Shake off the Euro Straitjacket', London: NEF, 13 September.
Mendelsohn, Matthew and Andrew, Parkin (eds) (2001), *Referendum Democracy: Citizens, Elites and Deliberation in Referendum Campaigns* (Basingstoke: Palgrave).
Menon, Anand (2003), 'Britain and the Convention on the Future of Europe', *International Affairs*, Vol. 79, No. 5, pp. 963–978.
Menon, Anand (2004), 'Leading from Behind: Britain and the European Constitutional Treaty', Notre Europe, Research and European Issues N°31, January.
Menon, Anand (2011), 'La politique de défense européenne après le traité de Lisbonne: beaucoup de bruit pour rien', *Politique Etrangère*, 2, pp. 375–387.
Menon, Anand (2014), 'Divided and Declining? Europe in a Changing World', JCMS Annual Review Lecture, *Journal of Common Market Studies*, Vol. 52, Annual Review, pp. 5–24.

Merkel, Angela (2012), Speech to the Bela Foundation: 'The Way Ahead for Europe', available at http://sylvie-goulard.eu/articles2012/Bela-Debate-2012.pdf.
Merler, Silvia and Pisani-Ferry, Jean (2012), 'Sudden Stops in the Euro Area', Breugel Policy Contribution 6, pp. 1–16, available at http://www.Bruegel.org/publications/publication-detail/publication/718-sudden-stops-in-the-euro-area/.
Miliband, Ed (2012), Speech on immigration at the Institute for Public Policy Research, 22 June, available at http://www.politics.co.uk/comment-analysis/2012/06/22/ed-miliband-s-immigration-speech-in-full.
Milward, Alan (1992), *The European Rescue of the Nation-State* (Berkeley: University of California Press).
Minkkinen, Petri and Patomaki, Heikki (eds) (1997), *The Politics of Economic and Monetary Union* (Dordrecht: Kluwer).
Minsky, Hyman (2008), *Stabilizing an Unstable Economy* (New York: McGraw-Hill).
Mirowski, Philip (2013), *Never Let a Good Crisis Go to Waste: How Neoliberalism Survived the Financial Meltdown* (London: Verso).
Mirowski, Philip and Plehwe, Dieter (eds) (2009), *The Road from Mont Pèlerin: The Making of the Neoliberal Thought Collective* (Cambridge, MA: Harvard University Press).
Moga, Teodor Lucian (2009), 'The Contribution of the Neofunctionalist and Intergovernmentalist Theories to the Evolution of the European Integration Process', *Journal of Alternative Perspectives in the Social Sciences*, Vol. 1, No. 3, pp. 796–807.
Monti, Mario (2010), 'A New Strategy for the Single Market', Report to the President of the European Commission, available at http://ec.europa.eu/bepa/pdf/monti_report_final_10_05_2010_en.pdf.
Moran, Michael (2007), *The British Regulatory State: High Modernism and Hyper-innovation* (Oxford: Oxford University Press).
Moravcsik, Andrew (1991), 'Negotiating the Single European Act: National Interests and Conventional Statecraft in the European Community', *International Organization*, Vol. 45, pp.19–56.
Moravcsik, Andrew (1993), 'Preferences and Power in the European Community: A Liberal Intergovernmentalist Approach', *Journal of Common Market Studies*, Vol. 31, No. 4, pp. 473–523.
Moravcsik, Andrew (1998), *The Choice for Europe: Social Purpose and State Power from Messina to Maastricht* (London, UCL Press, Ithaca, NY: Cornell University Press).
Moravcsik, Andrew (2002), 'In Defence of the "Democratic Deficit": Reassessing Legitimacy in the European Union', *Journal of Common Market Studies*, Vol. 40, No. 4, pp. 603–624.
Moravcsik, Andrew and Kalypso, Nicolaidis (1998), 'Keynote Article: Federal Ideals and Constitutional Realities in the Treaty of Amsterdam', *Journal of Common Market Studies*, Vol. 36, Annual Review, September.
Munchau, Wolfgang (2014), 'Britain and the EU: On the Way Out? The UK's Relations with the Rest of Europe are Unsustainable', *Prospect*, 17 July, available at http://www.prospectmagazine.co.uk/features/britain-and-the-eu-on-the-way-out.

Nairne, Patrick (1996), *Report of the Commission on the Conduct of Referendums* (London: Constitution Unit).
Nelson, Robert H. (2001), *Economics as Religion: From Samuelson to Chicago and Beyond* (University Park, PA: Pennsylvania State University Press).
Newman, Abraham (2010), 'Flight from Risk: Unified Germany and the Role of Beliefs in the European Response to the Financial Crisis', *German Politics and Society*, Vol. 28, No. 2, pp. 151–164.
Newman, Gerald (1987), *The Rise of English Nationalism: A Cultural History, 1740–1830* (London: St. Martin's Press).
Norman, Peter (2005), *The Accidental Constitution: The Making of Europe's Constitutional Treaty*, 2nd edn. (Brussels: EuroComment).
Norris, Pippa (1997), *Electoral Change since 1945* (Oxford: Blackwell).
Norris, Pippa (2000), *A Virtuous Circle: Political Communications in Postindustrial Societies* (Cambridge: Cambridge University Press).
Norris, Pippa (2001), 'Apathetic Landslide: The 2001 British General Election', *Parliamentary Affairs*, Vol. 54, pp. 565–589.
Norris, Pippa (2002), *Democratic Phoenix: Reinventing Political Activism* (Cambridge: Cambridge University Press).
Norris, Pippa (2011), *Democratic Deficit: Critical Citizens Revisited* (Cambridge: Cambridge University Press).
Norris, Pippa and Lovenduski, Joni (2004), 'Why Parties Fail to Learn: Electoral Defeat, Selective Perception and British Party Politics', *Party Politics*, Vol. 10, No. 1, pp. 83–102.
Nugent, Neill and Phinemore, David (2010), 'United Kingdom: Red Lines Defended' in Maurizio Carbone (ed), *National Politics and European Integration: From the Constitution to the Lisbon Treaty* (Cheltenham: Edward Elgar Publishing), pp. 71–89.
Nijeboer, Arjen (2005), 'Peoples' Vengeances: The Dutch Referendum', *European Constitutional Law Review*, Vol. 1, pp. 393–405.
O'Grady, Sean (2010), 'Fear and Loathing as the Hedge Funds Take on the Euro', *The Independent*, 4 March.
O'Hara, Mary (2013), *Austerity Bites: A Journey to the Sharp End of Cuts in the UK* (London: Policy Press).
Ohmae, Kenichi (1995), *The End of the Nation-state: The Rise of Regional Economies* (London: Harper Collins).
Olsen, Johan P. (2001), 'Reforming European Institutions of Governance', ARENA Working Papers, WP 01/7.
Open Europe (2011), 'Continental Shift: Safeguarding the UK's Financial Trade', Changing Europe, December, available at http://www.openeurope.org.uk/Content/Documents/Pdfs/continentalshift.pdf.
Open Europe (2012), 'Trading Places: Is EU membership Still the Best Option for UK Trade?' by Stephen Booth and Christopher Howarth, available at http://openeurope.org.uk/intelligence/britain-and-the-eu/eu-membership/.
Oppermann, Kai (2008), 'The Blair Government and Europe: The Policy of Containing the Salience of European Integration, *British Politics*, Vol. 3, No. 2, pp. 156–182.
Owen, David (2012), *Europe Restructured: The Euro Zone Crisis and Its Aftermath* (London: Methuen).

Owen, Geoffrey (2000), *From Empire to Europe: the Decline and Revival of British Industry since the Second World War* (London: Harper Collins).

Packer, George (2011), 'The Broken Contract', *Foreign Affairs*, Vol. 90, No. 6, pp. 20–31.

Padgett, Stephen (2003): 'Political Economy: The German Model under Stress', in Stephen Padgett, William E. Paterson, Gordon Smith (eds), *Developments in German Politics 3* (Basingstoke: Palgrave), pp. 126–127.

Palley, Thomas I. (1998), 'Restoring Prosperity: Why the U.S. Model Is Not the Right Answer for the U.S. or Europe', *Journal of Post Keynesian Economics*, Vol. 20, pp. 337–354.

Palley, Thomas I. (2009), 'America's Exhausted Paradigm: Macroeconomic Causes of the Financial Crisis and Great Recession', New American Contract Policy Paper (Washington, DC: New America Foundation), 22 July.

Palley, Thomas. I. (2011), 'The European Union Needs a Government Banker', *Challenge*, Vol. 54, pp. 5–21.

Palley, Thomas I. (2012), *From Financial Crisis to Stagnation: The Destruction of Shared Prosperity and the Role of Economics* (Cambridge: Cambridge University Press).

Palley, Thomas, I. (2013), 'Europe's Crisis without End: The Consequences of Neoliberalism', *Contributions to Political Economy*, Vol. 32, No. 1, pp. 29–50.

Parkin, Frank (1968), *Middle-Class Radicalism* (Manchester: Manchester University Press).

Paterson, Lindsay (2002), 'Is Britain Disintegrating? Changing Views of "Britain" after Devolution', *Regional and Federal Studies*, Vol. 12, No. 1, pp. 21–42.

Paterson, William E. (2011), 'The Reluctant Hegemon? Germany Moves Centre Stage in the European Union', *Journal of Common Market Studies*, Vol. 49, Annual Review, pp. 57–75.

Patomaki, Heikki (2001), *Democratising Globalisation: The Leverage of the Tobin Tax* (London: Zed Books).

Patomaki, Heikki (2009), 'Neoliberalism and the Global Financial Crisis', *New Political Science*, Vol. 31, No. 4, pp. 431–442.

Patomäki, Heikki (2013), *The Great Eurozone Disaster: From Crisis to Global New Deal* (London: Zed Books).

Payne, Anthony (ed) (2006), *Key Debates in New Political Economy* (Abingdon: Routledge).

Peck, Jamie and Tickell, Adam (2002), 'Neoliberalizing space,' *Antipode*, Vol. 34, No. 3, pp. 380–404.

Peet, John and Guardia, Anton La (2014), Unhappy Union: How the Euro Crisis – and Europe – Can be Fixed, *The Economist* (London: Profile Books).

Perraton, Jonathan, Goldblatt, David, Held, David and McGrew, Anthony (1997), 'The globalisation of economic activity', *New Political Economy*, Vol. 2, No. 2, pp. 257–278.

Peter, Jochen (2007), 'Media Effects on Attitudes Toward Europan Integration' in Wouter van der Brug and Cees van der Eijk (eds), *European Elections and Domestic Politics* (Notre Dame, IN: University of Notre Dame Press), pp. 131–144.

Peterson, V. Spike (2006), 'How the Meaning of Gender Patters in Political Economy' in Anthony Payne (ed), *Key Debates in New Political Economy* (Abingdon: Routledge), pp. 78–105.

Peterson, John (1996), *Europe and America: The Prospects for Partnership* (Abingdon: Routledge).
PewResearch (2014), 'A Fragile Rebound for EU image on Eve of European Parliament Elections', Global Attitudes Project, 12 May, available at http://www.pewglobal.org/2014/05/12/a-fragile-rebound-for-eu-image-on-eve-of-european-parliament-elections/, accessed 4 June 2014.
Pharr, Susan J. and Robert, D. Putnam (2000), *Disaffected Democracies: What's Troubling the Trilateral Countries?* (Princeton: Princeton University Press).
Pierson, Paul (1998), 'The Path of European Integration: A Historical Institutionalist Analysis' in Sandholtz, Wayne and Stone Sweey, Alec (eds), *European Integration and Supranational Governance* (Oxford: Oxford University Press), pp. 27–58.
Pierson, Paul (2000), 'Increasing Returns, Path Dependence and the Study of Politics', *American Political Science Review*, Vol. 94, No. 2, pp. 251–267.
Pierson, Paul (2004), *Politics in Time: History, Institutions and Social Analysis* (Princeton: Princeton University Press).
Pisani-Ferry, Jean, Sapir, Andre and Wolff, Guntram (2013), 'EU-IMF Assistance to Euro-Area Countries: An Early Assessment' (Brussels: Bruegel), available at: http://www.bruegel.org/publications/publication-detail/publication/779-eu-imf-assistance-to-euro-area-countries-an-early-assessment/.
Polidori, Elena (2010), Interview with Jean-Claude Trichet: *la Repubblica*, 16 June, available at http://www.bis.org/review/r100625a.pdf.
Pop, Valentina (2011), 'Germany Estimated to Have Made 9bn Profit Out of Crisis', *EUobserver.Com*, 9 November.
Portillo, Michael (1998), *Democratic Values and the Currency* (London: IEA).
Posen, Adam (2013), 'Germany Is Being Crushed by Its Export Obsession', *Financial Times*, 3 September.
Powell, Enoch (1972), Speech on the Second Reading of the European Communities Bill, 17 February.
Powell, Jonathan (2010), *The New Machiavelli: How to Wield Power in the Modern World* (London: The Bodley Head).
Pryce, Vicky (2013), *Greekonomics: The Euro Crisis and Why Politicians Don't Get It* (London: Biteback Publishing).
Ptak, Ralf (2009), 'Neoliberalism in Germany: Revisiting the Ordoliberal Foundations of the Social Market Economy' in Philip Mirowski and Dieter Plehwe (eds), *The Road from Mont Pèlerin: The Making of the Neoliberal Thought Collective* (Cambridge, MA: Harvard University Press), pp. 89–138.
Quinn, Adam (2011), 'The Art of Declining Politely: Obama's Prudent Presidency and the Waning of Power', *International Affairs*, Vol. 87, No. 4, 803–824.
Quinn, Thomas, Bara, Judith and Bartle, John (2011), 'The UK Coalition Agreement: Who Won?' *Journal of Public Opinion, Elections and Parties*, Vol. 21, No. 2, pp. 295–312.
Qvortrup, Matt (2005), *Government by the People: A Comparative Study of Referendums*, 2nd edn. (Manchester: Manchester University Press).
Qvortrup, Matt (2006), 'The Three Referendums on the European Constitution Treaty in 2005', *The Political Quarterly*, Vol. 77, No. 1, pp. 89–97.
Rachman, Gideon (2011), 'This Time It's for Real', *Foreign Policy*, January–February, 59–63.

Radice, Hugo (2013), 'Reshaping Fiscal Policies in Europe: Enforcing Austerity, Attacking Democracy', *Social Europe Journal*, 11 February.
Raffenne, Coralie (2015), 'The European Citizens' Initiative' in Emmanuelle Avril and Johan Neem (eds), *Democracy, Participation and Contestation: Civil Society, Governance and the Future of Liberal Democracy* (London: Routledge).
Ram, Vidya (2006), 'Public Attitudes to Politics, Politicians and Parliament', *Parliamentary Affairs*, Vol. 59, No. 1, pp. 188–197.
Rasmus, Jack (2010), *Epic Recession: Prelude to Global Depression* (London: Pluto Press).
Rawnsley, Andrew (2010), *The End of the Party: The Rise and Fall of New Labour* (London: Penguin).
Reich, Robert (2011), 'Follow the money: behind Europe's debt crisis lurks another giant bailout of Wall Street', *Huffingtonpost*, 4 October, available at http://www.huffingtonpost.com/robert-reich/europe-debt-crisis_b_996528.html.
Reif, Karlheinz and Schmitt, Hermann (1980), 'Nine Second-order National Elections – A Conceptual Framework for the Analysis of European Election Results', *European Journal of Political Research*, Vol. 8, pp. 3–44.
Reinhart, Carmen M. and Rogoff, Kenneth S. (2010), 'Growth in a Time of Debt', *American Economic Review*, Vol. 100, No. 2, pp. 573–578.
Rhodes, R. A. W. (1997), *Understanding Governance: Policy Networks, Governance, Reflexivity and Accountability* (Buckingham: Open University Press).
Riddell, Peter (1998), 'EMU and the Press', in A. Duff (ed), *Understanding the Euro* (London: Federal Trust), pp. 105–16.
Riddell, Peter (2005), 'Europe' in Anthony Seldon and Dennis Kavanagh (eds), *The Blair Effect 2001–2005* (Cambridge: Cambridge University Press), pp. 362–383.
Ridley, Nicholas (1990), 'Saying the Unsayable about the Germans', Dominic Lawson, 14 July 1990, Spectator Archives, available at http://blogs.spectator.co.uk/coffeehouse/2011/09/from-the-archives-ridley-was-right/.
Rodrik, Dani (2007), *One Economics, Many Recipes* (Princeton: Princeton University Press).
Rosamond, Ben (1998), 'The Integration of Labour? British Trade Union Attitudes to European Integration', in Baker David and David Seawright (eds), *Britain For and Against Europe: British Politics and the Question of European Integration* (Oxford: Clarendon Press), pp. 130–147.
Rosamond, Ben (2000), *Theories of European Integration* (Basingstoke: Palgrave).
Rosamond, Ben (2008), 'The Discursive Construction of Neoliberalism: The EU and the Contested Substance of European Economic Space', International Studies Association Annual Conference, San Francisco.
Rosamond, Ben and Wincott, D. (2005), 'Constitutionalism, European Integration and British Political Economy', *British Journal of Politics and International Relations*, Vol. 8, No. 1, pp. 1–14.
Rosanvallon, Pierre (2006), *La contre-démocratie: La politique à l'âge de la défiance* (Paris: Seuil).
Rose, Richard and McAllister, Ian (1990), *The Loyalties of Voters* (London: Sage).
Roth, Felix, Nowak-Lehmann, Felicitas D. and Otter, Thomas (2013), 'Crisis and Trust in the National and European Governmental Institutions' in Bruno de Witte, Adrienne Héritier and Alexander H. Trechsel (eds), *The Eurocrisis and the*

State of European Democracy, European University Institute, available at www.EUROcrisis-29–05.pdf, accessed 4 June 2014.

Roubini, Nouriel (2012), 'Economic Insecurity and Inequality Breed Political Instability', in Janet Byrne (ed), *The Occupy Handbook* (New York: Back Bay Books).

Roubini, Nouriel and Stephen, Mihm (2011), *Crisis Economics: A Crash Course in the Future of Finance* (London: Penguin).

Rt.com (2013), 'EU debt reaches all-time high of $11.4 trillion', July, available at http://rt.com/business/eu-debt-high-q1–459/.

Saerlvik, Bo and Crewe, Ivor (1983), *Decade of Dealignment: The Conservative Victory of 1979 and Electoral Trends in the 1970s* (Cambridge: Cambridge University Press).

Sally, Razeen (1996), 'Ordoliberalism and the Social Market: Classical Political Economy from Germany', *New Political Economy*, Vol. 1, No. 2, pp. 233–257.

Salmond, Alex (2013), speech to the SNP conference, 20 October, available at http://www.newstatesman.com/politics/2013/10/alex-salmonds-speech-2013-snp-conference-full-text.

Sartori, Giovanni (1976), *Parties and Party Systems: A Framework for Analysis* (London: Cambridge University Press).

Sartori, Giovanni (1987), *The Theory of Democracy Revisited* (London: Chatham House).

Sassen, Saskia (2006), 'When National Territory Is Home to the Global: Old Borders to Novel Borderings', in Anthony Payne (ed), *Key Debates in New Political Economy* (Abingdon: Routledge), pp. 106–127.

Schambaugh, Jay (2012), 'The Euro's Three Crises', Brookings Papers on Economic Activity, Washington, DC, Spring, No. 24, available at http://www.brookings.edu/~/media/Projects/BPEA/Spring%202012/2012a_Shambaugh.pdf.

Scharpf, F. W. (1999), *Governing in Europe: Effective and Democratic?* (Oxford: Oxford University Press).

Scharpf, F. W. (2002), 'The European Social Model: Coping with the Challenges of Diversity', *Journal of Common Market Studies*, Vol. 40, No. 4, pp. 645–670.

Schäuble, Wolfgang (2013), 'Ignore the Doomsayers: Europe Is Being Fixed', *Financial Times*, 16 September, available at http://www.ft.com/cms/s/0/e88c842a–1c67–11e3–8a3–00144feab7de.html#axzz3FUrqZzrb.

Schmidt, Vivien A. (2006), *Democracy in Europe: the European Union and National Politics* (Oxford: Oxford University Press).

Schmidt, Vivien A. (2008a): 'Discursive Institutionalism: The Explanatory Power of Discourse', *Annual Review of Political Science*, Vol. 11, pp. 303–326.

Schmidt, Vivien A. (2008b), 'Délibération publique et discours de légitimation en France et en Grande-Bretagne face à l'intégration européenne', *Revue Internationale de Politique Comparée*, Vol. 15, No. 4, pp. 555–571.

Schmidt, Vivien A. and Thatcher, Mark (2013), *Resilient Liberalism in Europe's Political Economy* (Cambridge: Cambridge University Press).

Schmidt, Vivien A. and Woll, Cornella (2013), 'The State: The Bête Noire of Neoliberalism or Its Greatest Conquest?' in Vivien A. Schmidt, and Mark Thatcher (eds), *Resilient Liberalism in Europe's Political Economy* (Cambridge: Cambridge University Press), pp. 112–141.

Schnapper, Pauline (2005), 'L'impact de la guerre en Irak sur les élections de 2005', *Revue Française de Civilisation Britannique*, Vol. 13, No. 3, 2005.

Schnapper, Pauline (2011), *British Political Parties and National Identity: A Changing Discourse 1997–2010* (Newcastle: Cambridge Scholars).

Schnapper, Pauline (2012), 'La politique européenne de la coalition: nouvelle donne ou maintien de la tradition?', *Observatoire de la Société Britannique*, No. 12, pp. 273–292.

Scruton Roger (2014), 'A Point of View: Should the English Have a Say on Scottish Independence?'*BBC News Magazine* 23 February, available at http://www.bbc.co.uk/news/magazine-26173128.

Scholte, Jan Aart (2005), *Globalization: A Critical Introduction* (Basingstoke: Palgrave).

Seawright, David (2010), *The British Conservative Party and One Nation Politics* (New York: Continuum).

Sedlacek, Tomas (2013), *Economics of Good and Evil: The Quest for Economic Meaning from Gilgamesh to Wall Street* (Oxford: Oxford University Press).

Seldon, Anthony and Lodge, Guy (2010), *Brown at Ten* (London: Biteback Publishing).

Setälä, Maija (2006), 'On the Problems of Responsibility and Accountability in Referendums', *European Journal of Political Research*, Vol. 45, No. 4, pp. 699–721.

Shaxson, Nicholas, Christensen, John and Mathiason, Nick (2012), *Inequality: You Don't Know the Half of It* (London: Tax Justice Network).

Shiller, Robert J. (2011), 'Debt and Delusion', *Project Syndicate*, 21 July.

Siedentop, Larry (2001), *Democracy in Europe* (New York: Columbia University Press).

Sikorski, Radoslaw (2011), 'Deutsche Macht furchte ich heute weniger als deutsche Untatigkeit', *Deutsche Gesellschaft fur Auswartige Politik*, 28 November.

Smith, Helena (2012), 'German "hypocrisy" over Greek Military Spending Has Critics up in Arms', *The Guardian*, 19 April.

Sinnott, Richard (2002), 'Attitudes and Behaviour of the Irish Electorate in the Referendum on the Treaty of Nice', results of a survey of public opinion carried out for the European Commission Representation in Ireland, available at http://www.ucd.ie/dempart/workingpapers/nice1.pdf, accessed 21 May 2014.

Smith, Julie (2005), 'A Missed Opportunity? New Labour's European Policy 1997–2005', *International Affairs*, Vol. 81, No. 4, pp. 703–721.

Smith, Anthony A. and Stolbert, Caroline J. (2010), 'Direct Democracy, Public Opinion and Candidate Choice', *Public Opinion Quarterly*, Vol. 74, No. 1, pp. 85–108.

Sørensen, Catharina (2004), 'Danish and British Popular Euroscepticism Compared: A Sceptical Assessment of the Concept', Working Paper 2004/25 (Copenhagen: Danish Institute for International Studies).

Soros, George (2012a), Transcript of Remarks at the Festival of Economics, Trento, 2 June, available at http://www.georgesoros.com/interviews-speeches/entry/remarks_at_the_festival_of_economics_trento_italy/.

Soros, George (2012b), 'The Tragedy of the European Union and How to Resolve It', *New York Review of Books*, 10 September.

Soros, George (2012c), *Financial Turmoil: Essays in Europe and the United States* (New York: Public Affairs).
Soros, George (2013), 'How to Save the European Union', *The Guardian*, 9 April.
Spicer, Michael (1992), *A Treaty Too Far: A New Policy for Europe* (London: Fourth Estate).
Startin, Nick and Krouwel, André (2013), 'Euroscepticism Re-galvanized: The Consequences of the French and Dutch Rejections of the EU constitution', *Journal of Common Market Studies*, Vol. 51, No. 1, pp. 65–84.
Stavrou, Protesilaos (2013), 'Single Supervisory Mechanism: How It Relates to the Institutional Morphology of the European Union', 7 February, available at http://www.protesilaos.com/euroblog/single-supervisory-mechanism-how-it-relates-to-the-institutional-morphology-of-the-european-union/.
Stoker, Gerry (2006), 'Explaining Political Disenchantment: Finding Pathways to Democratic Renewal', *The Political Quarterly*, Vol. 77, No. 2, pp. 184–194.
Stoker, Gerry (2011), 'Anti-Politics in Britain' in Richard Heffernan, Philip Cowley and Colin Hay (eds), *Developments in British Politics 9* (Basingstoke: Palgrave Macmillan), pp. 152–173.
Stokes, Donald (1963), 'Spatial Models of Party Competition', *The American Political Science Review*, Vol. 57, No. 2, pp. 368–377.
Strange, Gerard (2009), 'World Order and EU Regionalism: Towards an open Approach to New Constitutionalism', Asia Research Center: Working Paper No.162, Murdoch University.
Strange, Susan (1971), *Sterling and British Policy* (Oxford: Oxford University Press).
Strange, Susan (1988), *States and Markets: An Introduction to International Political Economy* (London: Pinter).
Stephens, Philip (1996), *Politics and the Pound: The Conservatives Struggle with Sterling* (Basingstoke: Macmillan).
Stephens, Philip (2001), 'Blair and Europe', *Political Quarterly*, Vol. 72, No. 1, pp. 67–75.
Stevens, Philip (2013), 'Germany Should Face the German Question', available at http://www.ft.com/cms/s/0/3517ad4c-a74c-11e2-9fbe-00144feabdc0.html#axzz3EzBFD9Jm.
Story, Louise (2010), 'A Secretive Banking Elite Rules Trading in Derivatives', *New York Times*, 11 December.
Stubbs, Alexander (2002), *Negotiating Flexibility in the European Union: Amsterdam, Nice and Beyond* (Basingstoke: Palgrave).
Sverdrup, Ulf (2001), 'Institutional Perspective on Treaty Reform: Contextualising the Amsterdam and Nice treaties', ARENA Working Papers, WP 01/27.
Swank, Duane and Hans-Georg, Betz (2003), 'Globalization, the Welfare State and Right-wing Populism in Western Europe', *Socio-Economic Review*, Vol. 1, No. 2, pp. 215–245.
Szczerbiak, Aleks and Paul, Taggart (2002), *The Party Politics of Euroscepticism in EU Member and Candidate States*, Sussex European Institute Working Paper No. 51.
Szczerbiak, Aleks and Paul, Taggart (eds) (2008), *Opposing Europe? The Comparative Party Politics of Euroscepticism* (Oxford: Oxford University Press).
Taggart, Paul (2004), 'Populism and Representative Politics in Contemporary Europe', *Journal of Political Ideologies*, Vol. 9, No. 3, pp. 269–288.
Taggart, Paul (2006), 'Keynote Article: Questions of Europe – The Domestic Politics of the 2005 French and Dutch referendums and Their Challenge for the

Study of European Integration', *Journal of Common Market Studies*, Vol. 44, Annual Review, pp. 7–25.

Taggart, Paul and Szczerbiak, Alex (2004), 'Contemporary Euroscepticism in the Party Systems of the European Union Candidate States of Central and Eastern Europe', *European Journal of Political Research*, Vol. 43, No. 1, pp. 1–27.

Tax Justice Network: Financial Secrecy Index 2013: http://www.financialsecrecyindex.com/

Telo, Mario (2007), *European Union and the New Regionalism: Regional Actors in a Post-Hegemonic Era* (Aldershot: Ashgate).

Temperton, Paul (2001), *The UK and the Euro* (London: John Wiley).

Tempest, Matthew (2005), 'Treasury papers reveal cost of Black Wednesday', *The Guardian*, http://www.theguardian.com/politics/2005/feb/09/freedomofinformation.uk1.

Thatcher, Margaret (1993), *The Downing Street Years* (London: HarperCollins).

Thatcher, Margaret (1995), *The Path to Power* (London: HarperCollins).

Tierney, Stephen (2009), 'Constitutional Referendums: A Theoretical Enquiry', *The Modern Law Review*, Vol. 72, No. 3, pp. 360–383.

Tilford, Simon and Whyte, Philip (2011), 'Why Stricter Rules Threaten the Eurozone', Center for European Reform, London, 2011, pp. 5–6.

Torreblanca, Jose Ignacio and Leonard, Mark (2013), 'The Continent-wide Rise of Euroscepticism', European Council on Foreign Relations, No. 79, May.

Traynor, Ian (2012), 'Germany to Set the Terms for Saving the Euro', *The Guardian*, 31 January.

Traynor, Ian (2014), 'Eurozone Fears of Stagnation Grow as France and Italy Suffer', *The Guardian*, 30 August, available at http://www.theguardian.com/world/2014/aug/30/france-germany-austerity-straitjacket-hollande.

Treaty establishing the European Economic Community, Rome 1957 original text (non-consolidated version), available at http://europa.eu/legislation_summaries/institutional_affairs/treaties/treaties_eec_en.htm.

US Department of the Treasury (2013), *Report to Congress on International Economic and Exchange Rate Policies*, 30 October, available at http://www.treasury.gov/resource-center/international/exchange-rate-policies/Documents/2013-10-30_FULL%20FX%20REPORT_FINAL.pdf.

Usherwood, Simon (2002), 'Opposition to the European Union in the UK: The Dilemma of Public Opinion and Party Management', *Government and Opposition*, Vol. 37, No. 2, pp. 211–230.

Usherwood, Simon and Startin, Nick (2013), 'Euroscepticism as a Persistent Phenomenon', *Journal of Common Market Studies*, Vol. 51, No. 1, pp. 1–16.

Van Apeldoorn, Bastian (2002) *Transnational Capitalism and the Struggle over European Integration* (London: Routledge).

Van Apeldoorn, Bastian (2009), 'The Contradictions of 'Embedded Neoliberalism' and Europe's Multi-level Legitimacy Crisis: The European Project and its Limits', in Bastiaan Van Apeldoorn, Jan Drahokoupil, and Laura Horn (eds), *Contradictions and Limits of Neoliberal European Governance– From Lisbon to Lisbon* (Basingstoke: Palgrave).

Van Apeldoorn, Bastiaan and Horn, Laura (2007), 'The Transformation of Corporate Governance Regulation in the European Union: From Harmonization to Marketization', in Henk Overbeek, B. Van Apeldoorn and Andreas Nölke

(eds), *The Transnational Politics of Corporate Governance Regulation* (London: Routledge), pp. 76–97.
Van Apeldoorn, Bastian, Drahokoupil, Jan and Horn, Laura (2009), *Contradictions and Limits of Neoliberal Governance: From Lisbon to Lisbon* (Basingstoke: Palgrave).
Van Ark, Bart, O'Mahony, Mary and Timmer, Marcel P. (2008), 'The Productivity Gap between Europe and the United States: Trends and Causes', *Journal of Economic Perspectives*, Vol. 22, No. 1, Winter, pp. 25–44.
Van der Pijl, Kees (1984), *The Making of an Atlantic Ruling Class* (London: Verso).
Van der Pijl, Kees (2004), 'Two faces of the Transnational Cadre under Neo-liberalism', *Journal of International Relations and Development*, Vol. 7, pp. 177–207.
Van der Pijl, Kees (2006), 'A Lockean Europe?', *New Left Review*, Vol. 37, pp. 9–37.
Van Treeck, Till (2009), 'The Political Economy Debate on 'financialization': A Macroeconomic Perspective', *Review of International Political Economy*, Vol. 16, No. 5, pp. 907–944.
Varoufakis, Yanis, Holland, Stuart and Galbraith, James K. (2013), 'A modest proposal for resolving the eurozone crisis' – Version 4.0', July, available at http://varoufakis.files.wordpress.com/2013/07/a-modest-proposal-for-resolving-the-eurozone-crisis-version-4-0-final1.pdf.
Verney, Susannah (2011), 'Euroscepticism in Europe: A Diachronic Perspective', *South European Society and Politics*, Vol. 16, No. 1, pp. 1–30.
Vitali, Stefania, Glattfelder, James B. and Battiston, Stefano (2011), *The Network of Global Corporate Control*, ETH Zurich, September.
Vreese, Claes H. de, Lauf, Edmund and Peter, Jochen (2007), 'The Media and European Parliament Elections: Second-rate Coverage of a Second-order Event?' in Wouter van der Brug and Cees van der Eijk (eds), *European Elections and Domestic Politics* (Notre Dame, IN: University of Notre Dame Press), pp. 116–130.
Vreese, Claes H. de (ed) (2007), *The Dynamics of Referendum Campaigns An International Perspective* (Basingstoke: Palgrave).
Vucheva, Elitsa (2009), 'EU governments committed 3 trillion for bank bailouts', *EUobserver.com*, 9 April.
Wall, Stephen (2008), *A Stranger in Europe: Britain and the EU from Thatcher to Blair* (Oxford: Oxford University Press).
Wallace, William (2005), 'The Collapse of British Foreign Policy', *International Affairs*, Vol. 82, No. 1, pp. 53–68.
Watson, Matthew (2010), 'House Price Keynesianism and the Contradictions of the Modern Investor Subject', *Housing Studies*, Vol. 25, No.3, pp. 413–426.
Webb, Paul (2005), 'The Continuing Advance of the Minor Parties', *Parliamentary Affairs*, Vol. 58, No. 4, pp. 7757–7775.
Welsh, Irvine (2014), 'This Glorious Failure Could Yet Be Scotland's Finest Hour', *The Guardian*, 20 September, available at http://www.theguardian.com/commentisfree/2014/sep/20/irvine-welsh-scottish-independence-glorious-failure.
Wendt, Alexander (1992), 'Anarchy Is What States Make of It: The Social Construction of Power Polities', *International Organization*, Vol. 46, No. 2, pp. 391–425.

Whiteley, Paul, Clarke, Harold, Sanders, David and Stewart, Marianne (2001), 'Turnout' in *Parliamentary Affairs*, Vol. 54, October, pp. 775–788.
Whiteley, Paul (2011), *Political Participation in Britain: The Decline and Revival of Civic Culture* (Basingstoke: Palgrave Macmillan).
Whiteley, Paul, Clarke, Harold D., Sanders, David and Stewart, Marianne C. (2012), 'Britain Says No: Voting in the AV ballot referendum', *Parliamentary Affairs*, Vol. 65, pp. 301–322.
Whittaker, John (2011), 'Eurosystem Debts, Greece, and the Role of Banknotes', Lancaster University Management School Paper, 14 November.
Wilks, Stuart (1996), 'Britain and Europe: An Awkward Partner or an Awkward State?' *Politics*, Vol. 16, No. 3, pp. 159–167.
Williamson, Andy (2010), 'Digital Citizens and Democratic Participation' (London: Hansard Society), available at http://www.hansardsociety.org.uk/wp-content/uploads/2012/10/Digital-Citizens-and-Democratic-Participation-2010.pdf, accessed 10 June 2014.
Wintour, Patrick (2013), 'Ukip Threat to Tories Revealed by Poll of Voters in Key Marginal Seat', *The Guardian*, 26 November.
Wolf, Martin (2004), *Why Globalization Works* (New Haven: Yale University Press).
Wolf, Martin (2011), 'Thinking through the Unthinkable: Fundamental Difficulty Has Been Failure to Understand the Crisis', *Financial Times*, 8 November.
Wolin, Sheldon S. (2008), *Democracy Incorporated: Managed Democracy and the Specter of Inverted Totalitarianism* (Princeton NJ: Princeton University Press).
Young, Brigitte and Semmler, Willi (2011), 'The European Sovereign Debt Crisis: Is Germany to Blame?', *German Politics and Society*, Vol. 97, No. 1, pp. 1–24.
Young, Brigitte and Semmler, Willi (2012), 'Germany's New Vision for the Eurozone: Rule-based Ordoliberalism?', Lecture at the Central European University, 15 February.
Young, Brigitte (2013), 'Financialization, Neoliberalism and the German Ordoliberalism in the EU-Crisis Management', in Marcel Heires and Andreas Nölke (eds), *Politische Ökonomie der Finanzialisierung* (*The Political Economy of Financialization*) (Wiesbaden: Springer VS), pp. 63–77.
Young, Brigitte (2013), 'Ordoliberalism – Neoliberalism – Laissez-Faire-Liberalism' in Joscha Wullweber, Antonia Graf, and Maria Behrens (eds), *Theorien der Internationalen Politischen Ökonomie* (*Theories of International Political Economy*) (Wiesbaden: SpringerVS), pp. 33–48.
Young, Brigitte (2014), 'The Role of German Ordoliberalism in the Euro Crisis' in Nicholas Petropoulos (ed), *The Debt Crisis in the Eurozone: Social Impact* (Newcastle upon Tyne: Cambridge Scholars Publishing).
Young, Brigitte (2014), 'The Power of German Ordoliberalism in the Eurozone Crisis Management 2013' in L. Stein Jerome, Daniel Daianu and Rajeesh Kumar (eds), *Eurozone Crisis* (Basingstoke: Palgrave Macmillan).
Young, Hugo (1989), *One of Us: A Biography of Mrs Thatcher* (Basingstoke: Macmillan).
Young, Hugo (1998), *This Blessed Plot: Britain and Europe from Churchill to Blair* (Basingstoke: Macmillan).
Youngs, Richard (2014), *The Uncertain Legacy of the Crisis: European Foreign Policy Faces the Future* (Washington: Carnegie Endowment for Peace).
Zacune, Joseph (2013), *Privatising Europe: Using the Crisis to Entrench Neoliberalism*, Amsterdam: TNI, March.

Zakaria, Fareed (2009), *The Post-American World and the Rise of the Rest* (London: Penguin).
Zalewska, Marta and Josef Gstrein, Oskar (2013), 'National Parliaments and Their Role in European Integration: The EU's Democratic Deficit in Times of Economic Hardship and Political Insecurity', Bruges Political Research Papers, No. 28, available at https://www.coleurope.eu/sites/default/files/research-paper/wp28_zalewskagstrein.pdf.
Zielonka, Jan (2006), *Europe as Empire: The Nature of an Enlarged European Union* (Oxford: Oxford University Press).
Zysman, J. (1983), *Governments, Markets and Growth: Financial Systems and the Politics of Industrial Change* (Ithaca, NY: Cornell University Press).

Index

Note: The locators followed by 'n' refer to note numbers

Abdelal, Rawi E, 30
Agenda 2010, 121
Alexander, Douglas, 78, 79
Alexandre-Collier, Agnès, 61, 65, 69, 70
Almond, Gabriel, 93, 97, 98, 110, 174
Alternative für Deutschland (AfD), 123–4
Alternative Vote (AV), 96
Amsterdam Treaty, 51–2, 54
Anderson, Peter, 74
Angela, Merkel, 26, 33, 39, 128, 136, 178
  see also Germany
Anglo-American model
  debt-led financialisation, 19
  deregulated finance capitalism, 36
  European integration process, 35
  informal member-state groupings, 167
  investment banking, 30
  political culture, 170
  shared values, 139
  Single Market neoliberalisation, 29
anti-Europeanism, 48, 61, 67, 70–1, 74, 79, 117, 123, 131, 148
anti-immigration campaign, 102, 117
Aspinwall, Mark, 65
Atlanticism, 10, 51, 57, 137–40, 160
Attlee, Clement, 45
Audit of Political Engagement, 97
Avril, Emmanuelle, 99
Axis powers, 45

Bache, Ian, 51
Baker, David, 1, 9, 13, 19, 52, 61, 65, 66, 68, 69, 70, 71, 72, 75, 81, 82, 111, 137, 139, 142, 143, 144, 148, 149, 171, 172
Bale, Tim, 79, 80, 156
Balls, Edward, 75, 77, 79, 187n. 1

Balsom, Denis, 106
banking
  European system, 19–20
  German system, 28, 36, 39
  G20 reforms, 78
  international, 174
  investment lobbies, 30
  offshore interest (Britain), 75
  overseas earnings, 182
  private, 18, 164
  2008 crisis, 169
Barber, Benjamin, 107
Bates, Thomas R., 3
Benn, Tony, 64, 67, 68, 106, 142, 188n. 1
Berger, Peter L., 12
Bergsten, C., 17
Betz, Hans-Georg, 131, 132
Black, Conrad, 74
Blair, Tony, 187n. 1
  Amsterdam Treaty, 51, 54
  Atlanticism, 57
  constitutional treaty negotiation, 58–9, 119–20
  election of May 1997, 52
  EU policy, 52
  on European constitution, 56
  on European Council, 55
  foreign policy, 8–9
  immigration policies, 105
  in-out decision, 180
  open regionalism, 148, 151
  opposition to the euro, 51, 54
  Warsaw speech in 2000, 55, 57, 128
Blumler, Jay G., 99
Blunkett, David, 73
Blyth, Mark, 12, 13, 18, 19, 20, 21, 22, 23, 27, 28, 29, 38, 140, 170, 172
Bogdanor, Vernon, 95, 96, 118
Bohle, Dorothy, 146
Bourlanges, Jean-Louis, 55, 116

Bozo, Frédéric, 7
Brazil, Russia, India, China, South Africa (BRICS), 7, 136, 144
Bréchon, Pierre, 94
Bretton Woods financial system, 144
Brexit deal, 161–4, 172–3, 175–6, 179, 181, 183
British economy, 46, 75, 147, 159, 164
British Election Survey, 98
British national identity, 139–41
British National Party (BNP), 63, 95, 101–3
British political system, 1, 16, 45, 65, 109, 112
British Social Attitudes poll, 97, 111
Bromley, Catherine, 97
Brown, George, 68
Brown, Gordon
  Cabinet divisions, 71–3
  economic issues, 54, 76–7
  euro-enthusiasm, 75
  on European Constitution (constitutional treaty), 56, 59, 106–7
  foreign policy, 8
  immigration policy, 105
  view on CAP reform, 78
Budge, Ian, 107
Buffet, Warren, 19
Bull, Martin J., 121
Buller, Jim, 154, 155
Bulpitt, Jim, 109, 141, 155, 171
Burton, Jonathan, 74
Butler, David, 93
Byrne, Paul, 98, 99, 100

Callaghan, Jim, 47
Cameron, David, 188n. 10, 188n. 17
  Bloomberg speech 2013, 64–5, 128–9, 152–3, 177
  British Treasury under, 158
  coalition's economic policies, 90
  EU Treaty modifications, 175
  fiscal compact, veto, 81
  immigration issue, EU member states, 2, 178–9
  in/out referendum, 84–5, 134–5, 159, 173
  intergovernmentalism, 124, 155–6

Junker's appointment, 160–1, 168
'liberal Conservatism,' 9
May 2014 election (EPP), 127
new Lisbon Treaty, 60, 107
open regionalism, 148
2005 election, 80
UKIP and, 104–5
Canovan, Margaret, 101
Cardinal, Mario, 179
Carey, Sean, 74
Carswell, Douglas, 84
Cash, Bill, 64, 71, 81
Charter, David, 135, 157, 163, 164, 181, 182
Charter of Fundamental Rights, 56, 58, 134
Chiaramonte, Alessandro, 123
Chirac, Jacques, 54, 57
Christian Democratic parties, 161
City of London, 76, 137, 139, 145, 157, 163–4, 173, 182
civil society, 42–3, 125–6, 138
Clarke, Charles, 73
Clarke, H.D., 100
Clarke, Kenneth, 71, 79–80
Clegg, Nick, 81, 92, 107, 153, 188n. 9, 190n. 3
Clift, Ben, 14, 29
coalition government
  anti-European populist parties, 117
  Conservative/Liberal Democrat (2010), 9, 15, 44, 60, 62, 81
  constitutional reforms, 107
  European, 67
  1997 and 2007, 1
  voter turnout (youth), 94
Cockfield, Arthur, 49
Coggan, Philip, 92
Cold War, 6, 10, 49, 86, 117, 139–40, 144
Coleman, Stephen, 99
Colley, Linda, 65, 141, 143
common agricultural policy (CAP), 52, 75, 78, 104, 127
Common Foreign and Security Policy (CFSP), 50–1, 53, 55–6, 58

Conservative Party
  anti-constitution campaign, 59
  anti-European wing, 61, 71
  Atlanticism, 137
  Blair government, 56, 58, 72
  Cameron government, 107, 159, 161–2
  electorate expansion, 155
  EU decision-making process, 128
  European integration, 44
  foreign policy, 9
  FPTP electoral system, 94
  governments 1979–1997, 47–52
  Howard, Michael, 104
  internal party divisions, 108
  middle-class voting, 93
  national interest, 15, 87, 134–5, 140–2, 144
  new Lisbon Treaty, 60, 77
  after 1997, 79–85
  political crisis (statecraft failure), 157–62, 171
  political rift with Scotland, 110
  Powell, Enoch, 67
  pro-European wing, 148
  referendum in 1975, 46
  referendum on EU membership, 103
  strategic decisions, 143, 155
  traditional values, 103
  2010 general election, 95–6
  2010 manifesto, 156
  between 2010 and 2012, 98
  2015 election, 6, 10, 176
constitutional treaty, 56–9, 73, 75–6, 81, 106–7, 119, 126, 132
Continuous Monitoring Survey, 98
Cook, Robin, 73
Cooper, Robert, 8
Copus, Colin, 101, 103
Corbetta, Piergiorgio, 123
Council of Ministers, 11, 161
Cowley, Philip, 71, 92, 95, 96, 98
Cox, Michael, 6
Crewe, Ivor, 93
crisis, 3, 22–4, 29, 33, 37–8, 113, 153, 169
Crouch, Colin, 32
Crozier, Michel, 91

currency union, 24, 28, 39, 47, 120, 135, 180
Curtice, John, 74, 83, 93, 96, 97, 100, 110, 111, 112
Cygan, Adam, 125

Daddow, Oliver, 8, 9, 75
Dalton, Russell J., 91
Daniels, Philip, 70
Davis, David, 51
Debomy, Daniel, 89
de Gaulle, General, 45–6, 113
Delors, Jacques, 30, 48, 70, 149
Delwitt, Pascal, 94
democratic deficit, 16, 19, 40, 51, 86, 114–15, 125, 127–8, 132
Denver, David, 93, 95
devolution process, 109–12
deVreese, Claes H. de, 179
Di Mauro, Danilo, 89
Dooge committee, 48
Draghi, Mario, 28, 33
Duchêne, François, 8
Dullien, Sebastian, 31, 32, 34
Dumenil, Gerard, 140
Dutch draft treaty, 50
Dyson, Kenneth, 23, 24, 32, 34, 167

East European member-states, 41, 105, 132, 172
EU membership, 1–2, 8, 81, 87, 101, 112, 134, 147, 178–9
European Central Bank (ECB), 21, 25–6, 34, 69, 114
European Coal and Steel Community (ECSC), 44–5
European Community (EC), 11, 47
European Council, 11, 38–9, 48, 51, 53, 55–9, 69, 74, 78, 81, 114, 125, 127–8, 159, 180
European Defence Community (EDC), 44–5
European Economic Community (EEC), 24, 44–5, 66–8, 96, 106, 143
European elections, 83, 93, 102–3, 114, 124, 127, 130, 133, 178
European Exchange Rate Mechanism, 180

Index 227

European integration
  British euroscepticism, 62–3, 65, 70
  embedded liberalism to variegated neoliberalism, 34–7
  globalisation context, 72, 92
  legitimate form, 158
  'Luxembourg Compromise,' 46
  member-states, 87–8, 116
  national interests, 11, 97
  in the 1950s, 44
  populist parties, 124
  QMV and, 55
  referendums, 118–19, 130
  state actors, 13
  theories, 11
  UK's position, 11, 114, 117, 148
European law, 2, 35, 45
European Monetary System (EMS), 29–30, 47, 49, 68
European Monetary Union (EMU), 14, 18, 21, 23, 25, 27–9, 31, 34, 36–7, 44, 50, 69, 71, 106, 113, 118, 121, 137
European Parliament (EP), 19, 40, 47, 49, 51–3, 55, 68, 75, 80, 87, 102, 114, 116, 118–19, 121, 124, 126–30, 160–1
European People's Party (EPP), 80, 161
European project, 1, 16, 62–3, 65–6, 89, 92, 113, 116–17, 120–1, 124, 180
EU Act 2011, 107
European Union Bill (2010), 81
EU budget, 43, 57, 75, 119, 129
Europe Restructured (Owen), 152
euroscepticism, 1–2, 12–13, 38, 60–70, 82–3, 88–90, 98, 105–6, 134–6, 165, 168–9, 173, 175, 179, 181
Eurozone
  analytical chronology, 24–6
  banking system, 22
  currency union, 24–6
  embedded liberalism, 34–7
  fiscal coordination, 153
  in and out choice (Britain), 180
  separation of responsibility, 41
  single currency logic, 158
  sovereign debt crisis, 26–8
  treaty changes, 178
  two-tier EU, 181
  see also neoliberalism; ordoliberalism
EU Scrutiny Committee, 81
Exchange Rate Mechanism (ERM), 25, 86

Farage, Nigel, 98, 103, 153, 174, 183
financial crisis
  deregulation of finance, 78
  EU, 77, 118
  global, 37
  negative interest rates (Germany), 39
  2007–8, 7, 78, 120
  2008–9, 22, 86
  UK–EU relations, 157
Financial Services Action Plan, 36
Financial Transactions Tax (FTT), 147
Fine, Ben, 185n. 5
first-past-the-post (FPTP) electoral system, 65, 83, 94–5
Fiscal Compact, 33, 39, 60, 81, 135, 137, 159
Fiscal Union, 20, 39, 159
Fitzgibbon, John, 86
Five-Star Movement (M5S, Italy), 4, 123
Follesdal, Andreas, 114
Ford, Robert, 18, 90, 102, 103, 104, 131, 172, 173, 174, 178, 179, 188n. 14
Forster, Anthony, 52, 61, 63, 65, 70
Foucault, Michel, 185n. 6, 186n. 1
Fraile, Maria, 89
France
  austerity measures, 7, 29
  Chirac (President), 57
  constitutional treaty referendum, 75, 77, 119–20, 130–2
  EEC domination, 45
  EMS membership, 30
  EP elections 2014, 116
  euro currency, 25
  fiscal stimulus 2008, 78
  FN in, 123–4
  German alliance, 11, 23, 25, 69, 82, 168
  Germany, comparison with, 168

France – *continued*
  haute administration, 46
  intergovernmentalism, 43
  interstate trade, 11
  Maastricht Treaty, 117
  mainstream parties, 88, 117
  national tropes, 141
  'Paris Consensus,' 30
  private financial sector, 36
  pro-European electorates, 118
  sovereign debt crisis, 121
  voting weight, 55, 94, 167
  Western European Union (WEU), 50, 52
Franco-British summit, 72
Franco–German alliance, 11, 23, 25, 69, 82, 168
Franklin, Mark N., 129, 130
Freedom Party (FPÖ, Haider), 117, 124
free-trade, 42, 48, 139
Friedman, Thomas L., 145
Front National (FN), 117, 123–4

Gabel, Matthew J., 85
Gamble, Andrew, 2, 3, 9, 10, 13, 14, 20, 37, 51, 65, 74, 138, 139, 140, 141, 142, 143, 144, 145, 148, 154, 163, 165, 170, 172, 182
Garry, John, 119
Geddes, Andrew, 19, 25, 160, 165, 182, 183
Genscher-Colombo plan, 48
George, Stephen, 1, 44, 61, 65
Germany
  austerity measures, 7, 15, 120–1, 167
  Bismarkian, 139
  'Brexit deal,' 181
  Bundesbank, 25–6, 49, 135–6
  Cameron's proposal, 179
  civic culture, 141
  economic aims, 39
  EP elections, 118
  EU's governance, 41, 46
  EU's troika, 148
  EZ game, 19, 21–2, 79
  Merkel's promises, 161, 175
  monetary policy, 27–8, 69
  national interests, 11, 43, 168
  post-crisis primacy, 40

  private financial sector, 36
  reunification, 34, 55, 144
  Single Market, 25, 49, 136
  2014 European elections, 7, 15, 124
  voting weight, 55, 167
  WEU, incorporation, 52
  zero-sum game, 178
Gifford, Chris, 44, 64, 65, 67, 82
Gill, Stephen, 146
global financial markets, 22, 30, 148, 163
globalisation
  Anglophone countries, 65
  Britain, 6–10, 71–2, 82
  domestic crises, 129–32, 172
  down-side impact, 103
  economic benefits, 109, 133
  emerging economies, 154
  Europe, 6–10, 75–8, 92
  European citizens' concerns, 114
  exogenous factors, 100
  Germany, 40
  ideological shifts, 100
  investment banking, 30
  party membership and, 98
  regionalisation *vs.,* 144, 149, 150–1
  see also hyperglobalism
Golden Dawn (Greece), 4, 58, 123, 166–7
Goldsmith, James, 66, 83, 106
Goodwin, Matthew, 18, 90, 103, 104, 131, 172, 173, 174, 178, 179, 188n. 14
Gowland, David, 44, 61
Grant, Charles, 7
Great Depression, 7
Great Recession, 2, 18, 37, 103
Green, Jane, 100
Green Party, 63, 95, 104
Greskovitz, Bela, 146
Grice, Andrew, 105
Grillo, Beppe, 4, 123
G7 economies, 4
Gstrein, Oskar Josef, 128
G20 economies, 78
Guardia, Anton La, 28, 33, 38, 41, 47
Guérot, Ulrike, 31, 32, 34, 121, 135, 136

Hague, William, 9, 79, 80, 81, 174
Haider, Jörg, 117
Hain, Peter, 57–8, 128
Hall, Peter, 99
Hamann, Trent H., 186n. 2
Hanley, Seβn, 87
Hannan, Daniel, 81
Hansard Society, 97, 99
Haseler, Stephen, 141
Hay, Colin, 12, 36, 72, 100, 145, 170
Hayward, Jack, 12, 23, 38, 116
Health & Safety and Employment legislation, 147
Heath, Anthony, 83
Held, David, 145
Heppell, Tim, 154, 156, 160, 173
Heseltine, Michael, 69, 71, 79
Hewitt, Gavin, 159
Hirst, Paul, 152
historical institutionalism, 11–13
Hix, Simon, 114
Hodges, Michael, 36
Hoffmann, Stanley, 42
Holman, Otto, 35
Holmes, M., 144, 147
Home and Justice Affairs (HJA), 50–1, 53, 55, 59
Hooghe, Liesbet, 12, 16, 64, 87, 113, 117
House of Commons, 54, 84, 94–5, 103, 107–8
Hurd, Douglas, 8
hyperglobalism, 111, 144–6, 153, 172
anti-EU, 149
British euroscepticism *vs.*, 62
Brown's, 76
Cameron's, 156, 176
Conservatives, 1, 82–3, 111, 144–8, 153–4, 157, 166, 172
EU level policies, 13
European project, rejection, 16
financial, 13
globalization effect, 100, 151
intergovernmentalism *vs.*, 151–3
open regionalism *vs.*, 148
Thatcher's, 74, 144–5
ultra-free market, 1
see also Conservative Party

Ichijo, Atsuko, 187n. 1
Ikenberry, G. John, 7
IMF, 18, 30, 158, 174
Inglehart, Ronald, 91, 99
institutionalism
historical, 11–13
neo-, 11
intergovernmental conference (IGC), 50–4, 57–8, 125
intergovernmentalism, 1, 11–13, 15, 25, 40–3, 124, 134, 141, 144, 151–3, 156, 169–70, 176
IPSOS/MORI poll, 5, 87, 97
Ivaldi, Gilles, 130

Jenkins, Roy, 47, 68
Joffe, Josef, 6, 7
Johal, Sukhdev, 157
Junker, Jean Claude, 160–1, 168, 173, 176, 180

Kagan, Robert, 7
Kavanagh, Denis, 91, 92, 93, 95, 96
Keating, Michael, 111
Kornelius, Stefan, 33
Kriesi, Hanspeter, 131
Krouwel, André, 130, 132
Krugman, Paul, 18, 21
Kwarteng, Kwasi, 144, 156
Kynaston, David, 137

Labour Party
Atlanticism, 137
constitutional reforms/treaty negotiations, 73, 92
devolution policy, 109
on EC membership, 86
electoral victory in 1997, 96
EU policies, 44, 52, 62, 72, 89
May 1997 victory, 52
Murdoch papers, 73
1997 manifesto, 106
open regionalism, 144
2001 general election, 80
see also Blair, Tony
Laeken declaration, 57, 119
Laeken European Council, 56
Lamers, Karl, 52
Lamfalussy Process, 36

Lapavitsas, Costas, 29, 38
Larsen, Henrik, 55
Lassalle, Didier, 105
Laursen, Finn, 51
Layard, Richard, 21
Leconte, Cécile, 61, 62, 88
Lee, Lucy, 97, 98
Lega Nord (Italy), 117, 132
Leonard, Mark, 121, 135, 136
Lequesne, Christian, 55, 56
Leuffen, Dirk, 12
Levy, Dominique, 140
Liddle, Roger, 109, 156, 181
Lilley, Peter, 71
Lindberg, Leon, 113
Lipietz, A., 150
Lipset, Seymour Martin, 13, 93, 130
Lisbon treaty (Agenda), 36, 59–60, 77, 80, 107, 119, 126–8, 159
Lodge, Guy, 78
Lombardo, Emanuela, 126
Los Indignados (social movement), 123
Lovenduski, Joni, 71
Luckmann, Thomas, 12
Ludlam, Steve, 171, 172
Lukes, Steven, 185n. 6
Lynch, Philip, 81, 82, 87, 104, 141

Maastricht Treaty, 22, 24–5, 34, 42, 44, 50–2, 61, 64, 69, 72, 82–3, 85–6, 88, 106, 117–18, 127, 129, 132, 135, 147, 167, 180
Macartney, Hugh, 12, 29, 30, 31, 35, 36, 37
Magnette, Paul, 126
Mahendran, Kesi, 85, 187n. 1
Maier, Charles, S., 14
Mair, Peter, 94, 114
Majone, Giandomenico, 113, 114, 116, 127
Major, John
 attitude towards EC, 61
 diplomacy, 49–51
 flexibility views, 52
 foreign policy, 8, 44
 in-out decision, 180
 intra-party management, European issue, 85

Maastricht Treaty, signing, 69–70
 party divisions, 71
Mandelson, Peter, 73, 79, 109, 187n. 7
Mann, Michael, 26, 29, 40
Marks, Gary, 12, 16, 64, 87, 113, 117
Marquand, David, 114, 175
Marsh, David, 19, 22, 25, 26, 27, 39, 145, 182
Marsh, Michael, 129
Marshall, Geoffrey, 107
Martell, Luke, 145
Mason, Rowena, 105
Mauro, Paolo, 89
McAllister, Ian, 93
McCormick, John, 177
McIver, Iain, 85, 187n. 1
McLaren, Lauren, 129
Mendelsohn, Matthew, 106, 108
Menon, Anand, 8, 56, 57, 58, 73, 126, 128
Merkel, Angela
 EU budget negotiations, 128
 on euro, 26
 on European (political) union, 39–40, 136
 federalist response, 41
 Franco–German relationship, 23
 Junker's appointment, 161, 176
 mercantile advantage, 38
 zero-sum game, 178–9
middle-class voters, 96, 131
Miliband, David, 57
Miliband, Ed, 72, 78, 105, 173
Milonakis, Dimitris, 185n. 5
Milward, Alan, 131
Mirowski, Philip, 13, 186n. 1
Moga, Teodor Lucian, 11
Monti, Mario, 33
Moravcsik, Andrew, 11, 13, 53
Morrison, Herbert, 45
Munchau, Wolfgang, 175, 180, 181
Murdoch, Rupert, 54, 74
Murdoch papers, 73

Nairne, Patrick, 107
National Assembly of Wales, 95
national law, 58, 72, 145
National Security Strategy (NSS), 9

NATO, 43, 50–1, 53, 69, 75
neo-institutionalism, 11
neoliberalism, 12, 35, 37, 41, 71, 82, 100, 146, 148, 157–8
   Anglo-American, 29–30, 144
   anti-EU hyperglobalism, 149
   authoritarian views, 87
   Blair's, 9
   British model, 76, 78, 103, 135, 157
   'efficient market hypothesis,' 14, 170
   EU/EZ development, 5, 20
   European integration, 130
   free-trade, 48
   German model, 78
   globalization context, 71, 148, 166
   individual actors, 12
   left scepticism, 137
   open regionalism, 75, 151
   orthodox governments, 167
   progressive model, 150
   Single Market, 29–30
   social groups, 12
   social market model, 29
   Thatcher's, 69, 82, 100, 158
   Tory's, 171
   US leadership, 90
   variegated, 31, 34–7
Newman, Gerald, 141
new political economy (NPE), 14
Nice Treaty, 55–6, 72, 119, 127
Nicolaidis, Kalypso, 53
Nijeboer, Arjen, 119
Norman, Peter, 57, 58
Norris, Pippa, 71, 74, 93, 94, 95, 96, 97, 98, 100
Nugent, Neill, 59

O'Hara, Mary, 172
Ohmae, Kenichi, 145
Olsen, Johan P., 43
open regionalism, 9, 42, 72, 75, 89, 111, 134, 144, 148–52, 156
open-seas policies, 139–40
ordoliberalism, 5, 29, 31–4
   austerity measures, 167
   EU/EZ development, 5, 14, 20
   European solutions, 34
   German, 23, 26–7, 29, 31–2, 35, 37, 39, 135, 168
   governing competence, 166
Ormston, Rachel, 110
Osborne, George, 90, 158
Owen, David, 137, 152

Packer, George, 7
Padgett, Stephen, 32
Palley, Thomas I., 18, 20, 22, 23, 29, 38
Parkin, Andrew, 106
Parkin, Frank, 99
Paterson, Lindsay, 109
path dependency, 13, 20, 137
Patomaki, Heikki, 22
Payne, Anthony, 14, 144, 148
Peck, Jamie, 35, 36
Peet, John, 28, 33, 38, 41, 47
People's Party (Denmark), 88, 124
Perraton, Jonathan, 145, 148
Pharr, Susan J., 91
Pierson, Paul, 13
Plehwe, Dieter, 140
Podemos (party), 123
political crisis, 2, 16, 41, 92, 114, 119–20, 124–5, 129, 171–2
political economy
   Anglo-American model, 138–9, 170
   Atlanticism, 139–40, 142
   British vision, 144
   economic model, 65
   fiscal and monetary sovereignty, 163
   Gamble's model, 3, 163
   geopolitical dominance, 1
   global, 142–3, 145, 165
   Gramscian model, 3
   historical models, 11, 13–14
   imagined community, 139, 141
   international, 143
   'Sado-Monetarist' solutions, 22
   strategic choices, 155, 163
Pop, Valentina, 39
populism, 101, 105, 131, 179
populist parties, 16, 91, 100–3, 105, 112, 116–17, 123–4, 133
Portillo, Michael, 71, 146
Portugal, Italy, Ireland, Greece and Spain (PIIGS), 5, 19, 21–2, 34, 136

Index

post-crisis EU/EZ, 29, 40, 166, 168, 177
Powell, Enoch, 64, 67
Powell, Jonathan, 73, 74
power, 1–3, 6–9, 11, 15, 23–5, 34, 37, 39, 41, 45, 49, 52, 62, 66, 76, 78, 81, 85, 89–90, 93, 956, 101, 105, 108–10, 114, 117, 119, 121, 124, 127, 129, 135–8, 143, 147, 151, 153–5, 157, 159–60, 165–9, 172, 178, 181, 183
Prescott, John, 73
Prison Notebooks (Gramsc), 165
Pritchard, Mark, 84
PSOS/MORI poll, 5, 87, 97
Ptak, Ralf, 32
Putnam, Robert D., 91

qualified majority voting (QMV), 49, 52–5, 58
quantitative easing (QE), 4–5, 26, 33, 182
Quinn, Adam, 6
Qvortrup, Matt, 106, 130

Rachman, Gideon, 6
Radice, Hugo, 39, 137
Raffenne, Coralie, 126
Ram, Vidya, 97
Rawnsley, Andrew, 71, 73, 75, 78
Redwood, John, 64
Rees-Mogg, Jacob, 84
Referendum Party, 66, 83, 103, 106
Reflection Group, 51
representative democracy, 105, 109, 112–13, 127
Riddell, Peter, 54, 59, 74
Ridley, Nicholas, 136
Rokkan, Stein, 13, 93
Rome Treaty, 117, 135
Rosamond, Ben, 65, 72, 145, 149, 150
Rosanvallon, Pierre, 98
Rose, Richard, 93
Roth, Felix, 122
Rumsfeld, Donald, 76

Saerlvik, Bo, 93
Sally, Razeen, 186n. 1
Salmond, Alex, 110, 174
Sartori, Giovanni, 102, 108

Scharpf, F. W., 35
Schäuble, Wolfgang, 28, 52
Scheingold, Stuart, 113
Schengen agreement, 53, 60
Schmidt, Vivien A., 12, 29, 39, 47, 115, 116, 157, 158
Schnapper, Pauline, 8, 9, 19, 65, 81, 102, 109
Scholte, Jan Aart, 145
Scottish National Party (SNP), 95, 109–11
Scottish Parliament, 95, 108–10
Seawright, David, 65, 68, 81, 155, 171, 172
Second World War, 45, 65–7, 88–9
Sedlacek, Tomas, 176
Seldon, Anthony, 76, 78
Semmler, Willi, 121
Sepos, Angelos, 167
Seyd, Ben, 97
Siedentop, Larry, 114
Sikorski, Radoslaw, 162
single currency
  Blair on, 52, 54, 60, 72–4
  Brown on, 76
  deflationary pressures, 170
  European project, 117
  eurozone integration, 158
  EU treaties on, 88
  German benefits, 121
  globalisation context, 71
  Hague on, 80
  Major on, 50–1, 69–70, 79, 106
  media and political opposition, 61
  member-state economic policies, 25, 153
  sovereign debts crisis, 82
  Straw on, 78
Single European Act, 11, 48–9, 86, 118
Single Market
  Anglo-American process, 29
  Brexit deal, 181, 183
  British preferences, 43, 60, 79, 137, 156, 163, 166, 180, 182
  constitutional treaty, 57, 76
  cross-border trade and investment, 25
  EU budget negotiations, 129
  European project, 30

EU's investment banking, 36
EZ sovereign debt crises, 14, 19
Germany's economic growth, 136
intergovernmentalism, 152
Open Europe organisation, 84
open regionalism, 151–3
preferred options, EU states, 177
pro-European realism, 77
white paper on, 49
Smith, Anthony A., 107
Smith, Julie, 8, 73
Social Chapter, 50, 52, 60, 72
Social Charter, 44
Social Mobility and Child Poverty Commission, 4
Sørensen, Catharina, 63, 87
Soros, George, 38
sovereign debt crisis
  'austerity-led growth' models, 166
  Cameron administration, 158
  elite-driven solutions, 11
  EMU, 31, 34
  European, 29, 37, 120, 135, 154, 159
  EZ's, 17–18, 24, 82, 142, 144
  Germany's approach, 31, 38–9
  global banking collapse, 33, 169
  phase two, 26
  solutions, 40
  tax harmony, 147
  of 2010, 169, 175
  UK's position, 1, 158, 180
Spicer, Michael, 144
Spinelli draft treaty, 48
Startin, Nick, 124, 130, 132
Stavrou, Protesilaos, 40
Steed, Michael, 83
Stephens, Philip, 25
Stevens, Philip, 17
Stoker, Gerry, 94, 97, 98, 100
Stokes, Donald, 93, 100
Strange, Gerard, 150
Straw, Jack, 71, 73, 78
Stuart, Gisela, 57, 77, 98, 129
Stuart, Mark, 98
Stubbs, Alexander, 53
Suez debacle, 45, 139
supranational organisation, 26, 40, 42–3, 45, 47, 64, 113–14, 124, 131, 135–6, 157–8, 174

Sverdrup, Ulf, 43
Swank, Duane, 132
Sweden Democrats (SD), 124
Szczerbiak, Aleks, 133

Taggart, Paul, 62, 63, 64, 65, 87, 101, 117, 130, 133
Tempest, Matthew, 25
Thatcher, Margaret
  anti-European views, 74
  attitude towards the EC, 61–2
  Bruges speech, 80
  Conservative government 1979–1997, 47–49
  Delors' appointment, 30
  downfall in 1990, 69
  Exchange Rate Mechanism, 69
  foreign policy, 9, 51
  national interest, 13, 171–2
  referendum proposition, 108
  Single European Act (SEA), 68–9, 105
  social market model, 29
  statecraft, 155
  TUC conference (Delor's speech), 149–50
  voter turnout, 95–6
  see also Conservative Party
Thatcher, Mark, 12, 29, 157, 158
Thompson, Graham, 152
Tickell, Adam, 35, 36
Tierney, Stephen, 108
Torreblanca, Jose Ignacio, 121
Traynor, Ian, 168
Treaty of Rome, 24
'troika,' 15, 18–19, 22, 29, 121, 123, 148, 154, 168
TUC conference 1988, 149
Turner, Anthony, 44, 61
2017 referendum, 180

Unionist parties, 95, 110
United Kingdom Independence Party (UKIP), 38, 59, 80, 83, 98, 104, 135, 145, 165, 171–2, 184
  anti-German policy, 157
  'Brexit' deal, 161
  Cameron's campaign, 173, 178

United Kingdom Independence Party (UKIP) – *continued*
  Conservative party *vs.*, 38, 59, 80, 83, 98, 104, 135, 145, 165, 171–2, 184
  European elections, 102–3
  populism, 101, 131
  referendum on EU membership, 103, 106, 112
  rise of, 1, 4–5
  splitting, right-wing vote, 179
  support group, 172
  2013 local elections, 104
  2014 European elections, 178
  2015 election, 180–1
  voter participation, 95, 105
  zero sum game, 174
USA
  federal system, 21
  financial crisis of 2007, 7
  military spending, 7
Usherwood, Simon, 65, 124, 133

Value Added Tax (VAT), 147
Van Apeldoorn, B., 29, 31, 35, 36
Van Ark, Bart, 8
Van der Pijl, Kees, 35, 37
Verba, Sidney, 93, 97, 98
Verney, Susannah, 117
Vignati, Rinaldo, 123
Vlaams Blok (VB, Belgium), 124

Wall, Stephen, 9, 48, 49, 54, 68
Wallace, William, 9
Watson, Matthew, 36
Webb, Paul, 94
Welsh, Irvine, 171
Western European Union (WEU), 50, 52–3
Weymouth, Tony, 74
Whiteley, Paul, 93, 97, 98
Wilks, Stuart, 65
Williams, Karel, 99
Williamson, Andy, 99
Wilson, Harold, 47, 68, 179
Wintour, Patrick, 104
Wolf, Martin, 145
Woolcock, Stephen, 36
working-class, 90, 93, 96, 99, 102–4, 130
Wurzel, Rüdiger, 23, 38, 116

Young, Brigitte, 7, 8, 97, 98, 121
Young, Hugo, 44, 45, 46, 47, 48, 49, 61, 65
Young, Penny, 97, 98
Youngs, Richard, 7, 8

Zacune, Joseph, 29
Zakaria, Fareed, 7
Zalewska, Marta, 128
zero-sum game, 64, 178
Zielonka, Jan, 8

Printed and bound by CPI Group (UK) Ltd, Croydon, CR0 4YY